MW01484672

Armand Bayou Illustrated
A Life on the Bayou

Mark Kramer

Armand Bayou Illustrated: A Life on the Bayou by Mark Kramer

Copyright © 2021 by Mark Kramer

All rights reserved. No part of this book may be used or reproduced in any manner without written permission from the copyright holder.

ISBN: 978-1-7373787-0-9   paperback
ISBN: 978-1-7373787-2-3   hardback
ISBN: 978-1-7373787-1-6   ebook

Acknowledgements

The production of *Armand Bayou Illustrated* would not have been possible without a collaborative effort from my friends.

First and foremost, I want to thank Gary Seloff. The inclusion of his photographs completes the "Illustrated" component of the book. Gary's photographs capture wildlife in their most intimate behaviors. After 40 years on the bayou, I am still often amazed when Gary's images reveal wildlife in remarkable activities. They highlight the richness and beauty of life along the bayou. His additional contribution as editor was significant, with a light touch that produced a manuscript that sounds like my voice. Thank you, Gary.

I want to thank Julie Massey and Wendy Reistle for their words of encouragement to write. Thank you to George Regmund, my friend and colleague for sharing your vast body of Armand Bayou knowledge. Thanks to the Review Team of Candy Donahue and George Regmund for your comments. Thanks to Mary Beth Maher for her artwork on the book cover and for her friendship and support over the past decades.

Finally, to my wife, friend, and partner Jennifer who has been a rock of support through this writing process and my health challenges. I love you.

A squadron of Little Blue Herons crosses Lake Mark Kramer in morning fog. Photo by Gary Seloff

Tri-colored Heron on Horsepen Bayou. Photo by Gary Seloff

Contents

A coyote stalks waterfowl in the bulrushes on Horsepen Bayou. Photo by Gary Seloff

Foreword

Armand Bayou is a song that has lingered in my ears for a lifetime. Like a prayer of devotion, I'd like to sing it to you now. Much of what is of importance to me and my life's journey has happened on these sunny shores. Love, loss, joy, pain, sorrow and more joy have all happened in knee deep brackish water. This is my collection of thoughts regarding that journey. I hope these words will serve as a natural history of my moment in time. You might also find material for reflection on your own personal journey. I have found great pearls of love, friendship and adventure just a few miles from where I was born. Whether you visit for a day or explore for a lifetime I hope that this effort will deepen your appreciation of this beautiful place and all wilderness that is so rapidly vanishing under the footprint of humanity.

It's interesting to be both a historian and part of history. Once you reach a certain intimacy, person and landscape are one and the same. Like the familiarity of a lover's touch. This will be my biographical naturalist chronicle of days spent along the waters of Armand Bayou. As a Pasadena native, I've spent almost the entirety of my days in its watershed. It's an unusual perspective having been witness to so much change, through so much time. Today we so rarely stay in one place. We so rarely have the will, patience or interest in remembering. Now, as my algorithm unwinds, I want to remember everything. The book contains passages that are both personal and professional. I began writing soon after I got an unwelcome health diagnosis. The process started as a good distraction but I hope you may find it useful and interesting.

A Naturalist

A young naturalist begins to explore and experience the natural world wherever he or she can find it. For me and for many of us, we may find wonder by experiencing what's right in our own backyard. The open fields and ditches around my childhood home in Pasadena were rich with toads, crawfish and fireflies. I could as easily have been in the Amazon wilderness to measure my sense of curiosity and excitement.

Naturalists are disciples of experience. Wilderness experience can be found in the wilds of Yellowstone or the ditches around Pasadena. We seek out these places to observe life and the natural processes that surround us. We seek to sharpen observation skills to see more deeply into the process. These early observations are largely external, such as noticing the beauty of a wildflower or the flight of a bird. As we grow and travel deeply and more frequently into the wilderness and our mind grows more quiet, we may also observe what is happening within us. Many of our greatest naturalists have sought out solitary time in these quiet spaces of remote beauty to observe and reflect. Darwin, Thoreau and Muir are among those who have been inspirational to me.

A natural outcome of this wilderness experience and observation leads to curiosity. We ask what forces shaped the forest to create this cathedral of trees? Why is that coyote behaving in such an unusual fashion? We might experience the process of discovery directly by watching the coyote later catch a rabbit or maybe spending time with another observer of nature and sharing our insights.

The accumulation of wilderness experience, observation and curiosity leads the naturalist to a sense of passion. Sometimes unexpectedly we're captured by the beauty of a bird diving into the water to catch a fish, the marvel of a sprouting seed or the power of a redfish on your line. Naturalists study anatomy, physiology, taxonomy, niche and behavior to name just a few of the disciplines involved. Naturalists experience a warm richness in their life from the biodiversity around us (referred to as biophilia). The more we look, the more we see. The more we see the greater the depth of our experience. Sometimes the naturalist's passion may be ignited by another's passion. Encounters with remarkable people who have devoted themselves to heal injured wildlife, collect and grow rare plants, or restore disappearing habitats may spark a moment of insight within.

The ability to pass on our experiences and passion to another is the art of the interpretive naturalist. For most of us in today's modern life we have lost the language of the natural world. Those who still hear her song and want to interpret her message for those who have lost the melody are interpretive naturalists. If only you could see Armand Bayou through my eyes, you would understand her depth of beauty. For me, I've grown to appreciate her and her beauty in every light, from every angle, from every age. I've sought to experience her cold shoulder on the blowout tides of January, her hot breath on the hottest July floral-fragrance blazing-star wildflower-peak-bloom days of summer, epic droughts and frequent hurricanes.

She becomes the muse that drives our desire for experience, observation, curiosity, passion and expression.

This book is dedicated to the place that has so profoundly shaped my life.

Chapter One: *The Early Years*

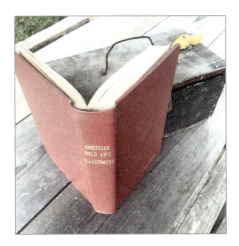

Growing up in the 1960s in Pasadena, Texas seems like a lifetime ago. This week in 2020, I suddenly realize that it was. I'm thankful to have this opportunity to reflect on it all. I had a book in those early years that shaped my days and nights: a book that had shown up in the house of my childhood with no explanation as to where it had come from. The book was titled *American Wildlife Illustrated* and it was filled with black and white photographs of various vertebrates–fish; amphibians; reptiles; birds; and mammals, with a short accompanying narrative about the species biology and life history. Included in the text were personal accounts of experiences associated with the author's observations of the animal. From that, the curiosity of a naturalist was born. My childhood on aptly named Prairie Street was surrounded by open fields and nearby ditches that were ripe for exploration. I was mainly interested in the adventure of loading my bucket with crawfish when the prairie wetlands filled with water after a summer rain or collecting as many Gulf Coast Toads as possible in my red wagon at night on a flashlight foray. Ditches in my

neighborhood were filled with turtles, snakes, and minnows, which were the daily quest to capture, identify and release.

The book was there with me in bed at night and I never grew tired of opening it to a page at random. If my eyes weren't tired, I would read. If I was sleepy, I would thumb through the pictures until lights out. The book was originally printed in 1933. It referenced bird names that were outdated. Rain Crow, Water Turkey, and Redbird were names in the book and were also the names that my father had used when we would see those species on our regular fishing trips. The book also made reference to species on the brink. Bald Eagle, Passenger Pigeon, Trumpeter Swan, and Ivory Billed Woodpecker were all noted as birds suffering from the plight of hunting pressure. It is sobering to think that just since the time the book was printed, two of those species no longer exist. Only recently did it dawn on me that the book had also been a guide book for my father. The names that he had used on those fishing trips were names that he learned from the book.

The new house on Prairie Street in 1961

In 1961, we moved into the house on Prairie Street. My grandfather had recently passed away in

Franklin, Louisiana and much of his belongings were transported to our house. Included was most of his life's collection of fishing equipment. I was only two years old at the time but when I grew older, I found his bamboo fly rods and level-wind reels in the garage.

He also left behind a handmade tackle box constructed of an empty Western Ammo box. Inside was a treasure of antique lures and most importantly, hand-tied flies that he had created. Flies of horsehair and rooster feathers that he probably collected from the neighbor's farm. I never met my grandfather but I imagined him fishing from his pirogue with those hand-tied flies in the old-growth, blackwater cypress swamps of south Louisiana. The lure in my young hand on Prairie Street had once been floating in those dark waters. It had probably been in the mouth of a bass that had fed my father as a child.

As I entered my teenage years, my explorations led me to Armand Bayou, named for the conservationist, Armand Yramategui, and the place of my real education as a naturalist. There, I was fortunate to meet a longtime friend of Mr. Yramategui's, Army Emmott. Army and Armand had known each other for a lifetime. Army had made his livelihood as the owner of a book binding company in Houston.

He was also a passionate fisherman so it was only natural that we should end up in a canoe together with fishing rods in our hands. Army was in his 80s when we fished together. I was in my 30s. He mostly fished and talked as I mostly paddled and listened to stories about him and Armand. As our stories drifted down the bayou, I recounted the history of my father, my grandfather and the book. By this time in the mid-1990s the book was in a deep state of deterioration. Pages were falling out and my heart was heavy with the loss of one of my most valued possessions. Army said, "Oh we can't let that happen." He took the book to his book binding company and completely re-bound it. He even embossed my name on the cover.

As I had it out this week in the fall of 2020, a flood of memories washed over me. I remembered falling asleep with the book in bed. I remembered the fishing trips with my father calling the bird names he learned from the book as he heard their calls. I remembered the book traveling with me when I did my road trip/walkabout across the country. How it lived with me in a tipi when I lived on the edge of Armand Bayou in 1979. I remembered bringing it home with me as I moved permanently onto the wildlife refuge in 1985. I remembered how I had relayed to a friend who happened to be a bookbinder, the family history of the book passing through three generations. I remembered how Army Emmott had saved the book from tatters in 1998.

The book was out this week sitting on the kitchen table. My wife walked past, catching a glimpse of the book. Noticing my name embossed on the front cover, she unexpectedly asked, "Is that your Bible?" It is hard bound, beautifully covered, and resembles a family Bible in every fashion. Still, it seemed like a silly question at first. She knows me well enough to have known better. But after further consideration I realized how important the book had been throughout every chapter of my life.

My hope is that these writings will be of similar interest to some. An easy read of how the beauty of the wilderness shapes the mind. Outstanding photography that captures intimate behaviors of wildlife. The joy of experiencing a wild animal's behavior in an unexpected act or moment of rare beauty. The moment of solitary awareness, in a wild place, that you are part of the natural processes universally unfolding in your body, the bayou, the planet, and the cosmos.

Early Days of a Young Naturalist

Landing on Earth in 1959, I enjoyed an idyllic early life. Post WWII was a prosperous time and my father bought a new brick home at 2707 Prairie Street on the salary of a baby food salesman. There were 24 kids within 4 years of age living on the 200-yard-long street and 3 of them were named Mark. The open fields surrounding the house were a place to fly kites with friends. They were also best described as coastal prairie. After a good rain, the prairie wetlands filled and became the site my early naturalist adventures. Following each flood, those wetlands teemed with crawfish. The day following the rain, the crustaceans emerge from their subterranean lair to forage in the flooded fields. It seemed like a very mysterious existence. There were aquifers below my feet in which the crawfish spent the majority of their life hidden underground. Only when the ephemeral prairie wetlands flooded did they appear.

I can remember when I was in elementary school begging my mother for my first pair of rubber boots after seeing them at K-Mart. They were the kind that laced up the front and seemed like a dream come true to a fourth grader. They allowed me to explore the prairie ponds around my house and find long, gelatinous strands of gulf coast toad eggs. Many a summer night was spent with a flashlight opening the lid of every neighbor's water meter looking for toads in their hidden hideouts. I filled my red wagon with gulf coast toads on several occasions. My mother was uncertain how to respond when I returned to the garage with a wagonload of toads.

There were also several ditches near the house that held deeper water and different species. Fish, amphibians, and reptiles inhabited the waters and were an adventure further afield. I learned that a string with bacon attached could catch even larger crawfish from the ditch. But the acquisition of a dip net opened a new world of fish. Of special interest was the elusive sailfin molly. On occasion a black morph was sighted and the chase continued throughout all of the surrounding ditches. The black molly was never caught. It may have been the antithesis of Moby Dick, the great white whale, but that small black minnow captivated the young mind of the elementary school kid clad in fine rubber boots, with a dip net.

My sister was 10 years older than me. When she got married at 18, we went to visit her and her new husband in Austin. There were huge live oak trees in a city park near her house. I saw my first squirrel. My first squirrel... Many years later I reflected on why I never saw squirrels in my youth on Prairie Street. In fact, I can't remember seeing squirrels anywhere in Pasadena. Then it dawned on me, squirrel habitat is forest. Pasadena was historically coastal prairie. It was grassland totally absent of trees...and squirrels. Eventually over the decades, people moved in, planted trees and the squirrels slowly entered the landscape.

This was also the era of the BB gun. Grassland songbirds were plentiful and I went on a brief quest to shoot and hold many of them. My pump-action Crossman shot pellets, but fortunately I was a poor shot. I wonder now, after killing my first Northern Mockingbird, if I lost the heart to kill more birds. I do remember holding a dead bird and being saddened by the affair, realizing that I'd killed a bird that was singing just a few minutes earlier. However, I kept shooting, just not killing. I remember an abundance of Loggerhead Shrikes and Eastern Meadowlarks. It began my foundation of understanding that I didn't have to hunt or kill to enjoy being outdoors.

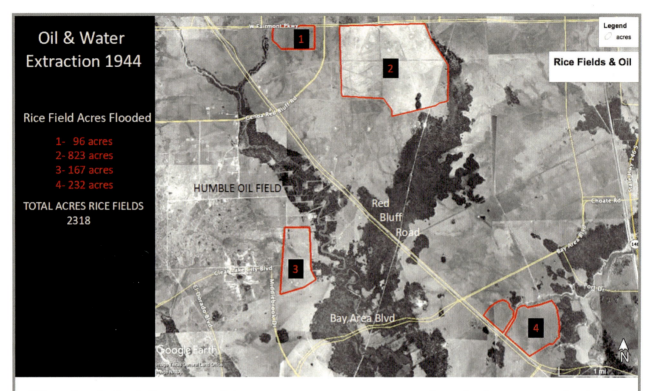

Oil & Water Extraction 1944

Rice Field Acres Flooded

1- 96 acres
2- 823 acres
3- 167 acres
4- 232 acres

TOTAL ACRES RICE FIELDS
2318

When Google Earth first appeared, it was an eye-opening experience. Going back in time on the Google Earth clock tool showed an aerial view of the pond area in 1944. Clearly visible were the curved contour lines of rice field levees. It was stunning to consider how much water must have been drawn to flood over 2,000 acres. Can you imagine flooding the whole of Armand Bayou Nature Center (ABNC) with a foot of water for several decades? The water withdrawal coupled with the massive extraction of oil along Armand Bayou account for nine feet of subsidence.

My dad called the shrikes butcher birds. Shrikes are best described as birds of prey that are without talons. They often catch prey (lizards, grasshoppers, small mice) and impale them on thorns or barbed-wire (butcher bird). The spines are used to kill prey in lieu of other raptors' talons. I even once saw a shrike flying with an English Sparrow in its mouth.

I also have a vivid memory of shooting at a Bob-white Quail near the corner of Red Bluff Road and San Augustine. If you stand at that corner now it seems impossible that there was once prairie habitat capable of supporting Bobwhite Quail.

My father first took me fishing on a pond in Pasadena, located where Fairmont Parkway and Underwood Road now lie. The pond was created by a huge water pump powered by a diesel engine built to flood the surrounding rice fields of the area. I brought my first tackle box with me. It came pre-stocked with lures. My mother had saved S&H Green Stamps from the grocery store to purchase it. It was a prized possession. I still have a lure from it, kept in my grandfather's homemade tackle box.

As years passed, I would ride my bike back to that pond. Before I was old enough to drive, I would make the long ride with all of my tackle lashed onto the bike frame. It was a long ride and I would stop at my friend Ray Morris's house, which was about halfway to the pond. Ray and I met in the sixth grade in Mrs. Broughton's English class. Ray and I looked very similar with dark hair and dark complexions. Mrs. Broughton started the semester by making certain that each of us had written our names in our textbook. She would start each class by walking the aisles and looking at the books on our desk. It helped her to learn students' names in the process. Ray and I had met because our desks were immediately across from each other. This made it easy for us to pass things across the aisle. It made it easy for us to pass things like our English textbook across the aisle. Every day during those first weeks of school we would trade our textbook, confusing Mrs. Broughton as to whether I was Mark or whether I was Ray. She eventually caught on to the game and we were marked men. But it was the beginning of our understanding that we could get away with more if we worked together. I have wondered how different my early years would have been if we hadn't been seated across from each other.

It is amazing now to think of all of the open space from my childhood. It's also amazing to think how far afield my bicycle took me. In the seventh grade my sister bought me a ten-speed cruiser. The bike changed my ability to range. Primarily it gave me access to three ponds within biking distance. The pond most frequented was located off of Beltway 8. Just south of where a present-day Target Store is located was a pond that had been dug as a cattle watering hole. It was only a half-acre in size but a prime summer destination for a 12-year-old. It was a fishing/swimming hole where we spent the first hour fishing, the second hour swimming and third hour pulling the mud out of our hair. There were occasional sightings of Wood Ducks and cottonmouths. Sometimes the cowboys would hang the carcasses of dead coyotes on the barbed wire fences. This was also one of the last strongholds of the red wolf. They are now extinct in the wild. In hindsight, I wonder if some of those carcasses might have been wolves. When I grew older and got a

driver's license my range expanded even further.

My connection to the natural world bloomed through monofilament fishing line attached to a topwater lure. I bought my first johnboat in middle school with money I'd earned from mowing neighbors' lawns. The Pineywoods of East Texas called out to the teenager who only wanted to be further in. Further into the woods. Further into the wilderness. Further into a system that was not a thought produced by the human mind. I saw the city, the culture, the system as something that had all been run through and processed by the mind of man. Surely there was a way to connect directly with the source. The mystical experience bypasses the need for religion. Ray and I were after determining how we might have that direct connection and were driven to find it in the wilderness of "the woods."

In eighth grade Ray and I had each attended a course on meditation. Transcendental meditation was being offered around the country in metropolitan areas. It was hip and cool to learn to meditate in that day. Even the Beatles were doing it. It's a simple technique that's been used for thousands of years to relax, promote clarity of thought, insight and personal growth. I remember my dad dropping me off at a motel for the half day course. It took me by surprise how much I was drawn to the practice. Twice every day no matter where I was, I found a way to carve out the half hour. During our high school years, we would meditate in the boat during fishing sessions. Meditation was a quiet practice of watching a single point of focus. Watch your breath rising, watch your breath falling. Thoughts will arise. Return to your mantra. Breath rising – breath falling. Only later did we recognize that our repetition of casting a lure and retrieving it was our own meditative practice. It was a practice that Ray and I shared for decades.

The Dolen Gravel Pits were a
favorite school weekend escape.

It was also the era of the Vietnam draft. Being forced to go to war was hard to grasp in the mind of a 16-year-old. Going to war in Asia for a cause I didn't understand. I remember seeing Joe Miller in uniform on Prairie Street the day he deployed. I remember thinking, is that going to be me? Somehow it seemed that if we could get far enough out into the wilderness, maybe we wouldn't have to come back. That became our goal. How far out could we go and how long could we stay?

We found places close to home to satisfy our need to be outdoors in high school. There were ponds and places to fish and dove hunt. I think back on the location near the corner where Genoa-Red Bluff Road and Beltway 8 is now. It was once our favorite place to dove hunt. Dove hunting was a short-lived affair. I consider myself a reformed bird hunter now. There was something about watching a bird fall from the sky and then walking over to break its neck that sucked all of the joy out of the experience. It is truly mind-blowing now to consider that the area was coastal prairie as far as the eye could see in every direction and that you could fire a shotgun with no concerns.

We soon discovered all of the access roads that ran into the lands surrounding Armand Bayou.

They all had locked gates, but we found an easy solution to entering. Ray's dad owned a pair of three-foot bolt cutters. We cut the chain on a number of gates and added our lock on to the series of other locks. We spent many a night around a campfire at various places along the bayou, plotting our escape to the woods.

The Water

Being around the water wasn't enough. I realized early that on and in the water was where I was meant to be. Mowing lawns in middle school allowed me to buy my first boat. A ten-foot johnboat was ordered from the Sears and Roebuck Catalogue. The boat was floated all around the lakes at Dayton Lakes Estates. Spending all day away from everyone allowed me to look around. It motivated a lifelong pursuit of boat ownership that includes two additional

Paddling the mangrove maze in Key Largo

johnboats, a Boston Whaler, a pontoon boat, a cedar strip canoe, an aluminum canoe, two fiberglass canoes, a solo fiberglass canoe and two kayaks.

Over the years, I've paddled in the Florida Keys; the Everglades; the Crystal River; Mobile Bay; the Pearl River; the Tchefuncte River; Lake Maurepas,

Grande Isle; The Amite River; Lake Sam Rayburn; Lake Steinhagen; Lake Conroe; the Angelina River; the Trinity River; the Brazos River; Village Creek; Lake Livingston; the Dolen Gravel Pits; Matagorda Island; Christmas Bay; Trinity Bay; Laguna Madre, and South Bay. And then there is Armand Bayou.

I first paddled Armand Bayou in high school with Ray. We were beginner bass fishermen. It was mostly a place to be away from our parents and everyone else. It was impossible for me to know what a lifelong influence the bayou would have on me. Love and intimacy have their own maturation process. At first Armand Bayou seemed like a girl that I barely noticed. Over the years as your depth of knowledge grows you see more. The more you know, the more you see. The more you see, the greater your depth of understanding. Today the most dangerous world view is from those who have never viewed the world. Intimacy cultivates love and a depth of understanding. We are all at our own different depth in the way we experience the world and each other. We all have our own depth of experience.

you're a hunter, birder, photographer, artist or fisherman, you've learned these things and have a built-in self-discipline to set your alarm for 5 a.m. You also know that the two hours after first light are when fish feed most and the biggest bite occurs.

For most of my adult life, sliding my kayak into the bayou at dawn has been one of my greatest pleasures. Early in the day you can see a multitude of fish-eating birds. The heron, egret, kingfisher, osprey and eagle watch me fish as I watch them fish. Raccoons work the marsh edge for blue crabs at low tide. River otters might be heard crunching the shell of a freshly caught crab like a hungry ten-year old child with a bag of potato chips. If your pace slows and you enter into the rhythm of the life along the water's edge, you find that life will welcome you in.

Dawn on Armand Bayou. Photo by Gary Seloff

The morning sun, a bent rod and a beautiful setting are a great start to a memorable day. Photo by Mark Kramer

For the last 35 years, I've tried to be on the bayou at least once a week. There is magic in being on the water before first light. The wind is light, the water is at its most calm, the temperature is cool, the water is at its clearest and wildlife is at its peak of activity. If

River otter on Horsepen Bayou. Photo by Gary Seloff

The Wind And The Water

By Mark Kramer

My love is the wind on the face of the water
The gentlest touch at dawn sends ripples
dancing to the other shore
Sparkling diamonds shine in an entranced
gaze of deep desire
My love is the wind on the face of the water
The song of her breath again and again
Until finally in a moment of stillness I see my
own reflection on her face

My love is the wind on the face of the water
The mystery of this unseen hand
Which guides the splashing of this impas-
sioned heart
Is as real as yesterday's dream of her breath
on my face

My love is the wind on the face of the water

After paddling widely across the Gulf coast, I found a greater concentration of wildlife on Armand Bayou than I have encountered anywhere else. The magnitude of the human footprint on the landscape in Harris County is profound. Finding any parcel not transformed into a home, road, business or industry is almost impossible. If you think that thought can't shape reality, come to Houston. It's the perfect example of how every viewscape originated as an idea in someone's mind. Shaped into a house or parking lot or drainage ditch. Entering into the wilds of Pasadena at Armand Bayou you feel the effects of both the human-built landscape and the landscape shaped by natural forces: those same forces that shape the lawful unfolding of the universe, this urban wilderness, and my declining body. Here, wildlife has been squozen into a single remaining parcel. The crucible of these remaining ecosystems concentrates life in a fashion I've seldom seen elsewhere.

I began fishing in earnest with my father on the Texas City Dike in the 1960s. We drove Red Bluff Road, which had recently been transformed from a shell surface to concrete. Beginning in the early 20th century, oyster and clam shells were harvested from Galveston Bay. A major commercial enterprise grew from dredging living oyster reefs in Galveston Bay. The three-mile-long road to my home at Armand Bayou Nature Center was also originally covered with shell.

Our fishing outings were on early Saturday mornings. We'd merge onto Highway 146 and head south over the Clear Creek Channel in Kemah. There was a draw bridge that would occasionally raise to allow boat traffic to pass through, remaining open for 10 to 20 minutes as the tension built to get our hooks in the water. We would stop at Curl's Bait Shop to buy our pound of bait shrimp, which lasted the day, but it was also a highlight to look at all of the other species of bait for sale.

**A day of family fishing from
the Texas City Dike in 1968**

For several decades, Galveston Bay was burdened with a heavy population of commercial shrimp boats. Some shrimpers caught table shrimp, others bait shrimp. The trawling activity also wreaked ecological havoc on the bay ecosystem. Trawlers have a short list of target species that are collected for sale. Everything else is returned to the bay, dead or alive. This *bycatch* was one of the major impacts from shrimping in the bay that was damaging to desirable juvenile fish populations as well as the ecosystem as a whole.

Once arriving at the fishing hole, I would bait up my Zebco 404, cast my line and wait for a bite. We were generally fishing for golden croaker. These small panfish are members of the drum family. On a good day we would catch a handful which would be enough for dinner. Croaker are one of the species that suffered population decline as a major

component of bycatch from shrimpers. In those days many people would look forward to the fall run of golden croaker when the fish were more readily caught during their seasonal migration. Those days are now mostly gone.

**A fine catch of golden croakers
from the Texas City Dike in 1969**

Local historians write that there was once a continuous oyster reef stretching from Eagle Point across the Bay to Smith Point. During extreme low tides of winter, cattlemen would drive cattle across the reef. These oysters were the critical filtration system of Galveston Bay. Oysters syphon water through their body and filter out the microorganisms that are their food. Each adult oyster filters approximately fifty gallons of bay water daily. Some ecologists theorize that much of Galveston Bay's waters may have passed through this filtration process every day. It's hard to comprehend now. Massive commercial operations were dredging living oyster reefs. It's the local equivalent to coral reefs being dredged and used as road base material. After fifty years of this ecological devastation, public outcry forced the practice to be banned in the 1970s.

My first redfish – 1969

My last redfish – June 4, 2020

The Redfish

One trip stands out as memorable when I hooked something new. Strong and fast, I knew this was different. When I got the fish onshore, I knew that I had caught my first redfish. Redfish are easy to identify by the single spot near the tail. My Cajun relatives tell the story of Jesus feeding redfish to the masses during the miracle of loaves and fishes. It is said that the redfish will forever bear the mark of where Jesus held the fish by its tail to bless the meal.

This redfish was a rare catch in Galveston Bay in the 1960s. Commercial fishermen using gillnets and long-line methods had significant impacts to finfishes, including speckled trout and redfish. To complicate the plight of the redfish further, a culinary craze was born from Cajun cuisine in the form of blackened redfish. The demand from restaurants and fish houses for redfish skyrocketed. Fortunately, these practices were banned by state regulators in 1981.

Redfish reach maturity after four years at approximately 30 inches and spend the adult portion of their life in the open Gulf of Mexico. The rough water created by the strong winds of September's peak tropical storm season and the first cool fronts call the fish to congregate near the major passes that enter the bay. Redfish like the water rough for spawning. From that point redfish larvae start their long journey, riding the tides. For several months the young are carried through the passes, into the bay and ultimately into the surrounding bayous and marshes where they spend the juvenile stage of life.

As a fisherman matures, the fishing experience unfolds. Many fishermen seek to catch fish on lures or flies instead of bait. I began lure fishing for redfish in Armand Bayou from a solo canoe when I moved onto the property in 1985. My favorite spot to fish was where the bayou met the East Bank Prairie of the nature center. There were a number of dead standing trees, which small crabs would cling to.

Redfish have "crushers" in the throat that enable the consuming of crabs. This three-inch blue crab was caught and crushed by a large redfish.

Small blue crabs are one of the redfish's favorite foods. Redfish have a special adaption to enable such an armored spiny item to be on the menu. Located in the throat are a set of crushers that pull the crab in and crack the shell. These *pharyngeal teeth* enable the fish to swallow a meal that would otherwise be impossible. In 1995 my favorite fishing spot became one of the largest tidal marsh creation projects on Armand Bayou. Sadly, I lost my spot but gained a beautiful marsh.

Much of Armand Bayou is shallow, lined with tidal marsh. The daily tide change averages about two feet between high and low tide. The high tide mark goes into the marsh grasses, flooding the vegetation. At low tide the water falls leaving the marsh dry. There are also areas that are unvegetated in this same tide zone. These tidal flats are important habitat for aquatic life. When flooded at high tide, tidal flats are only a two to three feet deep. This shallow depth allows sunlight to penetrate to the bayou bottom. Sunlight in this photic zone allows the luxurious growth of algae on the substrate. This algae attracts a diversity of small fish and crustaceans that feed on it. Particularly when the tide is flowing across tidal flats and abundant with small mullet, shrimp and crabs, the redfish hear the dinner bell ring.

Hooking a redfish in shallow water is a lot like being in love. You may be startled by the power. The power of the fish and the power of the experience. After catching all variety of fish on the Texas coast, most fishermen come to understand that the speed, power and fighting spirit of the redfish is unmatched. The power of the fish on light tackle may leave you feeling that you are no longer in control. They may make blistering runs stripping line from your reel and pulling the small boat through the water. If the fish are not running directly away from you, they can cover 40 yards left to right across the shallow flats in a few seconds, leaving a visible wake in the water and your jaw dropped wide. Redfish have shoulders and great stamina. I have released

many fish as I've been humbled by their spirit, never giving up the fight all the way to the boat. The excitement of this experience has been the primary force that keeps me on the water, keeps me connected to the bayou.

The Woods

In 1979, Ray Morris and I had enough of the path we were walking. I can remember the conversation starting slowly, as if we were each testing the water to explore just how serious the other was. Walking away from our current endeavors wasn't logical and we knew this would draw criticism from most who knew and loved us. After months of discussion, we were ready to move into the wilderness.

No single event in my life has shaped me in the way that living in the Big Thicket did. Ray and I wanted to get out. Out of the life that we were living. Maybe it was the post effects of wondering how to deal with the Vietnam War and the draft, for which registering ended the year before we were eligible, and which we'd narrowly escaped. Or maybe it was just that time of life transition from adolescence to adulthood that's always hard.

We felt that if we could get far enough out, we might not ever need to return. Ray's dad had exposed him to woods in the Sam Houston National Forest of East Texas. There was an area that at the turn of the century had been used to log the Longleaf Pine forest of the day. Lecher's Pond was a water stop for the steam-driven trains that were used to carry the timber off to the mills. The pond was about an acre in size and located deep in the piney woods. Most of the logging roads were in poor shape and filled with deep, wet holes, which made access a real challenge. We'd get stuck in the mud in the van and frequently spent several hours digging and hand-winching our way in or out. We spent our first adventure there when I was out of school for a four-week Christmas vacation in 1978. Ray was working as an insulator at Lubrizol with his dad, and I was studying the musculature of a formaldehyde-soaked cat on the floor of my garage for

Comparative Vertebrate Anatomy class at San Jacinto College.

That first campout during Christmas break was spent in Ray's van. It was an old Southwestern Bell van that been sold at the end of its service days. Ray and his dad had rebuilt the engine and it provided a good sleeping space for us. We spent three cold, rainy days and nights with temperatures that reached as low as 12 degrees. There was a nylon hiker's tarp pitched over the side door and a small table where we put small belongings and shotgun shells. As the cold rain continued, we decided to move the table and build a campfire under the tarp to stay warm. That night a hunter was hiking past just as the rain began to increase. He joined us under the tarp to warm up by the fire. Shortly after he sat down, we heard a sound similar to a bottle-rocket as ashes flew out of the fire. A minute or two later, another explosion. We soon realized that several shotgun shells had fallen off of the camp table onto the ground where we had built the campfire. When the fire heated the shells, they discharged, flying past us where we sat. The hunter determined that he'd prefer to hike out in the rain.

It was during that Christmas break campout that we began to seriously discuss moving to the woods for keeps. Dissatisfied with the present and prospects for the future, we discussed making a break. At the end of my final semester at San Jac, I went to work for the summer as a pool manager for the City of Houston at Beverly Hills Swimming Pool. We planned our escape through the summer and intended to head to the woods when the pool season ended in October.

We wanted to be mystics, to live as simply as possible with few of the trappings of the man-made world. We were religious converts in a congregation of two listening to the voice of God in its purest form as it sang through the canopy of pines. I brought every book that I could find by Thoreau and Ram Dass. We brought no tables, watches, chairs, mirrors or anything made of plastic. We had a small tent for rainy nights but otherwise slept directly on the ground under mosquito netting. There were nights when giant water bugs would land on the netting. These insects are large, fierce, flying predators. They spend most of the day underwater where they catch and eat small fish. They use an enzyme to liquefy their catches' innards and ingest the slurry. Their bite to a human can be very problematic. We had no refrigeration and cooked over an open fire for every meal. We hunted ducks with very little success, only shooting a few Mallards and Wood Ducks. Our encampment was located just west of Peach Creek on Lake Conroe. The creek was narrow, winding, and lined with pines and magnolias – like a river with a secret source. We'd take turns paddling each other in a cedar-strip wooden canoe in hopes that we might creep up on a Wood Duck for dinner.

We also hunted ducks on Lake Conroe. The national forest land that we were "squatting" in had many miles of remnant logging roads. The roads had been created in previous years when the area had been logged. We brought our bicycles (the same ones we'd used on our first pond fishing adventures) to get around when we wanted to cover some distance. One of the best duck hunting spots on Lake Conroe was several miles from the campsite. We would wake in the frosty mornings, an hour before dawn to allow time to get to the site and set out the decoys.

The only alarm clock that we had was set to 12 o'clock for sunrise. We agreed that we didn't want to "live by the clock" in the woods, but needed some means to help us track the time. The day was often started with a bong hit. It was a real experience just out of bed, an hour before first light.

We had made gun straps for our shotguns, which allowed us to carry the guns on our backs while we rode. One morning, about half-way to the hunting site, I hit a hole in the road and my shotgun fired while it was on my back. After that we began to ask ourselves if waking up in the pre-dawn hours was worth it, or maybe the bong was too early in the day. Either way, the next week we went back and shot our decoys. They're probably still on the bottom of Lake Conroe.

If we were lucky and shot a Wood Duck, the next four to five hours were spent cleaning the bird, building a fire and slowly baking the bird in a cast-iron Dutch oven. I remember what felt like a terrible dilemma: shooting and killing one of the most beautiful birds in North America to make an evening meal. There's a real art form to baking a duck for three hours in a Dutch oven. First an oak fire is built to produce the needed amount of coals. Then the coals are placed above and below the cooking pot in an effort to hold the temperature around 350 degrees. Constant monitoring, adjusting and patience are required. I could count on one hand all of the ducks that were shot during our six months in the wilderness.

Letcher's Pond 1979

Mostly we fished in the Letcher's Pond and Lake Conroe. That's what we were good at. Lake Conroe was a different place in 1979. The lake was newly formed and we seldom saw other fishermen or boats on the water. The cove leading into Peach Creek was filled with dead standing timber, which further served to prohibit any boats from navigating into our realm. It was very risky for a power boat to enter for fear of running hard aground on dead stumps just below the water's surface. We ate bass most every night cooked over an open fire. We'd fashion a cooking surface out of aluminum foil and sauté the fillets

in butter or a squeeze bottle of Parkay margarine. It was a meal that we never tired of.

We frequently smoked a joint before our fishing outings. We'd joke that "those fish will have nothing to worry about" as we'd imbibe before casting off. One afternoon after imbibing (maybe over-imbibing), Ray felt the need to lie down in the bottom of the canoe just as we were starting to catch fish. I was catching fish and in the process of swinging a bass into the boat, it came unhooked and fell into the bottom of the canoe and began to flap and thrash on top of Ray's sleeping face. He didn't wake up and I didn't stop fishing.

When we moved to the woods, we continued our meditation practice that we had learned in the eighth grade. I can remember several times when we stopped fishing to make time to meditate in the boat. I remember after one session in the johnboat, we returned to bass fishing. Bass fishing is an endeavor of repetitively casting a lure and retrieving it to lure a fish to strike. This is when, after a few meditation sessions in the boat, we realized that the act of fishing was another point of the meditative practice. "Cast and retrieve, cast and retrieve" was the mantra. There was an old-growth southern red cedar tree that had been left behind during the initial clear-cut logging of the Longleaf Pines where Ray and I would meditate. It was a huge tree with a twin trunk attached to a single trunk just above the ground that was maybe 200 years old. As people often thought that Ray and I were brothers, the symbolism of the meditations under that twin trunk leading down into the roots of the earth weren't lost on us. We were brothers branching from the same tree. In those quiet moments of solitude, we would sit together as one, many miles from the nearest road or person. We both climbed into that tree and cut walking sticks from its limbs. Yesterday, I went for a walk with Ray with his stick in my hand.

We spent our expedition in the woods in the coldest part of the winter. Several nights there were low temperatures in the teens. We had good sleeping bags and lots of time around the campfire. One night there was a mist as the temperature was falling. The canopy of the pine forest was glazed like a popsicle. As the wind began to increase the next morning, the limbs began to snap. When the sun rose, a shower of ice particles and small limbs began to rain around us.

We had purchased and refurbished a cedar-strip canoe for the trip. It was a fine beast of a boat. We used a grinder to remove old fiberglass from the outer shell. I can still remember itching for days. After we repaired the rotten wood, we replaced the fiberglass outer covering, which made the boat a heavy beast to paddle or carry. There was an artesian well located up the lake several miles. There was a "stand pipe" where spring water flowed out freely from its own pressure. We had an adventure every time we made the journey to fill our containers.

We moved to the woods to create a space to be free. A place where the noise, pace and pollution of the city would not be reflected in us. We moved to the woods to live at our own pace. We wanted to be one with the Earth. We moved to the woods because we wanted to see just how little we could get by on and prove our skills as outdoorsmen. We moved to the woods because we wanted to be mystic hermits who pushed away the trappings of the manmade world. We moved to the woods to be together. There has never been another person who I loved in that unique way. Since we met in middle school, it was as if we were identical twins. People would confuse us as blood brothers throughout our lives.

But as the months passed the isolation of being alone with one other person began to take its toll. We recognized that it was time to get out. While there were many lessons from the experience, I came away with the realization that no matter where you go, you can't escape yourself. In fact, much of the drive to go to the woods may have been to avoid dealing with issues that I wasn't prepared to look at directly. Living in the wilderness takes time and a lot of effort. While all of those outdoor tasks were interesting, they were also a diversion. Maybe, if you don't look directly at it, it might go away.

Back to Prairie Street

Returning from the woods was jolt. I had moved back with my parents on Prairie Street and felt like the adventure was over. Not sure where the next adventure would lead, I continued to explore around Armand Bayou. Things had changed with the opening of ABNC. Now there were new fences and a newly constructed facility. One day in 1979, I walked through the nature center building and heard music playing from behind a door. I thought to myself that this might be a nice place for the next phase of the adventure. I knocked on the door and naturalist George Regmund answered with a guitar in his hand. Indeed, it hit me, this might be a nice place to work.

A previous incarnation at ABNC circa 1980

I worked at ABNC for a year and was hired under grant funds from the federal jobs program, Comprehensive Employment Training Act (CETA). I was largely responsible for trail maintenance of the newly constructed Martyn Trail. While employed, I was given permission to raise and live in a tipi that I had purchased, in a location off of the Martyn Road. The Martyn Road present day runs from the Interpretive Building to the Boathouse and is part of the Karankawa Trail. In 1979 the Martyn Road was not part of any Trail system and was unsurfaced. I spent three months of winter/spring with my pregnant wife, Rachel, in the tipi. I fondly remember many a night lying on the floor with a campfire in the center of that tipi.

The King of Kramerville

There were several leftover pine poles that weren't needed for the tipi. I built a bentwood bench that graced the back porch of the Interpretive Building for nearly four decades. I sat on the bench today, 40 years after construction, as the King of Kramerville.

The beast is loaded and ready for cross country

After that first year at ABNC, Ray, Rachel and I loaded our cedar-strip canoe and tipi poles on top of a truck and headed off for an adventure into the unknown interior of the cosmos. Starting in the direction of upstate New York to meet with Rachel's friend Jenny. The truck burned a quart of oil for every tank of gas and we had 900 dollars in our pockets. At the time it seemed like a well-thought-out and fully-funded experiment. We arrived at the outskirts of Ithaca and pitched the tipi on the edge of Richard Bronca's pond. Ray and I caught fish every night and we hung our hammocks from the hemlock trees surrounding the pond. We toured the surrounding elite hippie communes and stayed a few nights at the "Yea God Community." It had recently been converted from a Buddhist Meditation Center into a tongue-in-cheek nod to the Almighty. After a month of hanging out, Ray parted ways with us. He hitchhiked from New York to Nova Scotia and from there to Guatemala. Rachel and I departed New York en route to New Mexico. Our destination was the Lama Foundation, which was a community founded by Ram Dass. Ram Dass was a spiritual teacher who created Lama to bring teachers from different paths together for spiritual retreat and meditation. It took less than a month for me to realize that I had a pregnant wife and only 400 dollars in my pocket.

Bay Area Park Team circa 1983

We moved back to Pasadena where I went to work for the Harris County Parks Department in 1981 as a horticulturist. I was hired to create wildflower beds in all of the parks for Precinct 1. Another part of the job was leading eco-tours on Armand Bayou aboard the Hana G electric pontoon boat. The county operated two boats. One boat gave tours and the other was on charge. This enabled the tour operation to deliver five free trips each day. The schedule was grueling but the experience definitely sharpened my public speaking skills and deepened my desire to be an interpretive naturalist.

Back to the land—day 1—June 20, 1985

In 1985 I pulled a 36-foot travel trailer on to the West Bank of ABNC. My son Aaron was three years old and he moved with me after Rachel and I divorced. It began the next chapter of the adventure. I had always wanted to homestead. I had gotten brochures from Alaska for a land grant program in the 1970s giving land to those who wanted to homestead. Alaska was too cold for me and too big a leap in general. I had never considered the option of homesteading in my hometown. It was very much like homesteading in that I had to clear the land and travel 3.5 miles of poorly kept shell-covered road/trail to get home. It was before the internet. There was also no telephone connection. There were times when I would get stuck in the mud while traveling the road home. I lived in the small trailer for 23 years before moving in a larger trailer in 2008.

There's a fine line between a rut and a groove.

The ruts in the road to the ABNC homestead held water most of the time and were so deep that I could drive much of the way without ever touching the steering wheel – like a carnival ride on tracks. This constant mud bath had consequences for the truck and I became an expert at doing brake jobs. It was common to need new brake pads two to three times each year.

A Dweller On Two Planets

It was an isolated life in the midst of the city. I like to say it's the best of both worlds. The wilderness homestead and the metropolitan life. I lived the first eight years on the property without a phone. I couldn't understand why this misunderstood hillbilly lifestyle was so criticized at the time. The area was so remote and the surrounding area was so little developed that there were frequent encounters with poachers. In the early days there was often gunfire. I would load the shotgun and hunt poachers. Not so much that I was hunting to shoot or kill them, but I was in a remote setting with no phone, no contact with the outside for law enforcement support. As I walked the woods, if I made contact with a poacher, I at least wanted to be able to look at him eye to eye – on even terms. With my shotgun in hand I at least expected to be taken seriously. And that almost happened several times when I saw poachers at a distance, always running away from me. I have to assume the shotgun promoted that running behavior.

I had been hired in Bay Area Park under Precinct 1 Commissioner Tom Bass, who was one of the early supporters of the effort to preserve Armand Bayou. After several years working there, the precinct lines were redrawn as result of the 10-year census. The new precinct lines moved the county parks located around the bay out of Precinct 1. The new delineation placed Bay Area Park and Clear Lake Park in Precinct 2 and under a different leader.

The new commissioner was an outdated, old-school, knuckleheaded fartknocker who saw no value in nature. He quickly abandoned the wildflower program and then sold the pontoon tour boats. One Friday afternoon I was told to have my hair cut before returning to work on Monday morning or not to expect to continue working for Harris County. After a long weekend in the hill country with friends I discovered my new hairdo. I returned to work with a Mandinka Warrior Braid similar to what Stevie Wonder wore at the time, complete with big, blue ceramic beads at the end of each braid. The Parks Supervisor was so shocked at my return with braids that it took several weeks to finally react. Shortly after I separated from the County the tour boats were sold.

I've lately been reflecting on how these twists of fate are defining moments that shape the story of our life. You never know what is around the next bend in the river that may be an unexpected change of course.

Ya Never Know

For several summers during my early teen years, we traveled to Louisiana to visit my Uncle Bubbie who lived in Ponchatoula, not far from Lake Ponchatrain. My parents would drop me off for the day in my johnboat to fish and explore the Manchac Swamp and every evening after dinner we would sit in my uncle's living room where he told jokes and stories. He was filled with the rich culture of south Louisiana and was a colorful storyteller. The family history runs back as far as the Civil War. His life spent growing up along the rivers and swamps were like music to my ears. His thick Cajun accent complimented the lyrical quality of his story telling. He told stories of hunting alligators so big that he had to return home for a second mule to drag them back. He told a story of a friend's pig that was trained to shuck oysters. One story seems particularly poignant as I reflect this week.

One day Uncle Bubbie's great grandfather Samuel was outside working on his farm when his only horse escaped and ran off into the woods. Later, as he talked to a neighbor about the loss, the neighbor sympathetically replied, "Oh that's terrible," to which Grandfather Samuel replied, "Ya never know."

Dedication of Lake Mark Kramer
in Clear Lake Park.

The next day the horse returned with six wild horses that followed it into the stable. Later, while talking to the neighbor, he said, "Oh that's wonderful," to which Grandfather Samuel replied, "Ya never know."

The next day Grandfather Samuel's only son was in the stable taming the wild horses when he fell and broke his leg. Later when talking to his neighbor who replied, "Oh that's terrible," Grandfather Samuel answered, "Ya never know."

The next day Confederate soldiers passed through the farm looking for conscripts to fight in the Civil War, but the son had a broken leg and couldn't fight. Later, talking to the neighbor who said, "Oh that's so fortunate', Grandfather Samuel replied...... "Ya never know."

It's said that life is best lived in fast forward and best understood in the rearview mirror. Today I've been reflecting. Today I attended a dedication ceremony to rename the southern portion of Armand Bayou. As of today, Armand Bayou now flows into Lake Mark Kramer. What an honor bestowed on me by Pasadena Mayor Jeff Wagner and Harris County Commissioner Adrian Garcia. The Commissioner even placed a beautiful commemorative sign honoring my work, located in the county park along the water's edge. The sign is placed in the same park that I was fired from 30 years earlier. If Uncle Bubbie were here, he would say.... "Ya Never Know."

Last of the good old days

The Passing of Ray

Ray had a passion for traveling to exotic international locations. That was something that we did not share. Central America was one of those places. Civil war and violence were on the news nightly. I was concerned with each new venture that he took. I got home from work one afternoon and found a note on my door from Ray's dad. It read, "Mark-Ray has been badly hurt in Guatemala." I had no home phone in that period (before cell phones) and drove directly to his parents' house. Ray's dad said that Ray had been in a bad accident while surfing and had broken his neck. His girlfriend had called, saying that Ray was asking for me to come. I booked a flight for the next day, but he passed away during the night.

It was a grief like I had never experienced. I guess that I had taken for granted we would share our deepest passions for the natural world together for the rest of our lives. It took months for me accept the loss. A poem from my sister captures the moment.

Mark & Ray

By Emily Moore

Now I know nobody told you
On that long, long ago day
That his friendship would unfold you
When you met him, "This is Ray"

And you learned a lot about him
Through your long and youthful play
That you never had to doubt him
Found him "true blue" Good ol' Ray

So the decades rocked right by you
And you both grew along the way

Sometimes separate, sometimes together
Seems like it was always "Mark & Ray"

But our time on earth is borrowed
Far too soon he was called away
To share his laughs with the angels
Leaving you oh so sorrowed... "I miss you Ray"

Cherish memories, deep inside you
Feel the sunshine, taste the ocean's salty spray
And you'll find him right beside you
And just think... "Well, that was Ray"

Jumping forward in Time

I began my second incarnation at Armand Bayou Nature Center in 1995. There was one building and four fulltime employees. George Regmund and I started playing music along with a couple of other environmental professional friends, forming the Bayouphyliacs. We were a bluegrass/smooth jazz fusion boy band and we were the idol of American youth for three to five years. We played at fundraisers or other environmental gatherings.

How fortunate I have been to experience it all from the beginning.

Remaining members of the Bayouphyliacs at
Fall Festival 2010 – Mark, Woody & George

Fledgling Least Bittern. Photo by Gary Seloff

Chapter Two: *History*

If Not for Hana: A Tribute to the Founders of Armand Bayou Nature Center

I have fond memories of Saturday mornings as a child in Pasadena during the 1960s. The Roadrunner, Bugs Bunny and Daffy Duck cartoons were regulars on shows that aired on local TV. In between cartoons, the KTRK TV station had personalities such as Cadette Don or Kitirik who hosted live programming. On occasion, in between all of these programs Armand Yramategui would appear. Armand would bring wildlife (turtles, rabbits, snakes, etc.) onto the program. He would show the animals and speak about the importance of wild places for animals to live. He also talked about the importance of open space for people to relax and connect with nature. As I reflect back on those years, I can't help but wonder what impact he may have had on the mind of a young Mark Kramer.

Armand Yramategui. from ABNC archives

Armand had earned a reputation as one who loved to share his passion for the natural world with children. He was a multi-dimensional, larger than life figure who had a wide range of knowledge and broad set of skills. He was the curator of Houston's Burke Baker Planetarium, a member of the Meteoritical Society, an electrical engineer by education and a self-trained naturalist. The 1960s were a time of great ecological awakening in America. Air and water quality were poor in the Houston area. Wetlands and wildlife habitat were generally not considered valuable. It seems hard to imagine that there was a time when the health of the environment was a minor issue on the minds of many. Armand Yramategui was the local environmental visionary leader who articulately championed many of these issues. His greatest effort focused on the preservation of open space and establishment of a parks system in the Houston area.

Passing like a comet. Photo from ABNC archives

Armand's passion for astronomy compelled him to drive to the edge of town for better viewing of the dark night sky. On the night of January 28, 1970, he loaded his telescopes and other optical equipment for the drive to view the Tago-Sato-Kosako comet. On his way out of town there was a flat tire. Passersby stopped to assist, but the helpers were actually thieves who spotted the valuable optical equipment in the backseat. Armand was robbed and murdered.

Photo from ABNC archives

Armand Yramategui was a local conservation figure who was also recognized as a national environmental leader. The following are quotes from the numerous letters assembled at his memorial:

"Through his appearances on radio and television, Armand imparted to each listener some of his own love and understanding of the finite and infinite parts of the world we share: The Big Thicket, the winter sky, a threatened estuary, an endangered live oak or the life cycle of a tiny spider. Through his eyes we were shown new wonders and the world was a little less wearisome. Through his heart we were made to feel the interdependent part of the throbbing life around us, and our lives were a little less lonely."

–J. Kent Hackleman, KTRH Radio

"It was a savage irony that Armand Yramategui should be shot to death on the concrete sprawl of a freeway while trying to get a glimpse of a comet. For while he chased the stars, Armand was more deeply concerned with man's unwitting desecration of his own planet and the resulting degradation of the human spirit. He worked in many quiet ways to improve his community, his world, and the life of his fellow man. He was a gentle but effective crusader. The very nature of his death was a brutal reminder that his work is still unfinished."

–Harold Scarlett, The Houston Post

"But Armand, day and night, accomplished enough for any one person in a full lifetime. His life was one of the factors in bringing mankind at last into the Age of the Environment."

–Edward C. Fritz, The Nature Conservancy

"Someone has suggested that a meaningful memorial be established in his name—perhaps a park, perhaps a stream, perhaps a quiet place somewhere. I would urge that such a memorial be established and I would love to have some small part in making it possible. Let me know what I can do."

–George H. W. Bush, House of Representatives

"At times a sentence or a paragraph will suddenly yield up a real insight into this man who was bigger than life while living. Everywhere I turn in the world of conservation, I find people who remember Armand. The thought slowly emerges, that this man, almost alone at first, ushered in the modern era of conservation in Texas."

–Rick Pratt, First Director of ABNC

The tragic loss of this beloved figure was a shock to the community and those who loved and knew him best. Hana Ginzbarg was one who had been a friend and colleague of Armand. His untimely passing at the age of 46 helped to produce the effort to memorialize his legacy. Armand had been a catalyst for the formation of many local groups, clubs and environmental actions, but one of his primary passions was advocating for open space. In fact, he was scheduled to speak the day after his murder in support for the establishment of a County Parks Department. Armand had campaigned for several large preservation efforts including The Big Thicket National Preserve, Padre Island National Seashore and the Texas Open Beaches Act. Of particular local preservation interest was the wild land along Middle Bayou (present day Armand Bayou). While Armand had only visited the area a few times, he made mention of the beauty of the area to several people. Slowly the idea emerged that a park named to memorialize Armand would be a very worthy cause.

The 1960s were a time of growth and upheaval in America. In addition to the environmental movement, the women's movement was also awakening. Hana Ginzbarg was a formative figure in both. Hana was no stranger to taking on a challenge. Born in Prague in 1925, she left Czechoslovakia at the age of 13 on one of the last Kindertransports before Hitler's occupation.

Late night planning on Hana's living room floor.
Photo from ABNC archives

So began Hana's campaign to raise funds and public support for the purchase of a parkland in the memory of Armand Yramategui. Hana's motto was "Wouldn't it be wonderful." Wouldn't it be wonderful if the Houston area had one of the largest pieces of wildland located in the middle of the city. Wouldn't it be wonderful if the area was a preserve large enough to provide habitat for many types of wildlife like deer, red wolves, prairie chickens, coyotes and alligators. Wouldn't it be wonderful if the area was a place for people of all ages to relax, learn, recreate and reconnect with nature.

Hana Ginzbarg - The founding mother of Armand Bayou Nature Center. Photo from ABNC archives

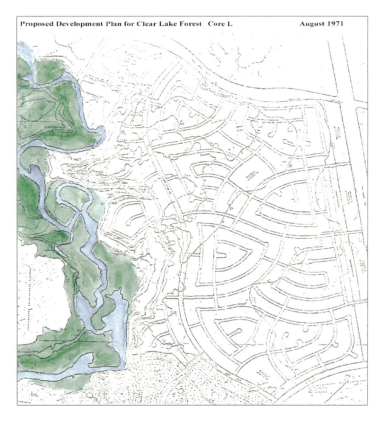

Armand Bayou
development plan map.
from ABNC archives

Hana drove the effort toward building a coalition of fundraising at the local, state and federal levels and was successful at all.

The sense of urgency grew as plans became public that suburbia was about to sprawl over what many considered to be the largest and most beautifully preserved piece of wild land remaining in Harris County: the Middle Bayou area.

Armand Bayou Day Celebrations were held at Bay Area Park for families to enjoy the bayou and raised local awareness. Photo from ABNC archives

Governor Preston Smith bears witness to community passion for preservation. Photo from ABNC archives

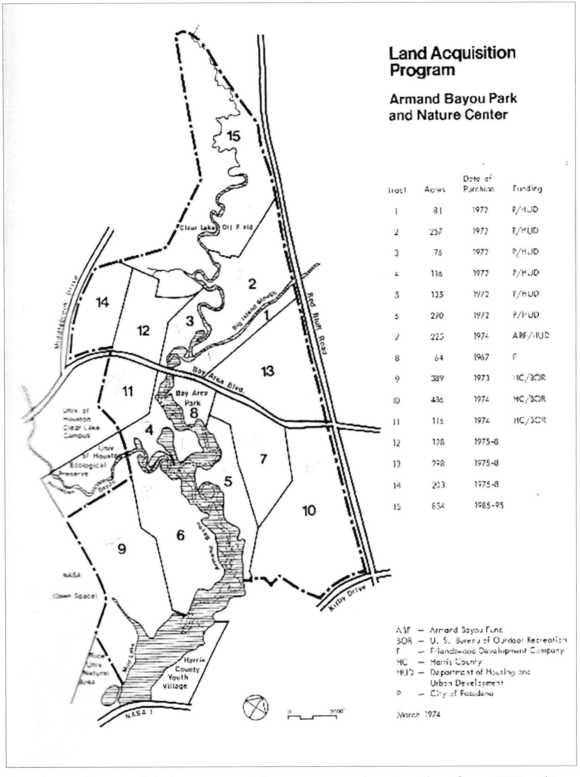

Land Acquisition Program

Armand Bayou Park and Nature Center

Tract	Acres	Date of Purchase	Funding
1	81	1972	P/HUD
2	257	1972	F/HUD
3	76	1972	P/HUD
4	116	1972	P/HUD
5	135	1972	F/HUD
6	270	1972	P/HUD
7	225	1974	ABF/HUD
8	64	1967	F
9	339	1973	HC/BOR
10	436	1974	HC/BOR
11	116	1974	HC/BOR
12	128	1975-8	
13	298	1975-8	
14	203	1975-8	
15	834	1985-95	

ABF — Armand Bayou Fund
BOR — U. S. Bureau of Outdoor Recreation
F — Friendswood Development Company
HC — Harris County
HUD — Department of Housing and Urban Development
P — City of Pasadena

March 1974

A herculean task, accomplished at warp speed due to a supreme champion. Photo from ABNC archives

We urgently need money to build absolutely nothing here.

Armand Bayou. A rare, untouched 3,000 acres we ask you to help us preserve. Because there can still be a wilderness, a place for nature — for peace and quiet — in the midst of one of the fastest growing metropolitan areas in our nation.

Armand Bayou is a living museum of our ecological past, now partially safe from bulldozers and civilization. The City of Pasadena, encouraged by conservation groups, is acquiring a part of the proposed park site with the help of matching funds from the Department of Housing and Urban Development. But Pasadena's 956 acres will not be enough to preserve the natural character of the bayou. More land is needed.

The next step in our 3,000-acre dream is to add an additional 450-acre tract as an interpretive nature study area and a native plant arboretum. Here in this living laboratory along the bayou, city-bred school children by the thousands will discover soft shell turtle, Louisiana heron, ringneck snake, devil's walking stick, and salt marsh morning glory. Here they will learn to love the natural world and understand from an early age the dependence of man on other living things.

Funds for the 450-acre arboretum will come from a one million grant from HUD

— *IF matching private funds can be raised by December 1972.*

Time is running out. Your help and financial support is desperately needed. Please send your tax exempt contribution today to Armand Bayou Fund.

Among the thousands who have endorsed the Armand Bayou project are the following: Congressman Bill Archer · Les Bennett · Bernard Bentch · Senator Lloyd Bentsen · State Senator Chet Brooks · Congressman Jack Brooks · Congressman Bob Casey · William W. Caudill Mr. and Mrs. John H. Cooper · Mr. and Mrs. J. Rorick Cravens · Miss Nina Cullinan · Mr. and Mrs. Tom Martin Davis Mr. and Mrs. L. N. Dexter · Mayor Clyde Doyal · Congressman Bob Eckhardt · County Judge Bill Elliot · Victor L. Emanuel Mr. and Mrs. A. V. Emmott · Mr. and Mrs. Albert B. Fay · Mr. and Mrs. Ernest B. Fay · The Most Rev. Patrick S. Flores · The Rev. William J. Fogleman · Dr. and Mrs. Robert R. Gilruth · Dr. and Mrs. Arthur S. Ginzbarg · Leroy Gloger · Mr. and Mrs. J. Kent Hackleman Andy L. Helms · Mr. and Mrs. J. W. Hershey · Mrs. Oveta Culp Hobby · Mr. and Mrs. William P. Hobby · Dr. and Mrs. Phillip G. Hoffman · Miss Ima Hogg · County Judge C. Ray Holbrook · Mr. and Mrs. Charles G. Hooks, Jr. · Don Horn · Mr. and Mrs. Palmer Hutcheson, Jr. · Mrs. Ruth Jobes · Mr. and Mrs. John T. Jones, Jr. · State Senator Barbara Jordan · Rabbi Robert I. Kahn · Mr. and Mrs. Harris L. Kempner · Mr. and Mrs. David H. Knapp · Mr. and Mrs. Robert C. Lanier · The Rev. Bill Lawson · Mr. and Mrs. S. M. McAshan Dr. and Mrs. Dan G. McNamara · Lawrence E. Marcus · S. R. (Buddy) Jones · Mr. and Mrs. George P. Mitchell · Mr. and Mrs. Harvin C. Moore · The Most Rev. John L. Morkovsky · Mr. and Mrs. Immanuel Olshan · Mr. and Mrs. Alvin M. Owsley, Jr. Mr. and Mrs. Merrick W. Phelps · The Rt. Rev. J. Milton Richardson · Mayor M. L. Ross · Mr. and Mrs. Robert T. Sakowitz · Mr. and Mrs. E. K. Salls · Harold Scarlett · Rabbi Hyman Judah Schachtel · Mr. and Mrs. Pierre M. Schlumberger · State Senator A. R. Schwartz Mr. and Mrs. Russell L. Schweickart · Mr. and Mrs. Percy Selden · Mr. and Mrs. Dudley C. Sharp Jr. · The Rev. and Mrs. Benjamin H. Skyles · C. Cabanne Smith · Mr. and Mrs. David B. Smith · Mr. and Mrs. Frank C. Smith Jr. · Dr. Thomas M. Spencer · Mr. and Mrs. Harwood Taylor · Mrs. James A. Tinsley · Mr. and Mrs. Laurence Tobin · Senator John G. Tower · Mr. and Mrs. Harvey Turner · Dr. and Mrs. Frank E. Vandiver · Robert A. Vines · Mr. and Mrs. David B. Warren · Mayor Louie Welch · Mr. and Mrs. Andrew Jackson Wray Mr. and Mrs. Newton Wray · Mrs. Frank Wozencraft · Maria E. Yramategui

Preservation of Armand Bayou Committee
P. O. Box 2000 Pasadena, Texas 77501 (713) 473-8090

HO/8 *New York Times 11/13/72*

This full-page advertisement was run in the
New York Times. Photo from ABNC archives

Four years later Hana and her coalition had raised the 6.5 million dollars needed toward the purchase of property along the bayou. The original acquisition purchased 1900 acres and consisted of coastal prairie and flatwoods forest adjacent to the bayou waters. Funding contributors included The City of Pasadena, Harris County, The Armand Bayou Fund, Bureau of Outdoor Recreation and Department of Housing and Urban Development (HUD). An important stipulation from HUD was that the lands must be retained as parkland in perpetuity. It was agreed that Harris County would serve as the property owner and that Armand Bayou Nature Center would hold a 99-year lease on the property that automatically renews.

Mission accomplished! (almost)

Original efforts targeted the preservation of 3000 acres along Armand Bayou. Original fund raising fell short of this goal and preserved 1900 acres. Efforts are well underway now (2020) to *complete her vision,* which will add an estimated 1000 acres of prairie and forest in the upper watershed of the bayou. The area is shown as Track 15 on the previous map.

Hana leading an early ABNC trail hike from Bay Area Park 1974. Photo from ABNC archives

In these early years there were no buildings on the property. However, Hana and other leading Houston naturalists, university professors and astronauts led hikes entering the property from Bay Area Park. The original trail led from Bay Area Park to where the current Boathouse is located. These were my high school years where I hiked and swam from the rope swing where today's ABNC Boathouse is located. In 1974, ABNC was established as a not-for-profit corporation and became the second "nature center" in all of Texas.

This sign marked the entrance to the first ABNC trail, which entered through Bay Area Park. Photo from ABNC archives

Do your part! Photo from ABNC archives

On July 4, 1976 ABNC held the official dedication of the Interpretive Building to the public. With an innovative design the building housed all staff, held public displays, and offered an auditorium for events and educational programs. It remained the only building at ABNC to perform these functions for 20 years.

Hana sits with officials during recognition and dedication ceremony. Photo from ABNC archives

In one of my last conversations with Hana we discussed that rope swing. In 1972, Hana had managed to assemble several Texas State Representatives to tour the bayou in hopes of securing funding. They boated past the rope swing, which was surrounded by teenage swimmers having fun in the summer sun. The State Reps said to her, "This place looks like it's used and enjoyed by the community. We should support it!" To which Hana said to me, "Looks like you and I were both doing our part for the preservation of the bayou on that day!"

Interpretive Building construction 1976. Photo from ABNC archives

Hana gave a presentation at the ABNC Volunteer Meeting in October 2005. She recounted much of what I've stated above, but also left us a written record, her personal memoire of the monumental effort. The title of her writings is "Setting the Record Straight." It's an in-depth history of the beginnings of ABNC. I have recounted one of her memoire quotes on many of my speaking engagements which reads, **"Although Armand never campaigned to preserve lands along the bayou, his spirit was felt throughout the effort."** Reading that sentence stopped me. It was an "aha" moment of realization. First, I realized that much of our story (our history) of ABNC had been mis-quoted through the years. Armand was not the champion who had campaigned and fundraised for preservation of the bayou. **In fact, Armand had only visited the bayou a very few times in his life.** It was Hana. She was the one who drove the effort of fundraising to preserve the lands. The second realization was that the title of her memoire, "Setting the Record Straight," was her attempt to gently announce that fact.

Hana addresses the ABNC Volunteer Meeting in October 2005. Photo from ABNC archives

Hana walks among the Armand Bayou cedars.

Hana last visited ABNC in March 2013. I had called her in hopes that she might attend the retirement party for my dear friend, ABNC Director and Chief Naturalist, George Regmund. It was an evening filled with memories of the early days and I felt a profound sense of wonder that such an extraordinary chain of events had come to pass that had led us all to be together for our moment in time. I could not know then that it would be our last.

Hana died on October 22, 2013. Her memorial service was a tribute to a life of personal commitment and dedication to local conservation. Her dogged persistence contributed to one speaker saying, "When we saw Hana coming down the sidewalk, we would try to cross the street." There were many memorable quotes from people who knew and loved her. I was honored to speak on behalf of Armand Bayou Nature Center. The following are my notes from the occasion:

"For the last 40 years I have worked and played in that park and natural area that she was devoted to. As an employee of Harris County Parks Department, I piloted an eco-tour boat named the Hana G, for the last 20 some odd years I have served at Armand Bayou Nature Center as biologist and naturalist.

Because of Hana – I like so many others have discovered the natural world and the beauty of the wilderness.

Because of Hana – I like so many others have found a quiet place to contemplate the beauty of the prairie sunset and the mystery of the night sky.

Because of Hana – Hundreds of thousands of children have seen their first caterpillars become butterflies and hundreds of thousands of parents have seen that wonder in their children's eyes.

Because of Hana – the alligator, otter, pelican, osprey and eagle have returned to the bayou.

Because of these things, when I was with Hana I felt like I was with a giant, a hero, and she leaves a legacy that generations of humans and wild creatures alike will be the better for all that she did."

The writing of these notes has increasingly revealed the essential nature within each moment. As I read these writings, I realize how the disconnection of any one of the above events could have unraveled the tapestry of life that has interwoven the connections with everyone I know who might read this. One different turn at any point along the story could have led to an entirely different destiny. I think how different my life would be without an Armand or Hana or Armand Bayou Nature Center. I know that many others feel this too. How profoundly different the trajectory of my life would have been, if not for Hana.

More of the story may be viewed at:

Dr. Deanna Schmidt-Hana's Urban Wilderness 2017

youtu.be/-ivAwntXDOM

Chapter Three: *Armand Bayou Nature Center*

An Introduction

Armand Bayou Nature Center (ABNC) opened its doors over forty years ago as one of the first nature centers in the state of Texas. Located in what was the rapidly growing urban and industrial Houston metropolitan area, ABNC preserves the best representative of bayou, prairie and forested wildlands remaining in Harris County. Armand Bayou Nature Center is proudly named after the famed local environmental visionary Armand Yramategui. It's fitting that ABNC bears his name due to his dedication to conservation of the natural world, and also to his belief in environmental education and the improvement of life through contact with the outdoors. Armand's tragic murder in 1970 served to galvanize a diverse coalition of individuals, organizations and governments, which he had inspired to protect and preserve this jewel of the Texas coast and to carry on his vision.

The nature center comprises three ecosystems that are rapidly disappearing around the Houston area. The 2,500 acres managed by ABNC qualify the preserve as one of the largest urban wildlife refuges in America. Houston is known as the "Bayou City." Armand Bayou is among the last remaining unchannelized bayous around Houston with an original meandering, serpentine stream bed lined with abundant tidal wetlands and a great diversity of aquatic life. Coastal flatwoods forests line the bayou edge and provide habitat for resident and migrating songbirds. Coastal tallgrass prairie habitat occupies over 900 acres of ABNC and is considered critically imperiled by ecologists. Today less than one percent of coastal prairie survives. Decades of restoration and active management by ABNC Staff and volunteers have restored these dominant ecosystems to their former beauty. Today, many iconic wildlife species of coastal Texas have returned from near extinction to now reside in this urban wilderness. The American alligator, brown pelican, peregrine falcon, osprey and bald eagle are commonly sighted at the refuge. Visitors to this living museum are offered the opportunity to experience a genuine wilderness and step back in time for an ecological visit to the Houston area as it was.

MISSION

The mission of Armand Bayou Nature Center is twofold: to preserve the habitats with which we have been entrusted, and to provide opportunities for people to experience and understand local ecosystems

Since the founding of ABNC over forty years ago, Harris County has grown into the most densely populated county in Texas. During this time period, the value of this most beautifully preserved piece of wild land has increased both for wildlife and for people. The lists of ecosystem services provided by these areas are numerous. The services provided by these types of green infrastructure include storm water retention and flood abatement, water quality improvement, a living laboratory educational resource, human recreation and wildlife habitat. Today, ABNC is home to more than 370 species of birds, mammals, reptiles and amphibians including several federally protected endangered species. A carefully planned approach of restoration and management is seasonally required to maintain this ecological jewel of coastal Texas.

Native Plant Society- ABNC 3 Plant Communities

youtu.be/hd34mxFt45o

ABNC is a private-public partnership 501c-3 nonprofit organization. Harris County serves as the property owner and ABNC holds a 99-year automatic rollover lease agreement and is solely responsible for all operations and funding. The mission of Armand Bayou Nature Center is to preserve the unique natural area under our care and to provide environmental education opportunities which focus on local ecology to people of all ages. More than 40,000 individuals visit the site annually to take advantage of education programs, nature trails, pontoon boat eco-tours, bird and wildlife watching and much more.

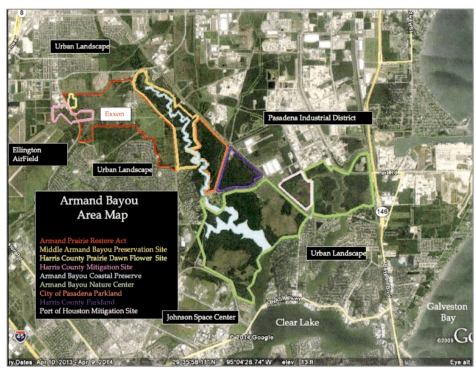

The mosaic of land ownership has enabled the success of one of America's unique conservation success stories.

Initial efforts to preserve open space along Armand Bayou were led by a small group of environmental leaders. During the 1960s and 1970s as Houston was rapidly growing, these environmental visionaries recognized the value of conservation both for wildlife and for people. These leaders were successful in stitching together a patchwork of funding and public support that enabled the purchase of the original 1,900-acre urban refuge.

Harris County's 4,589,928 people (as of 2016) are jammed into 1,777-square-miles, making the county population larger than that of 25 states. The Houston area is anticipating a similar growth event to that which occurred in the 1970s with an additional four million people expected by 2040. This increase is equivalent to having everyone in Dallas, Austin, San Antonio and Corpus Christi moving to Houston in the next twenty years. A similar preservation strategy is required today for the conservation of the remaining wildland north of Bay Area Boulevard.

The natural area, parkland and waters of Armand Bayou are a unique amenity to be found in one of the most densely populated metropolitan areas in America.

Rewilding the Urban Wilderness

Do you ever want to go back? I mean back in time. Rocky and Bullwinkle had the Way Back Machine. Marty McFly had the time traveling DeLorean in *Back to the Future*. Bill and Ted's *Excellent Adventure* had the time traveling phone booth. Another of my favorites is the *Hot Tub Time Machine.* For most of us, pondering time travel is more practical. Through the power of imagination, we can take a trip and never leave the farm. Einstein said that imagination is more important than knowledge. Most agree they are both needed. I've recently been thinking of my first bike ride (without training wheels) and the first fish I ever caught.

H abitat Loss
I nvasive Species
P ollution
P opulation
O ver Hunting

HIPPO is the acronym used to remember the important ecological issues facing the planet. These issues may contribute to a species' population declining.

At their peak an estimated one million Attwater's Prairie Chicken occupied the coastal prairie of Texas and Louisiana. Today they rank as one of the most critically endangered species in the world with less than 50 birds living in the wild due to a list of environmental issues. Photo by Gary Seloff

It turns out that ecologists think about going back in time too. We think back to the time before Europeans first explored North America. Back before the introduction of exotic diseases, which decimated Native American populations. We think back to the time before *habitat loss*, before *invasive species*, before *pollution*, before *over-hunting*, before human *population* exploded and before

climate change. Environmental educators use the acronym HIPPO to remember this list of the most pressing concerns for the planet. For an ecologist, going back to that time, riding in Mark's Ecological Time Traveling Helicopter brings the power of life into clear view as we look out over the landscape in the year 1500. It's the highest expression of art created by the hand of Nature.

We humans stumble in our attempt to translate the feeling and emotion of being immersed in such natural beauty. We splash color on canvas and write words on a page in an effort to capture the direct experience of these rare moments of reverie. The most powerful of all human experiences is to lose yourself in the flow of these powerful creative forces at play.

Today, these historic pre-European landscapes are one valuable tool used by ecologists to guide planning for ecological restoration. If I had the Conservation Director's Magic Wand, I would transform ABNC's habitats back to the year 1500 with a flick of my wrist.

Imagining ABNC that long ago, there were verdant fields of tall grass, lush marshes nourished by the rising tide and ribbons of deciduous riparian hardwoods converging here. In addition to the current wildlife species, black bear, whooping crane, ivory-billed woodpecker, trumpeter swan, mountain lion and red wolf abound. Winter populations of waterfowl darken the sky as if they were a cloud at sunrise. Bison herds 100 square miles in size slowly graze across the prairie towards the horizon. Prairie chickens and bobwhite quail were commonly heard *booming* at the first light of day. The Akokisa Indians followed the seasonal shifts in abundance of these plants and animals for over 8,000 years, until Europeans arrived.

The first settlers began to arrive on Armand Bayou in the mid-1800s. The Martyn family occupied their 80-acre farm until 1964 when Jimmy Martyn (shown above) passed away. Photo from ABNC archives

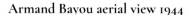
Armand Bayou aerial view 1944

There was a great ecological awakening in the American culture in the 1960s. As air and water quality declined and species were threatened with extinction, a new era was born. As a child, I remember it as the age of Mother Nature. Even television advertisements had slogans like "It's not nice to fool Mother Nature." You can Google that phrase for a glimpse back in time in the You Tube Time Machine.

The settlers began to colonize their new territory, which left a permanent mark, shifting the ecological balance that had been in place since the last ice age. Agriculture, logging, intensive cattle grazing, Native American eradication, invasive species introduction and an exploding human population began to impact the upper Texas coast as they do to this day.

The Houston area underwent a tremendous growth in population as is shown here with added homes, roads and businesses.

In 1972, Apollo 17 sent Earth's residents the first full planet view of home.
Photo credit NASA, crew of Apollo 17

In 1976, the first naturalists (George Regmund and Wayne Clark) contemplate the Rewilding of ABNC.

Not only was ecological crisis taking place on a grand scale, but we also saw ourselves for the first time. The first view of home on Earth occurred with space flight to the moon. Young children are often confused by seeing themselves for the first time in a mirror. Not so for us humans seeing ourselves from afar: we recognized that we were witnessing a profound truth. Never before had humans witnessed the small fragility of our shared biosphere and there was a brief cultural shift in recognition.

We take space flight for granted now and the image's impact has faded, but it hasn't faded for present day astronauts. A large number of astronauts report being overwhelmed with witnessing firsthand the beauty of Earth. Many describe it as being life changing. The *Overview Effect* produces a cognitive shift, an "ah ha" moment where Earth is seen as a small, blue marble hanging in the blackness of deep space. From a distance, state and national boundaries vanish, conflicts between people seem less important and we understand that we're all in this together. From the beginning, all of life has been on a parallel trajectory. Interdependent and coevolving as if the Earth were one living organism.

It was in this era that ABNC opened its doors in 1976. We had thought and hoped that if we could purchase this beautiful piece of property and build a fence around it that Mother Nature would do the rest. We were still learning.

Who Do You Think You Are

That's a question not a statement. Who do you think you are? Who do you think that you are in relation to the Earth – the natural world? Maybe you've never considered it. It's been said that the most dangerous world view is to have never viewed the world. An equally important question is who do *we* think *we* are? Cultural anthropologist Florence Kluckohn's research describes our cultural relation to nature as one of three possibilities.

1. *Man under nature* suggests that cultural belief towards nature is solely an outcome of an unseen power. We make offerings to the gods in hopes that the rains will come to water the fields. We believe

that all outcomes derive from an external force beyond our control - destiny or fate.

2. *Man over nature* suggests that our human challenge is to control and dominate nature. The environment is viewed only as a natural resource to be controlled and exploited. We need to insist that nature works with us, not that we should work with nature.

3. *Man in nature* describes a cultural belief that we not only live in harmony with natural systems, but that we work to sustain, enhance and restore them. Man crafting a culture that looks to nature's time-tested adaptations and processes to sustainably live with the natural world. It's a belief that our survival depends on those very systems.

In 1995, ABNC began more ambitious strategies to restore ecosystem health. Photo by Mark Kramer

Over time the landscape slowly began to change. The grasslands were encroached upon by invasive woody plants, marshes disappeared, and many forms of iconic wildlife vanished. All of these impacts were human caused, but it turns out that humans are also part of the solution. Restoration ecology is the branch of science that seeks to bring back the natives. To bring back the native plants, the native animals and also to bring back the historic ecological processes that shaped the region.

It might be thought of as gardening at the ecosystem scale. We remove invasive species (weeds), plant native species of grasses and wildflowers (nursery plants) and encourage predators

(beneficial insects) to keep the garden in balance. A patchwork of management techniques is stitched together. This patchwork creates a mosaic of microhabitats where each prairie specialist form of wildlife fills its unique set of needs, thus supporting the greatest diversity of wildlife. Originally this patchwork would have played out over huge areas on coastal Texas with vast acreages being burned by wildfire, grazed by bison or left untouched with standing tall grass. Today management at ABNC recreates those landscapes on a smaller scale. However, it comes at significant effort as shown above.

Photo of the author by Trudy LeDoux

Looking through the lens of science, we focus our vision and consciousness. Sometimes focusing on the tiny unseen microscopic life through the microscope. Conversely, we survey the depths of the cosmos through the telescope. This shifting of perspective is a useful thought experiment when we consider invasive species. At the level of the organism (such as my body), we may become sick. A microorganism invades our body making us feel poorly and we go to visit the doctor. The doctor will run tests and take vital signs to determine the nature of the illness and may prescribe medicine to treat the illness. After a couple of weeks if there is no improvement, we return for more tests. Now the doctor may determine that you are sicker than originally thought. In fact, you have cancer and the treatment plan has changed to more intensive therapy, chemotherapy.

Now let's shift the scientific lens of our consciousness to view the same scenario, not at the organism level, but now at the ecosystem level. When an invasive species enters an ecosystem, it behaves much like a biological toxin. If it is a particularly aggressive ecological invader it will begin to affect the vital signs of the environment. On occasion the treatment plan may include chemicals (chemotherapy).

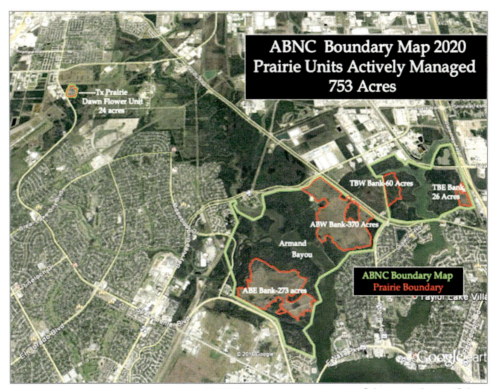

ABNC manages 2500 acres of the most beautiful wild land in the Houston area, including over 750 acres of critically imperiled coastal prairie.

It's difficult to imagine that in 1995, the prairie adjacent to the ABNC entry road (The Grimes Prairie) was a Chinese tallow forest. Collection of Mark Kramer

The Chinese tallow tree is the most damaging invasive species to coastal prairie habitats at Armand Bayou Nature Center. As aggressive invasive species begin to dominate an ecosystem, the measurements of these indicators decline. In some cases, the ecosystem completely collapses under the strain. What was once a thriving diverse ecosystem has been transformed by the invasive species into a biological desert.

In 2001 the Five Star Grant partnered ABNC, Texas Parks & Wildlife Department, Houston Lighting & Power, U.S. Fish and Wildlife Service and Tx Agri-Life Extension for one of the largest tallow eradication projects ever. With help from the "Team of Conservation Doctors," the environment may recover. Implementing proven techniques of restoration ecology, invasive species are suppressed and species diversity returns.

Some of these biological indictors (vital signs) of ecosystem health are assessed by measuring species diversity, ecosystem function, climax plant communities and the presence of apex predators.

When it comes to the return of predators, size matters. Apex predators require a large territory as a home range. The urban wilderness of ABNC contains four square miles of restored habitat, which is large enough to support alligators, Bald Eagles, bob-cats, coyotes and river otters. Large enough if the habitat is healthy.

Habitat 101

Let's shift our lens of consciousness one last time to focus on habitat. First, let's examine our habitat (Habitat for Humanity). Each room in our home is specifically designed to meet our complex set of needs. Some rooms are designed for feeding habitat (kitchen), some for raising children (nursery habitat) and some for lounging habitat (the living room recliner). Each species of wildlife has a similar, yet unique set of habitat needs in order for the species to thrive through each stage of life.

Armand Bayou Nature Center has been an ongoing ecological fixer upper. As with any fixer upper, step one is to purchase the property and begin refurbishing the home (habitats). Our initial efforts raised 6.5 million dollars as the purchase price. For over twenty-five years the nature center has been a work in progress, slowly completing one ecological enhancement project after another.

Twenty years of bayou restoration
have created 26 acres of marsh habitat.

After decades of effort and significant investment, the refuge looks like a million bucks. Literally. This life's work has managed well over 1.5 million dollars of state and federal restoration grants as well as hosting numerous mitigation projects to further the mission.

Since 1995, ABNC has spent an estimated
$1,486,920 on ongoing ecological restoration.

Prescribed mowing is the single most important prairie management technique.

Mowing effects mimic the historic influences of grazing bison and wildfire which act to suppress the growth of invasive woody plants.

Long-term management is crucial to ensure
that all of the prior project investments
maintain ecological function.

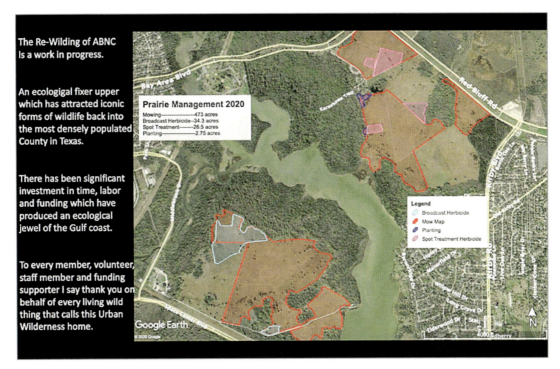

The Re-Wilding of ABNC
Is a work in progress.

An ecologigal fixer upper which has attracted iconic forms of wildlife back into the most densely populated County in Texas.

There has been significant investment in time, labor and funding which have produced an ecological jewel of the Gulf coast.

To every member, volunteer, staff member and funding supporter I say thank you on behalf of every living wild thing that calls this Urban Wilderness home.

The Rewilding of ABNC

These project dollars are similar to leveling the foundation of the house of our fixer upper. We've completed the ecological foundation repair. We've repaired the slab and frame of our habitat, but we can't walk away from our investment. If we do, the structure begins to rapidly decline.

Now, the most challenging chapter begins. The long-term management of our initial investment is crucial. State and federal grants are keen to fund the early foundational stages of restoration (house), but for some reason are reluctant to provide grants for long-term management (painting, toilet repair, flooring replacement etc.) Every day of the year, the Stewardship Team engages in implementing these long-term ecological management techniques as described in the ABNC Natural Resource Management Plan. Controlling invasive species, propagating locally rare native plants, mimicking the historic influence of keystone species like bison (through prescribed mowing), monitoring and training the Stewardship Alpha Elite Volunteer Strike Team.

The term for this lengthy process is known as *Rewilding*. Wikipedia defines Rewilding as "large-scale conservation aimed at restoring and protecting natural processes and core wilderness areas, providing connectivity between such areas, and protecting or reintroducing apex predators and keystone species." The human footprint has now stomped out most of the best wildlands that remain in our area. However, through the process of Rewilding these *human dependent natural areas* are now the *New Wild*. Armand Bayou Nature Center, The Katy Prairie Conservancy, The Bayou Land Conservancy and The Nature Conservancy manage some of the largest remnant habitats in the Houston area. We may never be able to go back in time, but we can use the power of imagination to remember, and we can appreciate what we have remaining in the New Wild of Armand Bayou Nature Center.

For a deep dive into the Rewilding of ABNC tune in to:

Native Plant Society of Texas 2016

Annual Meeting Keynote - Wildscaping at the Landscape Level

www.youtube.com/watch?v=S0XqcV1W5WI

Chapter Four: *Prairie Ecology*

Map courtesy of Katy Prairie Conservancy

Coastal tallgrass prairie exists in a very thin margin extending approximately fifty miles inland along the Gulf of Mexico from Corpus Christi, TX to the Louisiana coast. Its close proximity to the ocean results in frequent rainfall events, creating a prairie ecosystem that has more wetland features than prairies located in the Great Plains region. The coastal tallgrass prairie has one of the most diverse plant communities in North America. Remnant prairies may contain as many as 1,000 different plant species, many of which produce a changing array of colorful flowers throughout the growing season. Despite this, prairies continue to be one of the most underappreciated ecosystems. Throughout the country 99% of coastal tallgrass prairie has been lost, making it one of the most critically imperiled habitats in North America.

Historically, coastal tallgrass prairie was the prominent landscape throughout the Houston area. Due to

soil type and distribution, trees were mostly found directly adjacent to waterways. Harris County was once dominated by prairie. However, the reduction of prairie habitat in this area has been severe. Currently, Armand Bayou Nature Center is home to one of the largest remnant tallgrass prairies around Galveston Bay.

Prairies are Houston's ecological heritage. Chances are that where you live was once prairie. Map courtesy Katy Prairie Conservancy

Armand Bayou Nature Center actively manages 900 acres of coastal tallgrass prairie annually.

ABNC contains 2,500 acres of coastal tallgrass prairie, tidal marsh, and forested ecosystems. The mission of ABNC is to preserve these ecosystems and provide opportunities for visitors to experience the diverse flora and fauna found in these habitats.

ABNC Restoration History

Armand Bayou Nature Center has a lengthy history of restoring coastal prairie. Since 1979, a team of staff biologists and dedicated volunteers has implemented an integrated management strategy that includes prescribed burning, mowing, invasive species control, native plant cultivation and installation, vegetation monitoring and prairie education. Today, ABNC is a leader in prairie restoration in the Houston area. A typical year of prairie management includes applying prescribed fire to approximately 300 acres, mowing approximately 250 acres, controlling 50 acres of invasive species through selective herbicide treatments, cultivating and installing approximately 20,000 one gallon pots of locally rare grasses and wildflowers, installing those prairie plants through service learning projects, collecting important plant data every spring and fall from 32 vegetation transect lines and teaching the community to appreciate the subtle ecology and vanishing nature of this imperiled habitat. Through this assorted effort, ABNC prairies are healthier and more beautiful today than ever before!

ABNC Prairie Pandemonium – Pasadena Channel
www.youtube.com/watch?v=O73mNUaWZR4

What Is a Prairie?

Prairies are plant communities composed primarily of grass. The dominant grass species include big bluestem, eastern gamma grass, switchgrass, yellow Indiangrass, and little bluestem. Historically, most of the prairie would have been covered by these few species. If we could fly over a coastal prairie in our time traveling helicopter 300 years ago, when we look down, 80% of the prairie would be covered with only these handful of species. As indicated by the name, tallgrass prairies consist of grasses that can reach seven feet in height. Interestingly, prairies are known as "upside down" plant communities because the bulk of a prairie plant biomass exists below the soil surface in the form of the grasses' massive root systems.

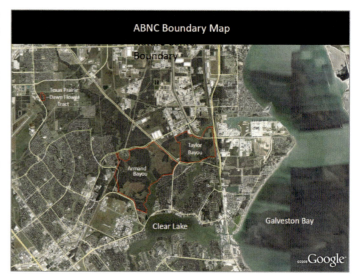

Two bayous run through ABNC property. Armand Bayou to the west and Taylor Bayou to the east.

Coastal tallgrass prairie. Photo collection of Mark Kramer

The Land that Was Built by Fire

Photo by Lyman Brown

Over many thousands of years prairie plants have evolved special growth strategies that enable them to endure the intense heat generated during prairie fires. Unlike prairie grasses, the bulk of the tissue of trees and shrubs is located above ground and is often severely damaged by fire. Conversely, grasses and prairie plants are considered fire-adapted and have the majority of their tissue located below the soil surface, where it is insulated from the heat. During the winter months, prairies are covered in dead dormant grass thatch and lack any above ground physiological activity. At this time, they are low in moisture content, which makes them very susceptible to fire. In turn, prairie plants are stimulated by fire. The blackened prairie absorbs the sun and warms the soil, promoting an abundance of nitrogen-fixing bacteria in the soil. Nitrogen is a growth limiting element for plants and is converted by these bacteria to a form useable by the prairie vegetation. As a result, prairie plants in a post-burn environment grow with vigor.

Before Europeans came to this country, an estimated 60 million bison roamed throughout North America. Some herds were thought to be as large as 20 miles wide and 60 miles in length. Bison would rub on trees and shrubs, pushing them down as they moved through. They created wallows for rolling in mud or dust bathing. The wallows created microhabitats used by other forms of wildlife. As these herds made their way across the country in search of green pastures, their grazing effects shaped the prairie landscape. The leading edge of the bison herd had access to the preference plants, those that tasted better and had a greater nutritional benefit for the animals. These grasses are sometimes described as "ice cream plants" due to their high sugar content and good palatability. The bison at the back of the herd were forced to graze on any vegetation remaining, including woody shrubs. This high intensity, low frequency grazing strategy was essential in keeping prairies free of woody vegetation.

Grazing animals are in constant search of greener pastures. As the bison pushed across the landscape, the area previously grazed was left to recover. This rest period enabled prairie plants to regrow, re-foliate and recover. It allowed them to photosynthesize and store sugars in their roots until the next wave of grazing bison returned.

Some bison herds may have been as large as Harris County!

As settlers began to occupy the region, they built fenced pastures, which kept cattle permanently fenced in the same area. Remember the ice cream plants? Remember the dominant grasses that covered 80% of the prairie surface? It turns out that they are the same species of grasses. The dominant grasses had high palatability and were repeatedly grazed by cattle within the permanently fenced pastures, only now they had no rest period. With the migrating bison herds the prairie had time to recover. Now, the ice cream plants were grazed again and again. Every new inch of foliage grown was quickly eaten as soon as it sprouted. This overgrazing pressure forced the grasses to rely on reserves stored in the roots, which were eventually exhausted. Over time, the grasses that once dominated the prairie landscape were grazed out of existence and disappeared one pasture at a time.

Prairie wetlands are an important filter improving water quality before it enters Galveston Bay.

Coastal tallgrass prairies are commonly categorized as wetlands. Subtle changes in the elevation create depressional wetlands, or prairie potholes. These shallow wetlands are temporary and change with the seasons. Due to short duration of standing water in these wetlands, it is difficult for fish to establish populations. Several species of amphibian use these ephemeral wetlands as reproductive habitat. No fish means better chances of survival for their offspring.

The Houston area experiences a predictable soil moisture cycle. During some seasons the soils are wet while in others they are dry. During the summer months, many of these wetlands are difficult to identify because they hold no water. The only rainfall occurs with isolated thunderstorms. Bright sun, hot summer temperatures and long day length promote rapid drying of the soil. Active summer prairie plant growth pulls further moisture from the soil, then releases it from leaf surfaces. This evapotranspiration and infrequent rainfall make summer soils

predictably dry. Digging a hole in Houston during the dry summer season is often like trying to dig concrete.

As the summer soils dry out, they begin to shrink. In fact, during prolonged periods the soils may become so dry that they begin to pull apart creating long deep cracks.

The first cool fronts arrive in late September, beginning the change of seasons. When the cool air of a frontal boundary collides with warm Gulf moisture, rain is produced. These fronts begin to produce rainfall and also reduce temperatures, slowing evaporation. As temperatures drop, prairie plants' growth also slows minimizing their effects of pulling moisture from the soil.

As prairie soils become more moist during the fall, they begin to swell. The moisture eventually swells the clayey soils closed, suppressing water from percolating downwards. As the soils become supersaturated, water begins to pool in low lying depressions creating prairie wetlands. These prairie wetlands most commonly hold standing water during the cold months of winter.

Houston area prairie soils are made mostly of fine clay particles, which expand and contract depending how wet they are.

This seasonal process of soil moisture increasing and decreasing causes prairie soils to shrink in the summer and swell in the winter. For this reason, they are often described as shrink swell soils.

These "here today–gone tomorrow" prairie wetlands are a great asset to people by providing storm water retention and flood reduction. In addition, they provide a water source for wildlife, and a habitat conducive to amphibian reproduction.

The character of coastal prairie visibly changes during the winter. Verdant green is replaced with russet brown. This color is driven by the absence of chlorophyll in the leaves and stems of prairie grasses. The entire life force of the prairie plant community retreats underground in winter. Everything above the soil surface is dead, dormant thatch from the growth of the previous summer.

Where Have All the Prairies Gone?

The significant reduction of coastal tallgrass prairie habitat over the past 200 years has made it one of the most endangered ecosystems in the country. The two key ecological processes that sustain prairies have, over many years, been altered by human influence, allowing trees and woody shrubs to invade areas that once supported a climax community of grasses and wildflowers.

Once bison began to disappear from the landscape, prairies began to change dramatically. Bison were a keystone species in the prairie ecosystem and as Europeans began to settle throughout North America, they were hunted and killed by the thousands at a time. Many accounts of the slaughter described how the bison continued to graze as bullets flew all around them. Adult bison had few natural enemies and nothing in their history had prepared them for humans armed with rifles. Bison populations prior to 1700 were estimated to be around 60 million individuals. Following the civil war, the commercial hide hunt known as "the Great Slaughter" began. Bison were skinned for their hides and the carcasses were left to rot on the prairie. By the late 1800s, American bison were nearly extinct.

The Great Slaughter not only decimated the population of an iconic American animal, but it also played a significant role in destroying prairie habitat throughout the country. Without the high intensity, low frequency grazing of bison—unlike that of domestic cattle—woody shrubs began to take over areas where trees had historically been absent.

The other essential ecological process that supports a healthy prairie habitat is fire. Grasslands are historically considered fire dependent ecosystems. Before humans occupied North America, fires were ignited by lightning strikes. These fires would often burn for days or weeks and cover hundreds of miles until they encountered a natural fire break, such as a river, lake, ocean, or bay. After the last ice age, Native Americans entered North America and were also responsible for igniting fires on the prairie. They recognized fire as a tool and used it to their advantage. The Native Americans were nomadic people and burning the tall grasses made traveling much easier. Can you imagine walking from Clear Lake to Galveston Island? Burning a prairie ahead of you eased the migration. Additionally, they understood that the tender, green re-growth of grasses following a burn would attract game animals.

As Europeans settled throughout North America, natural fire regimes were slowly halted. Native Americans gradually disappeared from the land and much of the natural prairie habitat was settled and converted into towns and agricultural fields. Any wildfires that now occur are quickly subdued to protect life and property. Without grazing and fire, much of the remaining prairie habitat was transformed into shrub land and forested ecosystems.

Peak Bloom

Prairie blazing star (*Liatris spp.*) paints one of the rarest views remaining in Texas. Photo by Ann Brinly

Stunning prairie landscapes inspire art and are moving to behold. Photo by Ann Brinly

Have you ever seen a landscape that was so beautiful that it stopped you, made you take another look or maybe made you sit down in admiration? We flat-lander Houstonians (not flat-Earthers) sometimes need a dose of that healing elixir. On occasion we even need to be taught "*that* is beautiful." I've had prairie classes hike through acres of blooming wild-flowers as if they were walking through the Walmart parking lot. Residents of coastal Texas don't get the grandeur of mountain vistas; we don't have the iconic plants of the Redwood Forest or the topography of the Grand Canyon. We do have beauty. The art of appreciating local nature is an exercise in valuing *subtle* beauty. The beauty of color in a field of grasses and wildflowers that is windswept to the horizon. The beauty of a landscape rich in hundreds of species of prairie grasses, flowers, insects, birds, reptiles and mammals. A diverse assembly of prairie life, seldom seen and seldom truly appreciated. The beauty of 10,000 human hands who have painted the colors of that landscape through decades of prairie restoration. The rare beauty that comes from being the last of your kind. Prairies today are critically imperiled hab-itat and now this prairie view is one of the rarest views remaining in Texas. The art of appreciating the beauty of coastal Texas is also the act of cultivating a deeper understanding.

As spring approaches summer, a sea of vibrant color swells over the landscape. The few weeks around mid-June are peak bloom for the Texas coneflower (*Rudbeckia texana*). Standing four to five feet tall with multiple large vivid yellow flowers, the plant can transform the prairie viewscape. A flower blooms, transforming the landscape, sets its seed and withdraws below the soil surface, not seen again until next year. It is replaced by a continuing rotation of successive beautiful blooming wildflow-ers. One peak bloom after another scattered across the field with each unfolding summer. My favorite spots to reflect on the beauty of this moment are from the ABNC Prairie Observation Platform and along the Prairie Hiking Trail.

Coastal prairies are people dependent habitats requiring long-term management and care. ABNC mows 1/3 of the prairie every year. Photo by Mark Kramer

People struggle to appreciate the view of *just* a field of grass. It turns out that prairies are much more than just grass. Wildflowers add a complex dimension of color which all people immediately relate to as beautiful. ABNC has used these "charismatic mega-flora" such as the Texas coneflower as an integral component of prairie restoration for decades. Beautiful blooming wildflowers are a gateway species that pull people into a deeper appreciation of the subtle beauty of our ecological heritage. Countless hours of dedicated management from ABNC staff and volunteers have produced a view worthy of reflection.

For a Deeper Dive into Coastal Prairies:

ABNC Prairie Coneflowers with Birdsong and Captions
www.youtube.com/watch?v=_NNQTSbtuhc

Bayou City Eco-Almanac Coastal Tallgrass Prairies Part 1
www.youtube.com/watch?v=k-hwFjo3B0s

Monarchs on the Move

Monarchs pass through ABNC in search of nectar plants and host plants like this Green Milkweed.
Photo by Lyman Brown

Imagine waking from a long winter's nap and beginning a journey, a long journey, a journey that would be left to your children to complete. In fact, it would also take their children and their children's children as well to complete it. With each of you weighing about half as much as a dollar bill and traveling on gossamer wings. To make it more remarkable, imagine the journey taking you and your descendants across three countries and from the southern part of the continent to the northern part of the continent–and then back again! Such is the odyssey of the monarch butterfly, the remarkable travelers of time and space that pass through the Houston area and stop over at ABNC in the spring and fall.

Monarch butterflies are also in trouble. Their populations have plummeted over the last 20 years. Experts believe there are a number of contributing factors in their decline. Habitat loss is recognized as a top global ecological issue and the monarch has suffered those consequences too. Across the nation, what was once open prairie is now subdivision, parking lot or shopping mall. Prairie habitats have been dramatically reduced. There has also been a radical change in agricultural practices over the past two decades. Our modern farming techniques now allow us to plant genetically modified crops that are resistant to herbicide. Corn, soy and many other food staples can be treated with herbicide and still thrive, while killing competitive "weeds." While this is a miracle for farmers, it has devastated nectar producing wildflowers and milkweed host plants along the monarch's vast migratory route. While experts continue to add to the list of human-caused threats contributing to the decline, it's clear that current numbers have dropped well below the threshold to prevent the population from potentially collapsing into extinction. They are in fact a local posterchild for the larger global extinction event that we have entered into.

These vulnerable travelers on the brink are still on view in the prairies of ABNC. Riding the southerly breezes monarchs are stopping in to refuel on the nectar rich prairie wildflowers and on critical milkweed host plants. The best viewing opportunities are from the Prairie Observation Platform. This panoramic view is one of the rarest remaining in

Harris County with a viewscape of 300 acres of coastal tallgrass prairie. Much of this view is rich with the prairie wildflowers grown in the ABNC native plant nursery. In fact, the coastal tallgrass prairies of ABNC are recognized by the U. S. Fish and Wildlife Service as a monarch "way station." Continued support of natural areas ensures that they have a chance for the future. Support future generations by considering ABNC membership. Enjoy this spectacle while you still have chance by visiting the nature center.

Invasive Prairie Species

Invasive species also play a role in degrading prairie habitat. Transportation of exotic plants from other parts of the world for agricultural and botanical uses has become commonplace. However, when plants from other parts of the country are introduced into a new area, they often lack the natural set of checks and balances necessary to keep a species under control. Certain species become invasive if they exhibit adaptive strategies that allow them to out-compete native plants.

Deep-rooted Sedge

Vaseygrass

Chinese Tallow

McCartney Rose

These invasive plants are among the most ecologically damaging plants in Armand Bayou prairies.

Plants are in constant competition for the resources they need. We don't often think about this competition because it happens so slowly. It's not as exciting as watching the NBA Playoffs because it happens in ultra-slow motion.

There is constant competition between woody plants and grasses.

The picture above is of a prairie, although at first glance it may not look like a prairie at all. This prairie has not been actively managed nor been exposed to the beneficial effects of fire or grazing bison. Notice, in the bottom of the image there are and shrubs. Chinese tallow, oak and yaupon can be seen. Over time, the trees and shrubs grow to a height where they harvest the available sunlight above the prairie plants that are growing below. Over several decades, the trees and shrubs will grow so closely together that the canopy closes. This closed canopy will harvest all available sunlight, essentially shading out the prairie plants that are below.

This is a natural process. However, in pre-European America coastal prairie maintained the integrity of grasslands through the beneficial effects of fire and huge herds of bison.

Today, prairies only exist where humans actively manage them, mimicking these processes critical to prairie ecology. Without management prairies are always converted into forest and shrublands.

This closed canopy Chinese tallow monoculture has replaced one of the most diverse plant communities in North America with a single, non-native species.

Chinese tallows were brought to the Houston area and widely used as a landscape plant. The trees have beautiful Fall color, grow in any soil type and are very difficult to kill, which made them very attractive to local landscapers.

One of the most harmful prairie invaders is the Chinese tallow tree. This tree was imported from China in the late 1700s for the purpose of making soap, candles, and oil from the seeds. Unfortunately, the Chinese tallow tree has a list of impressive adaptive growth strategies that allow it to out-compete most plant species native to the U.S. Chinese tallow trees grow rapidly in almost any type of soil. Additionally, they produce a large number of seeds that can be viable for up to 10 years.

Birds and other animals ingest the seeds and help spread this exotic invader throughout North American forests and prairies. These trees compete with native prairie plants for nutrients, moisture, and sunlight. In a short span of time, what was one of the most species rich ecosystems can be converted into a closed canopy Chinese tallow monoculture. The trees grow so close together that sunlight is unable to penetrate to the ground and reach the prairie grasses and wildflowers below, essentially creating a biological desert.

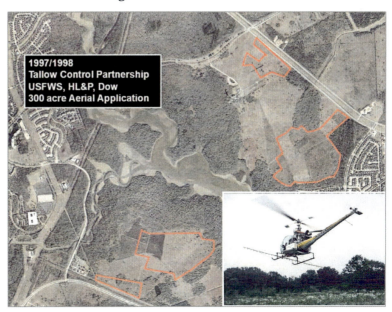

1997/1998
Tallow Control Partnership
USFWS, HL&P, Dow
300 acre Aerial Application

World's greatest tallow farmer – 1998.
Photo collection of Mark Kramer

Restoring hundreds of acres of prairie is a big job. By the mid-1990s, the Chinese tallow had overwhelmed much of the prairie ecosystem at ABNC. In order to reclaim these historic grasslands, ABNC took action. Three hundred acres of closed canopy tallow forest were aerially treated by helicopter with selective herbicides to kill woody plants.

As the adult trees began to decline and die, there was an unexpected surprise. A sea of Chinese tallow seedlings quickly emerged. Each adult tree produces thousands of seeds annually. Seeds may remain viable and dormant for 7 to 10 years. The seedlings were no longer languishing in the shaded understory and now had the benefit of full sunlight. This seed bank meant that treatment of the closed canopy was only the first step in a journey of restoration. In the picture above, I am standing in a sea of sprouting Chinese tallows.

Turning tallow trees into toothpicks.
Photo collection of Mark Kramer

As trees began to decline and die, a heavy-duty chipping machine was brought in to *mow them down.* The shredding of the trees produced a layer of wood mulch. Removal of the trees allowed for further equipment access. ATV access facilitates the use of herbicide spot treatment of any tallow resprout.

Over several decades, prairie restoration has included the efforts of many partners and various tools. The mechanical shredding of tallow forests with heavy equipment is an important control method. Additionally, the ground-based herbicide treatment has proven effective in controlling the carpet of tallow seedlings that may later emerge.

Tractor access allows for prescribed mowing, which mimics the effects of bison intensely grazing. Mowing is now an essential element of the integrated management approach.

Paradise Lost

Humans have no doubt altered the prairie landscape forever. Never again will bison roam freely across the country removing woody and invasive plant species. Fire is no longer allowed to naturally sweep across the prairie stimulating an abundance of new plant growth. Each day new plants are introduced into this country from abroad with the potential threat of becoming the next exotic invader capable of outcompeting native vegetation. Furthermore, destruction of prairies due to urbanization, industrialization, and commercialization continues to be an ongoing threat to the few prairie remnants that remain. Although the destruction of prairie habitat by humans has been extensive, it is also up to humans to protect what is left.

Restoration and Management

Today, prairies are a human dependent ecosystem. In the absence of active management, a prairie will always turn into a shrubland or forest. Faced with the threat of even more prairie habitat being lost and degraded, a new branch of science emerged called restoration ecology. Successful restoration is a human act to implement a well thought out plan to achieve certain ecological goals. Implementing the restoration plan involves securing adequate funding to acquire needed materials, equipment and personnel. For prairies, it involves removing invasive species and reintroducing native plants and animals. Additionally, in the absence of natural ecological processes, landowners and conservationists

must mimic the effects of grazing and fire to maintain prairie ecosystems.

ABNC actively manages 750 acres of coastal tallgrass prairie habitat throughout the preserve. Our prairie is divided into 25-acre or less management units that receive different annual treatments depending on location and habitat need. Many of the prairie units undergo manual removal of Chinese tallow trees with chainsaws or heavy machinery, and broadcast or spot treatment of invasive vegetation with herbicide. ABNC may mow specific prairie units in an attempt to mimic the grazing of bison. Additionally, certain units may be managed with prescribed fire.

ABNC Prescribed Fire Pasadena Channel

www.youtube.com/watch?v=_1TyHceRhmQ

The stewardship department has a larger goal to create a prairie habitat mosaic. The landscape is not managed uniformly, but rather with the intent of creating different habitat types for different wildlife species. A recently burned management unit will be attractive to certain types of birds that need direct access to the soil to probe for invertebrates. The short, green grass created by a recently mowed unit provides a good feeding habitat for browsing animals. Additionally, units with standing cover are important for migrating winter songbirds.

This habitat mosaic is a patchwork of landscapes supporting a great diversity of wildlife species.

Looking carefully at this image you can see the blackened area left after a prescribed fire. Snipe and ibis are some of the bird species found after a winter prairie fire. The fire removes the dead grass thatch allowing the birds access to moist prairie soils as feeding habitat.

In the lower right, a mow unit is shown. This area mimics the effects of grazing bison. The tender green grass regrowth is attractive to browsing animals such as rabbits and deer. In the center of the image is an area that has not been treated. This area of standing prairie thatch is ideal cover habitat for many species of songbirds that migrate to coastal Texas in winter to avoid the extreme temperature in northern latitudes.

If we could travel back in time, flying over Texas coastal prairies we would see a similar mosaic played out over the entire coastal plain. Huge areas would have been blackened by wildfire. Additionally, large areas would have been intensively grazed by roaming herds of bison. Some areas would have escaped disturbance from fire or grazing and been left standing intact. Certain species of wildlife evolved special adaptations over long periods of time to specialize in each of the areas of this habitat mosaic.

Today, ABNC conducts intensive management in order to produce this mosaic. What once occurred naturally over much of the upper Texas coast is now reproduced in this small remnant parcel of rare coastal tallgrass prairie. This habitat patchwork mosaic enables this prairie to support a greater variety of prairie-dependent wildlife species. However, it requires significant effort and funding.

During a typical year of prairie management, a tremendous amount of time, effort and funding are invested.

Texas Prairie Dawn Flower

Hidden away on one of the most remote tracts of nature center prairie grows the rarest of prairie plants.

The Texas Prairie Dawn Flower (Hymenoxys texana) is small and inconspicuous even to the expert eye. Our plants generally bloom from March through April. Listed on both the State and Federal Endangered Species List, the flower is the only endangered species plant occurring at ABNC. As an annual plant, it must regrow the next generation every year from seed. It only occurs in very specific prairie soils that have high salt content or are generally absent of other vegetation. It also prefers to grow in association with mima mounds in the prairie. These mounds may be one to three feet higher than average prairie topography and are made of sandy soils. The Harris County area holds some of the highest populations of remaining Texas Prairie Dawn Flower. As the Houston area has grown, habitat for the plant has largely disappeared. Sadly, the Endangered Species Act does not afford the same level of protection to plants as it does for animals. Plants on private lands have essentially no protection from the Endangered Species Act. Armand Bayou Nature Center provides some of the last refuge for this fragile remnant of the past. ABNC participates with the Federal Recovery Team to monitor the plant's population trends. An equally important element of the plant's survival is ABNC's ongoing prairie habitat management activities. Suppressing the growth of invasive woody plants and excluding feral hogs from the site are critical for the Texas Prairie Dawn to thrive. Even though the plants occur in an area of no public access, you can enjoy knowing that this critically endangered species' habitat is being conserved and restored at ABNC.

Bring Back the Natives

Spider lilies are among the most beautiful
and fragrant of all prairie wildflowers.
Photo by Lyman Brown

There is no wildflower finer in all of the prairie than the spider lily. Pure white and striking from across the field, with a fragrance that's intoxicating when close at hand, the spider lily is the largest and most handsome of all ABNC prairie wildflowers. They were once common in the prairie wetlands and open fields of Pasadena and surrounding area. Now

both the open fields and wildflowers are mostly gone. You can enjoy them (but please don't pick) along the Nature Center entry road. Many of those lilies were grown in the ABNC Native Plant Nursery and used for prairie habitat restoration (and your enjoyment).

ABNC native plant nursery produces
all plant material for restoration.

ABNC also reintroduces native plant species back into the prairie. Volunteers, schools and community groups from around the area frequently participate in our service learning projects, where they assist in planting native grasses and forbs that were propagated in ABNC's native plant nursery. Our goal is to reintroduce the dominant grasses back into the prairie, along with many other locally rare plant species. Staff and volunteers grow and install an average of 10,000 native grasses and wildflowers annually.

Armand Bayou Nature Center
Service Learning Program

Engaging students in meaningful and personally relevant environmental service activities to benefit their community.

Service Learning projects have enabled hundreds of thousands of locally rare plant species to be brought back to the prairie. The projects also provide an in-depth lecture of prairie ecology, engaging the next generation of nature lovers regarding their natural heritage.

With only a few staff members, ABNC's stewardship department relies on volunteers and school groups to help with the installation of native plants into the prairie.

Over the course of an entire year, numerous groups assist in planting thousands of prairie plants. As the years progress, positive changes occur at the landscape level.

In order to determine if ABNC's management efforts are successful, 32 transects are monitored in various prairie management units on a biannual basis. A transect is a study area where biologists collect data in order to better understand a species or an ecosystem.

The data is collected on field data sheets, which provides a snapshot of conditions in the field on a given day. The data is then added into the larger data set that is collected at intervals over time. The larger the data set (the more years that information is collected), the more reliable the information that is produced. ABNC has collected data from transect lines for over 20 years.

Service Learning Projects 2013 - 11,410 Plants

Photo from Google Earth Pro

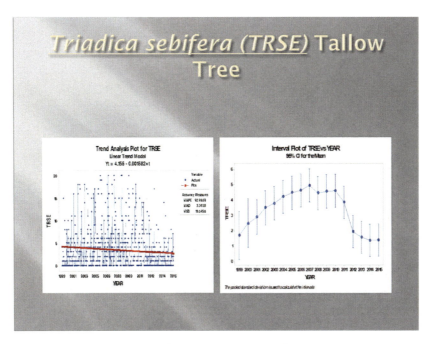

Graph courtesy Eric Combs

Collection of data over long periods of time may indicate trends. In this case we see the trend of Chinese tallow population decline over several decades. The data and trends are one tool used to help guide prairie management strategies. In this case we see that our management activities are succeeding as shown by the tallow decline on the above graph. If the graph shows an increasing tallow population, adjustments are needed to the strategy.

Prairie for the People

ABNC is home to one of the largest remnant prairie ecosystems around Galveston Bay. Furthermore, it is a publicly accessible prairie. Visitors may view this rare panorama from the Prairie Observation Platform, hike the prairie trail, or ride along on a Prairie Hayride Wildflower Tour. The success of ABNC's prairies is not only dependent on visitation by community members, but also by their participation in helping to restore them.

Prairie Rising: Get Involved!

Armand Bayou Nature Center has numerous opportunities for volunteers to join in and help restore coastal tallgrass prairie habitat. Our "Prairie Friday" team meets every Friday morning to conduct various activities such as plant propagation, seed collection, and installation of plants into the prairie. Our "Stewardship Saturday" group meets on the first and third Saturday of the month to conduct prairie activities, as well as other maintenance projects around the nature center. We also have an annual Prairie Pandemonium event occurring in October, where local residents join our volunteers in installing prairie plants.

For more information visit www.abnc.org or call 281-474-2551.

Benefits of Prairie Habitat: Prairie Dependent Wildlife

It is difficult for restoration to return prairie entirely back to its native, pristine state. However, the benefits of restoration are apparent when native wildlife species begin to reappear. Many species of wildlife are dependent upon coastal tallgrass prairie and entire populations can be extirpated from an area with the loss of this essential habitat.

Mottled Ducks

Mottled ducks are a non-migratory duck that depend on tall grass cover near a water source to nest and care for their young. They are endemic to Texas and Louisiana marshes and rely on adjacent tallgrass prairie habitat to reproduce. This species has experienced a 50 % population decline in the past 40 years to due habitat loss and hunting pressure.

Photo by Gary Seloff

Mottled ducks are one of only a few species of ducks that breed in Texas. The birds nest on the ground in coastal prairie habitat adjacent to bayou waters. Hatchlings follow their parents through the grass and into the bayou. Due to the loss of prairie habitat and tidal marsh habitat mottled duck populations have experienced a dramatic population decline. My last sighting of a mottled duck on Armand Bayou was in 2010.

Box Turtles

Ornate box turtles are a prairie dependent reptile. These softball sized turtles spend their entire lives in prairie habitats, feeding on insects, worms, snails, grasses, wildflowers, and berries. Ornate box turtles have declined throughout their range mostly due to loss of prairie habitat. They are listed as a species of concern throughout Texas. It seems that agricultural practices and habitat loss have diminished ornate box turtle populations throughout the area around ABNC. No ornate box turtles have been

seen recently within the nature center's prairies. However, the more forest dependent relative of the ornate box turtle, the three-toed box turtle frequently inhabits ABNC prairies. It is common to see three-toed box turtles in prairie habitat near the woods edge.

Box turtles have the ability to close themselves completely inside their shells. This is an advantage for a turtle species whose habitat is often completely consumed by fire.

Prairie Kingsnake

As their name implies, prairie kingsnakes are prairie dependent reptiles that play an important role in the prairie ecosystem. Prairie kingsnakes are considered dietary generalists and will consume mammals, birds, bird eggs, frogs, lizards, reptile eggs and snakes, including venomous snakes. It is because of this that their population numbers have remained stable. However, loss of prairie habitat is a continued threat to this unique grassland species.

Prairie Kingsnakes are non-venomous and may rattle their tail or emit a foul odor to deter predators.

Loggerhead Shrikes

Loggerhead shrikes are predatory songbirds that rely on prairie habitat for survival. This species feeds mainly on insects but will opportunistically take other prey species found in the prairie, including small mammals, birds, and snakes. Loggerhead shrike populations have experienced significant decline throughout their range as a result of habitat loss. The National Audubon Society estimates that this species has experienced an 80% decline in the past 40 years.

White-tailed Kites

Prairies provide essential foraging habitat for many birds of prey. One unique raptor, the white-tailed kite, is specifically adapted for hunting in the prairie. They have the ability to hover in place while scanning the landscape for their main diet of rodents and other small mammals. White-tailed kites were threatened with extinction in North America during the early twentieth century due to hunting and egg collection. Although populations are now stable, loss of prairie habitat is a threat to the long-term survival of the species.

Loggerhead shrikes are often referred to as "butcher birds". Because they lack talons, loggerhead shrikes will often impale their prey on thorns or even a barbed-wire fence to kill it. Photo by Gary Seloff

White-tailed kites are one of the only prairie-dependent birds of prey that nest at ABNC. Photo by Gary Seloff

Peregrine Falcon

Peregrine Falcon. Photo by Gary Seloff

Seeing the fastest animal that has ever lived leaves a lasting impression. There are occasional sightings over the open waters of lower Armand Bayou. Peregrines seek out wide open spaces. Space to view their prey from a distance and space to build intense speed to capture it. The falcon specializes in eating birds and is capable of diving at speeds approaching 200 miles per hour in pursuit. They are often described as a bird with a bad attitude. One of my most memorable pontoon boat Sunset Tours was with a boat load of Girl Scouts. The falcon gave a spectacular show of force chasing vultures and cormorants. One frantic cormorant flew full speed crashing headfirst into the bayou to escape the bully in pursuit. I assured the girls that I typically don't scream like that on most trips. Peregrine falcons were listed as an Endangered Species the year ABNC opened. Their populations have now recovered thanks in large part to the protection of the federal regulations of the Endangered Species Act. It's good to see that they've returned home.

For a deeper dive into Prairie Ecology:
www.youtube.com/watch?v=yKFeUXle2Vg

Chapter Five: *Bayou Ecology*

A Warm Winter's Night

By Mark Kramer

*There are stars upon the bayou on a warm
winter's night
Ancient rhythms fill the air and sing softly
to the light*

*The world is turning slowly as spring is
drawing near
Its vision to our dreaming eyes now is
growing clear*

*The warming soil, the sprouting seed, the
osprey's maiden flight
Are dreaming of the days to come on a
warm winter's night*

*There is lightning but no thunder and the
sky is growing clear
And my heart still knows the wonder of the
turning of the year*

*You bring to me this gift I see reflection to
my sight
To be touched by the beauty of the season
On a warm winter's night*

Armand Bayou is a rarity in the Bayou City.
Its original un-channelized streambed, tidal
connection to the bay, and wetland edge
promote a beautifully diverse urban oasis.

Armand Bayou is one of three tributaries that flow
into Clear Lake, originally called Middle Bayou because it's the central of the three. Taylor Bayou is to
the east, Clear Creek is to the west. The Clear Creek
Channel connects Clear Lake to Galveston Bay,
providing salty water through its connection to the
Gulf of Mexico.

What Is a Bayou?

Bayous are short, coastal, sluggish, moving water bodies. Unlike rivers and streams, which have steady
flow, bayou water's movement is subtle. Rising and
ebbing tides push the current in slow motion in
both directions. The exception to this gentle flow is
after significant rain. Major runoff events create
flow rates that reshape the deep-water streambed.

The term "bayou" is a colloquialism and only
used in certain locations. These coastal water bodies
are known as bayous throughout coastal Louisiana.
The term is also used to the south along the coast of

Texas until Mexican influences begin to dominate the language where other terms replace it.

Houston is known as the Bayou City due to their abundance. White Oak, Sims, Vince, Greens, Armand and Brays Bayou are familiar to local residents. Buffalo Bayou is the largest and most well-known bayou, which runs through downtown Houston and eventually becomes the Houston Ship Channel. When we drive over any of these others and look over the bridge into the bayou, what we see are man-made waterways. Armand Bayou even at a glance is much different.

Armand Bayou is more than a beautiful place, it's a living museum that serves as a laboratory for students. Rich with aquatic life, the bayou waters are an exciting place for exploration for naturalists of all ages.

What Is an Estuary?

Estuaries are places where rivers meet the sea. This mixing of rainwater and seawater create some of the most productive habitat on earth. Estuarine ecosystems rival tropical rainforests and coral reefs in the amount of life that they support. They are important nursery areas for many species of marine organisms. Spawning largely takes place in the waters of the Gulf of Mexico and Galveston Bay. In early Spring the developing larvae are trapped by the tides and are carried deep into the bayous where the young spend the first summer of their life. Over 90% of the important commercial and recreational

species harvested around Galveston Bay begin life in the protected estuarine nursery environment. This includes the young of redfish, speckled trout, flounder, mullet, drum, shrimp and blue crab. The young spend the first summer of life in this protected food-rich habitat. Feeding on algae and other available food, the young grow to several inches in length through the summer before the first fall cool fronts arrive. As the bayou water cools it signals the beginning of the return migration back to the salty waters of the bays and the Gulf where they spend the remainder of their adult life.

Gulf Fisheries Values
NOAA-2006

Shrimp – 65%
Menhaden – 8%
Blue Crabs – 6%

Estuaries and tidal marsh are the engine that drives the commercial and recreational fishery of the bay. Gulf menhaden in the millions spend the first few months of life feeding in the algae-rich waters of Armand Bayou.

Where Does the Water Come From?

There are three major sources of water that supply Armand Bayou. The tidal influence that connects the bayou to Clear Lake brings salty sea water to the bayou. Every day the tide rises and falls approximately two feet. The rising tide is an important source of salty seawater. This tidal influence reaches as far north as Genoa Red Bluff Road approximately six miles to the north. A second water source is produced with each rainfall and runoff event. The watershed of Armand Bayou captures rainfall from approximately 60 square miles of land. A third source of water is created from the water used in homes, business and industry. The water we use is held in surface reservoirs like Lake Houston. The water is used by people and then travels to an area waste-water treatment plant. The water is purified and then discharged into one of the bayous in Harris County. This water can be substantial and contributes a large volume of fresh water. The major waste-water treatment plant operated by Clear Lake City Water Authority is permitted to discharge ten million gallons of effluent into Horsepen Bayou daily.

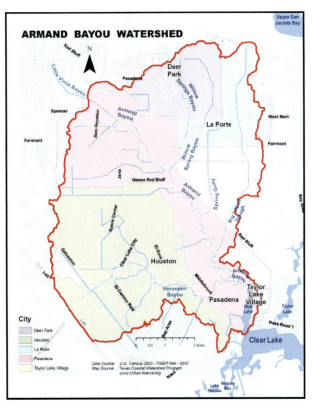

The bayou is the report card for its watershed.

What Is a Watershed?

If we were standing in Estes Park, Colorado, we could look around us for 360 degrees and see peaks of the Rocky Mountains. There is a tangible imagery of how rainwater travels downhill towards a receiving stream. Here in Houston, it's different. The coastal plain of Texas is relatively flat and featureless. It's more difficult to visualize how rainwater runoff

moves when the land is flat. Here topography is subtle. While it's not clearly visible to the naked eye, the Bayou City has a distinct watershed boundary for each bayou. Today Armand Bayou averages about 50 inches of rainfall per year. Climate change has altered weather patterns in the Houston area and today annual rainfall rates are increasing. This increases the need for individual awareness of which watershed that you live in.

Today most ecologists agree that the watershed is the single most effective unit of ecological management. The watershed of Armand Bayou captures approximately 60 square miles of rainfall and includes portions of Pasadena, Deer Park, La Porte, Houston and Taylor Lake Village. Landscapes are diverse and include suburban, industrial and wild lands. Approximately 125,000 people reside within its boundaries. So many people in such a small area compound the effects of each of our actions. It may not be an issue if one or two of us fertilize our lawns heavily, but if thousands follow a behavior the effects are cumulative.

Prairie Wetlands

There are several common wetland types in our area. Prairie wetlands were discussed in the previous chapter. However, there was little context as to their value to the water quality of Galveston Bay. Traveling back in time before Harris County became populated, prairies were the dominant feature in the landscape. There would have been tens of thousands of these wetland features scattered across the prairie landscape. They essentially absorb water like a sponge, then slowly release the water into local bayous. They may only be a few inches lower than the surrounding prairie and only a few inches deep, but during rainfall events they fill and temporarily hold the water. They may be dry much of the year but provide critical ecological functions and have significant value when full.

The Houston area experiences predictable seasonal cycles of rainfall, which impact soil moisture. During the heat of summer, rainfall is sporadic occurring only with isolated thunderstorms. Summer temperatures are high creating significant evaporation. Prairie plant physiology is active and the high plant metabolism pulls moisture from the soil and releases it to the atmosphere through evapotranspiration. Anyone who has ever tried to dig a hole in Houston in the summer knows that the soil can be bone dry and rock hard.

The seasonal cycle begins to shift as the first cool fronts arrive in late September. When warm air meets cool air, rainfall occurs. With each successive passing northerly weather system, rains bring change to soil moisture. Often by the end of the year the soils become so moist they are "super saturated" with standing water visible in most prairie wetlands.

Prairie wetlands are important habitat to many species. Amphibians seek these temporary wetlands as valuable reproductive habitat. Local frogs including the gulf coast toad, eastern narrow-mouth toad and eastern chorus frog require these ephemeral wetlands to breed and deposit their eggs. Fish are one of the primary predators of frog eggs. It's not possible for fish populations to establish with the short hydroperiod of prairie wetlands. These temporary wetlands completely dry out, regularly providing reproductive habitat that excludes the amphibian's main predator.

Armand Bayou watershed 1960. What do you see (or not see) when you look at this image?

Flooding and Green Infrastructure

Imagine you are flying over Harris County two hundred years ago, in our time traveling helicopter. When you look down, what you see is almost entirely coastal prairie. It contains many thousands of prairie wetland features. These are small depressions, just a few inches or a few feet lower than the surrounding topography. Imagine that there is a rain event that is slowly filling the wetlands. The rainwater is held in place and slowly released. This holding or *residence time* allows the water to be held and purified before entering the bay and bayou. Sediments settle out as a result of the water being held in place. Toxins are absorbed by prairie plants and into the soil. This *filtered* water is *slowly* released improving water quality in the bayous and bay.

Fast forward to present day and look down from our helicopter tour. The landscape has been completely transformed. This human built landscape is now mostly devoid of the abundant prairies and their associated wetlands. They have been replaced with roadways, parking lots, buildings and industry. These new features no longer capture and hold water. In fact, quite the opposite: they are referred to as *impermeable surfaces*. Where previously the water was held in wetlands, today these new surfaces usher the water quickly into local bayous. Without these filtering wetlands, water quality suffers.

Today, flooding is the top concern listed in polls by residents in the Houston area. In Houston we don't just have rain, we have *rain events*. We know that a rain event is imminent when the TV meteorologist questions whether we should leave home due to flooding concerns. Those concerns are reinforced when the news and weather preempt regular programming all day.

The era of the Anthropocene and human-driven climate change have magnified extremes in weather phenomenon. Houston has always been a wet area, but annual rainfall rates measured at both airports show an average annual rain increase of eight inches since 1970. This is in large part driven by the warming climate. The same airport weather stations also measured an average increase of three degrees Fahrenheit over the same time period. The warming atmosphere increases its ability to contain moisture by seven percent for every one degree of temperature rise. The resulting impact is that we now receive fifty-seven inches of rain per year on average. There is also an increase of rain events that release exceptionally large amounts of precipitation in a single day.

Compounding additional rainfall, rapid growth from the 1950s to 2020 has completely transformed the landscape. Without wetlands a rain event now creates a major pulse of rising water. Without wetlands the rapid rising water level may escape the bayou banks and enter our homes. Sadly, the Houston area has lost over 30,000 acres of prairie wetlands since 1950. Rapid growth over the past decades has altered the landscape and removed much of this valuable asset to the community.

These natural services that wetlands provide for wildlife habitat, water quality enhancement and flood reduction are referred to as *green infrastructure*. Open space, natural areas and especially wetlands produce valuable services at no cost to residents. In fact, wetlands are so valuable that they are the only ecosystem in the country that is federally protected.

The environmental success story that first preserved the wildlands along Armand Bayou is also a success story for the surrounding community. Greenspace (green infrastructure) along lower and middle Armand Bayou serves as a buffer. The lands surrounding the bayou's rising waters receives the flood without human impact. It's not just OK that the natural area floods, it's beneficial. In fact, the surrounding lands have evolved with and benefit from periodic flood events. Giving the bayou room to breathe has proven to be a good strategy to reduce the catastrophic human impacts of flooding while conserving our natural heritage.

What Is a Wetland?

Wetlands are composed of three elements. They may be identified by the presence of water, which is obvious. However, water needs to be present only for a portion of the year. Prairie wetlands as discussed may only contain visible water for a portion of the year and be dry the remainder. Some wetlands may be inundated and then dry every day, such as tidal wetlands. The amount of time that a wetland is inundated is referred to as the *hydroperiod*.

The second identifier is the presence of *wetland plants*. Plants require special adaptations to endure living in a wet area. Plants such as cattail, bulrush and cordgrass are biological indicators of wetlands. The final element required for a wetland are wetland soils. These *hydric soils* have been inundated for long periods and have experienced chemical changes to their structure. It takes all three elements (hydrology, wetland plants and hydric soils) to be a wetland.

This Great Egret dines on a moving buffet line of gulf menhaden. Photo by Gary Seloff

Tidal Wetlands

Tidal wetlands occur along the edges of Armand Bayou and Galveston Bay. As the name implies tidal marsh grows in the *tide zone*. In the Galveston Bay complex there is a *tidal fluctuation* of approximately two feet every day. When the tide is high the marshes are flooded. When the tide is low the marshes are dry. It's only within this critical margin of shallow water that the tidal marsh survives.

Tidal marshes are nursery grounds for many forms of fish and wildlife. At high tide they offer sanctuary from larger predators. The dense vegetation offers an escape from the pressures of open water where they are exposed and vulnerable.

Bayou City Eco-Almanac – Tidal Wetlands
www.youtube.com/watch?v=hwbrxigDUY8

Tidal Wetland Wildlife

Red-winged Blackbird

Red-winged Blackbird nest with eggs. Photo by Mark Kramer

Red-winged Blackbirds are icons of marshes and wetlands all across North America. Photo by Gary Seloff

These marshes are equally important to many species of birds. They provide feeding habitat along the marsh edge. More importantly they offer nesting habitat to marsh dependent species like the Redwinged Blackbird, Marsh Wren and Least Bittern.

Red-winged Blackbird chicks with four hungry mouths. Photo by Gary Seloff

Male Red-winged Blackbirds display vivid red shoulder patches which they flair and flutter in an effort to attract the attention of a female. Perched on the highest tree branch near the marsh, the male bird does his best song and dance. This marks the beginning of the nesting season for redwings in the marshes of Armand Bayou and throughout North America. After mating, females weave an incredibly intricate nest by pulling the tops of marsh grass together. ABNC has restored over 26 acres of tidal marsh habitat since 1995. Red-winged Blackbirds have taken notice.

Marsh Wren

Marsh Wren on bulrush. Photo by Gary Seloff

Wrens are small birds with huge voices. Difficult to see even under the best conditions, their call is an intricate melody that can mesmerize a drifting kayaker into a different world. The mouth of Horsepen Bayou is a marsh wren hotspot and ideal for paddlers (or Pontoon Boat Eco-Tourists) who come to hear their floating calls in every direction in the early morning hours. This biological hotspot contains acres of restored marshes, planted by ABNC, which provide critical habitat for numerous marsh dependent bird species.

The Swallows of Summer

Tree Swallow targeting flying insects above Horsepen Bayou. Photo by Gary Seloff

The skies above Armand Bayou host over 220 species of birds in an average year. Of that vast array, swallows more than any other bird typify the joy of flight. Swallows spend most of their life airborne and are capable of exhibiting spectacular displays of speed, maneuverability and endurance. Remarkably, these incredible flyers weigh only about a half ounce (two U.S. quarters).

Three swallow species occupy the summer skies of Armand Bayou. The Barn Swallow *(Hirundo rustica)* and Cliff Swallow *(Petrochelidon pyrrhonota)* are on view from around mid-March and are commonly sighted. My favorite spots to enjoy their precision flight maneuvers are from the prairie observation platform, boathouse bayou overlook, or best of all, while paddling. These aerial insectivores are birds of open space and require the expanse to demonstrate their extreme acrobatics while plucking bugs from mid-air. These species have expanded their nesting range over the past several decades. As the name implies, Cliff Swallows prefer to build their nests on the sides of cliffs. The nearest cliffs to the Bayou City are, well, a long way off. Twenty years ago, there were no nesting swallows on Armand Bayou. The birds have expanded their range throughout the Houston area and have learned to adapt to new nesting habitats. They now find suitable nesting sites on the underside of concrete bridges that cross over local bayous and rivers. The Bay Area Boulevard

Cliff Swallows collect mud for their nests. Photo by Ann Brinly

bridge crossing Armand Bayou holds the largest swallow nesting colony in the Armand Bayou watershed with approximately 100 nests and also provides an excellent viewing opportunity with binoculars from Bay Area Park.

Swallows return to the Texas coast in early

spring (mid-March) after the very long journey from their winter range in South America. Many birds fly directly over the Gulf of Mexico on their migration, from the Yucatan Peninsula to the Texas coast, an arduous, non-stop flight that saves them many travel miles. Once back, the first order of business is nest building. Cliff Swallows build a fascinating nest made of mud. Gently landing or hovering over the bayou mudflats at low tide, the birds collect a mouthful of mud. Mixed with saliva, the nest is created one mud ball at a time. Hundreds of trips are required to complete the construction.

Cliff Swallow nests under construction.
Photo by Lyman Brown

Adult Barn Swallow feeding newly fledged youngsters in restored bulrush marshes.
Photo by Gary Seloff

Early summer is the time of year that newly hatched swallows take first flight. But imagine when you look down from the nest! Water everywhere. The first flight for fledgling swallows has zero tolerance for error. Birds in the water don't recover. Swallow's tiny feet find perfect perching habitat in nearby restored bulrush marshes.

Aerial acrobats feed young on the wing.
Photo by Gary Seloff

Slowly the young birds will build their flight muscles and are well fed on abundant flying insects. Swallows are amongst the earliest of fall migrants to depart Texas. They leave Armand Bayou in late July or early August on the return flight to South America, which is where they spend our winter months.

All swallows are handsome birds, but the Tree Swallow (*Tachycineta bicolor*) is adorned in a tuxedo.
Photo by Gary Seloff

Tree swallows are the rarest of swallows on Armand Bayou: there are only two known nests on the refuge. As the name implies, they build their nests in tree cavities. One nest is located off of the Bay Area Park marsh boardwalk. A second nest is located in a nest box/birdhouse installed by ABNC Staff. The nest box is located on a dead tree over the bayou waters and is visible with binoculars from the bayou overlook on the Karankawa Trail. How exciting it was for me as I paddled past it in late spring and confirmed the box was in use!

On rare occasion, large flocks of migrating swallows drop in on their fall migration south and use ABNC as a rest stop. Photo by Gary Seloff.

Swallows are on a short list of birds that are celebrated by communities around the world. The swallows of San Juan Capistrano, California are welcomed every spring with one of the longest running celebrations in the country (80 years). Spring is the time for you to visit and celebrate these local masters of flight, right in your own backyard.

For a Deeper Dive Into Armand Bayou Swallows:

Bayou City Eco-Almanac – Swallows
youtu.be/sN3JQ-1efiI

Avian Acrobats

Least Bittern (*Ixobrychus exilis*).
Photo by Gary Seloff

Green Heron (*Butorides virescens*).
Photo by Gary Seloff

Most members of the heron family are long legged birds that spend much the day wading in the shallows pursuing their next meal. There are two notable exceptions to the family of wade feeding birds, which prefer to keep their feet dry. These are the smallest members of the heron family and when performing, put on a real show for those who appreciate a natural spectacle. Just as Olympic gymnasts are small in stature, so too are these elite avian athletes. Grace, speed, balance and strength characterize these marvels of the marsh.

Armand Bayou is unusual in the Bayou City in that it is one of the only bayous that has never been channelized. This process of straightening, widening and deepening the streambed has been employed for decades in the Houston area in an effort to minimize flooding. Unfortunately, the channelization process also creates a number of negative environmental impacts. The channelized bayou has been deepened with an abrupt drop off from the water's edge. The dredging of this shallow water margin also means no marsh occurs along the bayou edge. The channelized bayou has also been cleared of adjacent trees and shrubs in an effort to improve water flow rates during flood events. As we'll see, these two heron species have critical habitat requirements, which include emergent marsh and dense forest adjacent to the bayou, making the waters of Armand Bayou ideal.

In addition to Armand Bayou retaining its historic streambed and meandering serpentine path, there has been extensive restoration of tidal marsh. More than 26 acres of tidal marsh habitat has been replanted since 1995. For several decades the ABNC native plant nursery ponds cultivated California bulrush *(Schoenoplectus californicus)*. This plant material was used for restoration throughout the bayou. Bulrush marshes are important feeding and nesting habitat for the Least Bittern.

Yaktographer in his preferred habitat.
Photo by Randell Zerr

These species show only glimpses of their true abilities. Even for someone who has spent a lifetime admiring bayou fauna, getting a good look at these secretive hunters is rare. Their extreme maneuvers take place at lightning speed and are difficult for the naked eye to process or appreciate. I have said many times that the lens and artistry of Gary Seloff reveals images of wildlife behavior impossible to witness by any other means. These are among the species rarely seen, but now are captured on our photographic safari in close up freeze fame for your viewing pleasure.

Least Bitterns are the smallest member of the heron family. With feet specially adapted to walk from stem to stem, they occur primarily in the restored California bulrush marshes of Armand Bayou from April through October. Photo by Gary Seloff

ABNC Staff and volunteers cultivated much of the California bulrush used in our marsh restoration work at our on-site native plant nursery. Staff also developed an innovative bulrush planting technique called the bulrush bomb, which allows bulrush to be installed in a restoration site off of a boat and without getting in the water. Since the time the nature center was first established, least bitterns were not seen on Armand Bayou until California bulrush marshes were restored.

Fishing is easy in the food rich waters of summer. Schools of gulf menhaden ride the tides, drifting past hungry mouths. Photo by Gary Seloff

Dad is bringing home the groceries to the bittern family. Photo by Gary Seloff

In the excellent nesting habitat of California bulrush, this parent keeps watchful eyes on any who venture close. Photo by Gary Seloff

Green Herons are year-round residents on Armand Bayou. Photo by Gary Seloff

Green herons are typically found stalking through dense brush and vegetation along the bayou's edge. These opportunistic predators are fast and agile. At first glance the bird appears drab and camouflaged. But a closer view with good optics reveals hues that are both subtle and striking.

Green Heron colors revealed in morning light.
Photo by Gary Seloff

Tree limbs overhanging the protected waters
of Horsepen Bayou offer prime Green
Heron fishing perches. Photo by Gary Seloff

No other heron possesses the extreme athleticism
of the Green Heron. Photo by Gary Seloff

Great Egret and the Rising Tide

As the last of the cool fronts of early spring have blown past us, the winds of change are stirring. As if there was a flipping of a switch the onshore flow of coastal winds will dominate our weather for the next six months. Sweeping southerlies push warm salty seawater into Galveston Bay and deep into Armand Bayou. The rising gulf tides of spring are a living soup carrying an abundance and diversity of juvenile marine life. Over 90% of our local commercial and recreational seafood spends the juvenile portion of its life in these types of estuarine waters and tidal marshes. Tidal marshes are the engine that drives the commercial and recreational fishing industry. Born in the open waters of the gulf and Galveston Bay, young

Great Egret exploding a school of gulf menhaden.
Photo by Gary Seloff

redfish, speckled trout, flounder, black drum, shrimp, blue crab and gulf menhaden are riding the tides and seeking this nursery habitat. Does that sound like a seafood platter to you? Hiding, feeding and evading predators, the young will spend the first summer of their life in the protected estuarine waters of Armand Bayou before returning to bay waters in the fall.

Like a moving buffet line carried by the rising tide, the Great Egret has found dinner in a school of juvenile gulf menhaden. Gulf menhaden are not well known to most people and yet they are the third most important commercial fish species harvested from the Gulf of Mexico. Adult menhaden are 6 to 8 inches long and are harvested by huge fishing boats in the Gulf and used as a major component of animal food (dog, cat and chicken food). They are also among the most important forage fish in the bayou. This Great Egret is gathering groceries from the productive waters of the estuary to take home to the rookery to feed this year's offspring. Estuaries like Armand Bayou are among the most productive habitats on earth, providing food for seafood lovers of all types.

Living Water

If most people were asked to imagine a healthy productive waterway, they would probably visualize a clear mountain lake or salmon filled river. For most of us, clear water is associated with productive water. But while gin clear alpine lakes and West Coast rivers are beautiful, they pale in comparison to the volume and diversity of life found in the muddy waters of Gulf Coast estuaries. It turns out that the very nature of the turbid bayou water holds the secret ingredient to aquatic life.

Estuaries are defined by the ebb and flow of tidal exchange. Tide water mixes with rainwater from the surrounding watershed. Tidal streams, such as Armand Bayou are in a dynamic hydrological process. Freshwater rain runoff buffers high salinity levels pushed in by gulf tides. A Houston-sized rain event may drop bayou salinity from salty to fresh water overnight. Salinity levels drive the distribution of all plant and animal life in Armand Bayou. The magic

happens where rivers meet the sea, producing an abundance of life that few other ecosystems rival.

The algae rich bayou water of summer has a characteristic green color. Even alligators may begin to grow algae. Photo by Lou Wheatcraft

The abundance is built on a theme that plays itself out from the arctic to the equator. The Bayou food web foundation is built on algae. Algae and plankton are among the simplest plants on the planet. They chase the sun in a slow-motion, diurnal vertical migration, every day rising to the surface at dawn and then withdrawing into the night. Observant summer paddlers on Armand Bayou often find relatively clear water at first light until plankton travel to the surface, giving the water a green, cloudy appearance.

These single celled free-floating algae in the water column are consumed by fishes and add oxygen to the water.

Filamentous algae grow on the bayou bottom and on dead fallen trees. Photos by Mark Kramer

Sometimes these simple organisms link together forming long chains or strands. Filamentous algae grow in the shallows where sunlight penetrates to the bayou bottom. This photic zone only occurs in water less than a couple of feet deep on the tidal flats of Armand Bayou. These tidal flats support lush fields of filamentous algae and are important feeding habitat for many forms of marine organisms.

At low tide the dark stain of epiphytic algae is exposed on the stems of cordgrass. Photo by Mark Kramer

Sometimes algae may grow on other larger plants. Plants that grow attached to other plants are known as epiphytes. In Armand Bayou, epiphytic algae grow on the stems of marsh plants. Each stem of bulrush and cordgrass is a vertical reef where shrimp, crabs and mullet graze within the protected food rich environment.

Warm water, long days, abundant nutrients and bright sunlight promote prolific algal growth in the summer months. It's a beautifully meshed web of life where juvenile marine organisms drift in on the summer tide to find abundant algal nourishment during the most vulnerable stage of life.

Toxic Algae

There is increasing evidence that one form of algae may produce harmful toxins. *Blue-green algae* occur in fresh, brackish, and saltwater environments. Blue-green algae populations may explode in areas that receive large inputs of nitrogen and phosphorous. Phosphorous is used as fertilizer and is also found in many laundry detergents. Runoff events may carry phosphorus from fertilized lawns, throughout the watershed and ultimately into the bayou. Laundry detergents are carried from the washing machine, through the sewer system and into wastewater treatment plants. In Texas there are few regulations controlling the amount of treated *effluent* that enters into local bayous. For example, the wastewater treatment plant located on Horsepen Bayou is permitted to discharge as much as 10,000,000 gallons of treated wastewater every day. The water meets state standards but there are no state regulations which limit phosphorous discharge. This significant volume of discharge carries a heavy load of nutrients, especially nitrogen and phosphorus. This significant *nutrient load* provides elements essential for vigorous plant growth. Plankton and algae populations reproduce rapidly creating an *algae bloom*. On occasion during the summer months, bayou water is vivid green and resembles the color of electric split pea soup.

When blue-green algae populations explode, they may produce a toxic substance known as BMAA. BMAA is a potent neurotoxin. There is increasing evidence that suggests the compound may be a contributing factor to degenerative neuro-muscular disorders such as amyotrophic lateral sclerosis (ALS), Alzheimer's Disease and Parkinson's Disease.

Rangia clams thrive in Armand Bayou due to abundant food. Photo by Mark Kramer

Some algae eaters specialize in harvesting free floating plankton from the water. Special adaptations enable the filtering of these tiny plants where they are consumed. Some, such as the *Rangia* clam, are bivalves that siphon volumes of water through their system daily. During the lowest tides of winter, the mud flats where they live are dry and exposed for a uniquely rare viewing opportunity. This siphoning continues as they sip what water that they can from the surrounding mud. They squirt a jet of water toward the sky as if a child with a water pistol was shooting from below.

Other algae eaters, such as the bay anchovy, gizzard shad and gulf menhaden have a different filtering strategy. These filter feeders spend all day and most of their life swimming with their mouths open, gathering a meal from this super food.

Omnivores find ample grazing in the Bayou waters. Crustaceans such as shrimp and crabs use specially adapted pincers to snip bite size morsels of filamentous algae.

Barnacles on dead trees in Armand Bayou.
Photo by Mark Kramer

Barnacles are abundant on fallen trees and other hard structures in brackish water. These crustaceans use special feather-like appendages which sift floating algae from the water as the tide comes in. As the tide falls, the appendages withdraw and are protected inside the body until the next high tide.

A female fiddler crab

Bay anchovy   Gizzard shad
Photos by Mark Kramer

A male fiddler crab

Armored catfish are not native to Texas.
Photo by Gary Seloff

Striped mullet and armored catfish (aka Plecostomous) make a good living by feasting on epiphytic algae found on the stems of marsh plants. During the summer, smooth cordgrass stems dance as mullet lunge to grab a mouthful of living green velvet.

Armored catfish are sold through the aquarium trade as "Algae Eaters" to help keep aquarium glass clean. Home aquarium hobbyists contribute to the problematic spread of invasive species by releasing aquarium fish into public waters.

This gravid grass shrimp feasts on epiphytic algae along the marsh edge. As her young are born, they're eaten by one of the most unusual fish in Armand Bayou. Gulf pipefish are members of the seahorse family and are one of the most beautifully fragile of all bayou fish.

Grass shrimp and gulf pipefish. Notice the cluster of eggs attached to the shrimp's abdomen.
Photos by Mark Kramer

Predators galore reap the bounty as sunlit energy passes from algae to the top of the food chain. Many of the most sought-after coastal gamefish build their populations through this complex food web.

Photos by Mark Kramer

Flathead catfish circa 1973.
Collection of Mark Kramer

Scavengers are the clean-up crew. Numerous species of freshwater and saltwater catfish and gar make an easy living.

The long, elegant pectoral and dorsal fins make the gafftop catfish a beautiful and distinctive specimen. Photo by Mark Kramer

Salinity levels drive the distribution of all plant and animal life in estuaries such as Armand Bayou. Saltwater fishes such as the gafftop catfish are found in the extreme southern reach of the bayou adjacent to Clear Lake where salty tides enter.

Members of the sunfish family such as this longear sunfish get their name by displaying every color under the sun. Photo by Mark Kramer

Upper Armand Bayou is characteristic of any east Texas freshwater stream. Here, freshwater plants and animals comprise the assembly of life. Bass, sunfish, catfish, crappie, smallmouth buffalo and gar are some of the river species which occur.

Asian grass carp (aka white amur). Photo by Mark Kramer

Some aquatic species are newcomers to the bayou. Some of these animals found their way here accidently. Others were intentionally released into the waters of Texas. Asian grass carp were intentionally released into east Texas reservoirs by state agencies in an attempt to control invasive aquatic plants (hydrilla). Grass carp escaped from these lakes, migrated down rivers and entered into Galveston Bay. They migrated through the bay and entered Armand Bayou where I first encountered them in 1995. The fish have pharyngeal teeth, which enable them to consume large amounts of plant material. Asian grass carp are big fish which may weigh up to 60 pounds and may eat twice their body weight in plant material every day. This voracious appetite is known to have significant impacts to valuable wetland habitats.

In a relatively short stream section, there is a tremendous diversity of freshwater and saltwater aquatic life. Traveling just under seven river miles on Armand Bayou you'll encounter many species typically found in Galveston Bay and others that are associated with east Texas river systems.

If only somehow, we get could get a glimpse of what is below the surface. If only I could use my Naturalist Magic Wand and we could transform the water to the clarity of a mountain lake and be able to see down twenty feet into the water, even if only for a few minutes.

Fish of Armand Bayou

Sketches courtesy Dr. Earl Chilton

Looking below the surface. Photo by Mark Kramer

If we could have that clarity of vision, we would have a mind-blowing experience. We would see shrimp, and crabs clinging to the bulrush and cordgrass browsing on the epiphytic algae on their stems. We would see schools of striped mullet grazing on fields of filamentous algae covering the shallow floor of tidal flats. We would be shocked to see huge schools of gulf menhaden stretching shore to shore with hundreds of thousands of small fish in each school. Menhaden swimming choreographed like a huge flock of blackbirds, changing direction in unison. With our enhanced vision, we would see hundreds of ladyfish chasing those schools of menhaden into a tight ball, slashing through the water's surface, erupting from their pursuit. We would see the gulf pipefish, the bayou's only member of the seahorse family stalking through the marsh grasses, hoping to find tube worms or tiny grass shrimp for a meal. We would see wading birds of every shape hunting the marsh edge for an easy meal. We would see mullet just below the water's surface with a hovering osprey overhead, locked on its prey, preparing for a spectacular dive.

Looking into the depths of the bayou, there are large blue catfish and alligator gar cruising their domain for any scraps settling down from above. Shifting our gaze, we see the alligator quietly waiting. Patiently anticipating that a Great Blue Heron might land within striking distance. We would see the fast and agile American river otter gracefully catching blue crab along the marsh edge. That's all happening right now, typically hidden from view in this complex ecosystem.

Here, life is built layer upon layer, interconnected and co-dependent, just like all of the old Indian chiefs said. It turns out that we *are* all related. From sunlight to algae. From algae to fish. From fish to my dinner table. The abundance of life is hidden below the surface, obscured from human view in the rich, cloudy bayou water. Because of the veil of algae hiding the life below the water's surface, bayous don't get the ecological respect that they deserve. If only we could get a glimpse into the secret world, into these living waters.

For more bayou information:

Bayou City – TX Parks & Wildlife Dept
filmfreeway.com/BayouCity Password: Houston

Daily, Seasonal, and Long-term Cycles

Bayous and estuaries are dynamic systems. Change is the constant feature shaping all organisms. Daily cycles of tides ebb and flow, flooding tidal marshes. As the seasons change so do salinity and water temperatures. In the summer, infrequent rainfall and high evaporation rates mean little runoff and small amounts of freshwater inflow. As a result, summer salinities are higher. By contrast, the winter has abundant rainfall and frequent rain creating freshwater inflow. Due to this, salinities are lower in the winter months.

Jellyfish in Armand Bayou. Photo by Mark Kramer

On rare occasion a long-term change occurs. In 2011 Houston recorded its driest year ever. Estuaries are a mixing of fresh and saltwater. In Armand Bayou, no rain means no freshwater inflow. With no freshwater to dilute the daily rising of the salty tides, water became very salty, and seldom seen species marine species such as jellyfish were observed. Average summer salinities in open Galveston are 22 parts per thousand. This same salinity was recorded in the farthest upper reaches of the bayou during the drought.

Non-point source pollutants enter a waterway from a diffuse and ill-defined source. Point source pollutants are easy to identify such as a pipe discharge.

Non-point source pollutants are the primary contributor to water quality issues in Armand Bayou. Rain falls in the watershed and begins its journey across the land surface toward the bayou. As it travels across the land surface it picks up material and transports it in the flow. Chemicals, fertilizer and sediment are some of the pollutants that enter the water. Chemicals such as insecticide that are used in households are carried in the flow. Sediments are picked up in areas of construction and travel to the bayou. Bacteria are another problematic pollutant in all Houston bayous.

In nature balance is critical to ecosystem health. While algae are important for oxygenation and as food for aquatic organisms, there can be an overabundance. Plants need nutrients in order to thrive.

Commercial fertilizer available at the hardware store lists three numbers on the front of the bag. They indicate the ratio of nitrogen, phosphorous, and potassium. For example, a bag posting 20-20-20 has an equal ratio of the three nutrients. These elements are *growth limiting factors* in plants. When any of these elements are absent plants languish and grow slowly. When they are abundant plants grow with vigor.

Eutrophication can cause fish kills. These gulf menhaden died from low levels of dissolved oxygen. Photo by Mark Kramer

As rain falls in the watershed, fertilizers containing these nutrients are picked up from yards and make their way into the bayou. Remembering there are 125,000 watershed residents, *cumulative effects* compound the problem. This process is called *nutrient loading*. The abundance of nutrients promotes a "bloom" of algae. As algae populations explode, they consume the available dissolved gases (including oxygen) from the water column. Summer temperatures are especially problematic as warm water has less capacity to hold oxygen. Virtually all aquatic life as we know it depends on oxygen for survival. The term used for this low level of oxygen in a waterway is hypoxia. Without available oxygen, fish kills occur. Typically, more sensitive species such as gulf menhaden are primarily impacted. This process of nutrient loading, algae blooms, hypoxia and fish kills is known as *eutrophication*. While these events are rare, they can occur every year or two.

Tides
-What creates tidal movement?
-What role do tides play in the distribution of life?

Tides are the driving force in distributing all life in Armand Bayou

What are tides?

Tides are created by the gravitational pull of the moon and sun on the ocean waters of the planet. Twice per month usually during the full and new moon phases the tides are particularly high and especially low. These events are called *Spring tides* and are created when the gravitational pull of the sun and moon are in alignment working together to make extreme tidal events. This daily ebb and flow of the tide contributes more than water quantity, it is the source of salty seawater entering the bayou. The tidal connection occurs at the Armand Bayou's confluence with Clear Lake, where Lake Mark Kramer passes under NASA Parkway. Generally, the further north that you travel away from the tidal source, the lower the salinity. Saline water is critical to the recipe for estuaries.

In shallow bay systems wind may also play a role in pushing tidal water. For example, when Hurricane Ike made landfall the powerful southerly winds pushed a wall of water ahead of the hurricane. This is known as *storm surge* and it is dramatic.

Even lesser southerly winds of 15 to 25 miles per hour may create tides above normal high tide levels. These southerly wind-driven tides also play a role in pushing salty sea water deep into Galveston Bay.

By contrast, strong northerly winds have the opposite effect on tides. Northerly winds blow bay waters offshore. In a shallow bay or bayou this creates wind driven tide levels that are well below normal. For this reason, local fishermen refer to these events as *blowout tides.* As a strong cold front passes over Houston, it may create strong northerly winds sustained for several days. To the untrained eye, it appears that someone has pulled the drain plug on the bayou. The picture above is just such a blowout tide.

In coastal Texas, southerly winds dominate during summer making bayou water much saltier. Winter winds are predominately northerly making the waters less saline. The high levels of salt in summer mesh perfectly with the multitude of juvenile marine species that depend on estuaries for their first summer of life.

Salt is a toxic substance to virtually all life. Plants and animals that live in saltwater must have special adaptations. Those species of plants and animals adapted to tolerate salt occur at the southern end of the bayou near the tidal influence at Clear Lake. Those less adapted live further north in fresher water. Because of this gradient of salinity levels, the fishery of Armand Bayou is very diverse. In this relatively short six-mile stream, representatives of fish species from Galveston Bay as well as just about any East Texas lake of river can be found.

The Mega-Fish of Armand Bayou

Many a paddler has returned to the shores of Armand Bayou convinced that they have had a close encounter with an alligator or even worse a monster from the deep. A huge splash rocks the boat and soaks the person from head to toe. The culprit is most

certainly one of the three species of gar occurring in Armand Bayou. Gars are harmless to humans, yet a surprise encounter creates a moment that will be remembered. I have certainly had my share of these heart-stopping paddling adventures and they never fail to excite.

Gars are ancient fishes which are specially adapted for life in shallow sluggish moving bayou waters. They are among a group of fishes which predate bony fish and whose skeleton is composed largely of cartilage. Gar scales function as an interlocking armor plating. Their scales, called ganoid scales, are heavier and more protective than most other fish scales (called cycloid scales). It was once believed that gars were a fish which impacted sport fish populations. Today it is known that gars are primarily scavengers and have little impact on "desirable" sport fish species populations.

A gar surfaces to gulp air and also takes in some Armand Bayou bird watching. Photo by Gary Seloff

The key to gar success in bayou waters lies in their unusual adaption to breath air. Gars are able to absorb oxygen from the water through the use of gills as are most fish. However, they also have a specially adapted swim bladder that functions as a primitive lung. The swim bladder in most fish is a "balloon" type organ that helps to float or position the fish in the water column. Inflated, the fish rises nearer the water surface, deflated, the fish sinks. The gar's swim bladder when inflated also functions like a primitive lung. The swim bladder lining is rich with blood vessels and can absorb oxygen to supplement the gills' uptake of dissolved oxygen from the water. The gar's swim bladder is also attached to the esophagus. This allows the fish to surface and "gulp" air to inflate the bladder and "breathe." I occasionally witness a large gar surface near my kayak and there is a sound resembling a person taking a sudden gasp of air when the swim bladder is inflated.

During the hot summer months bayou water temperatures hover around 90 degrees. An important physical property of water to understand is that *the warmer the water temperature, the less dissolved oxygen the water is capable of holding.* Water quality may be further compromised by excessive populations of plankton and algae in bayou water. Long day length, bright sun and warm temperatures create perfect conditions for a "plankton bloom." Often bayou water resembles split pea soup during these peak algae bloom periods. These conditions further rob dissolved gases including oxygen from the water. Gars have evolved the unusual ability to supplement oxygen intake through the swim bladder allowing their species to thrive during these difficult periods.

Four species of gar occur in Texas. I have documented three species in Armand Bayou. Shortnose gar *(Lepisosteus platostomus)* is the only species not yet identified in Armand Bayou. The most common is the spotted gar. Spotted gars are the smallest gar species found in the bayou and average two to three feet long. Spotted gars prefer low salinity levels in the water and typically are found in upper Armand Bayou.

Longnose gar (*Lepisosteous osseus*).
Photo by Mark Kramer

Most people consider gar to be an ugly or frightful fish. Maybe this accounts in part for the general lack of respect the fish receives. I suggest that there is beauty in the enduring design of the fish, which has lived unchanged for millions of years. I would further disagree when discussing the longnose gar. Seldom seen, the long-nose gar is sleek with an extended slender snout that has beautiful black markings.

Spotted gar (*Lepisosteus oculatus*) are commonly seen at the water's surface during eco-tours on the Bayou Ranger. Photo by Mark Kramer

Alligator gar are the second largest freshwater fish in North America with a world record of 327 lbs.
Photo by Mark Kramer

Alligator gar are the largest freshwater fish in Texas. Adults average six feet in length but some have been known to grow 10 feet long and live for over 60 years! While they are classified as a freshwater fish, I have encountered them while paddling in waters ranging from Lake Livingston to San Luis Pass. The animal has a stout head that resembles the head of an alligator. It's large size and gruesome appearance have given it an ill-fated reputation. In fact, in 1933 the Texas Fish and Game Commission undertook a statewide effort to eradicate gars from many Texas water bodies. This philosophy endured for years around the country and today the alligator gar has been extirpated in Indiana, Illinois and Ohio due largely to lack of adequate harvest regulations. The species has been considered a "rough" or "trash" fish and only in recent years received the appropriate protection to promote its long-term survival.

Anonymous bow fishermen on Armand Bayou.

While this large, long lived, specially-adapted fish may seem invulnerable after surviving on earth for many millions of years, there are several chinks in its defenses. The fish are slow to reach maturity, taking about 10 years to reach reproductive age. This long maturation period makes for a lengthy recovery if the adult breeding population is removed. Alligator gars also have a very specific set of requirements needed to trigger spawning. Flood events motivate reproductive behavior, stimulating fish movement to adjacent flooded grassy fields where spawning occurs in the spring and summer. In the Bayou City most all of those bayous have now been channelized. This man-made alteration of bayou hydrology is designed to help minimize flooding, but has also largely eliminated those adjacent fields needed for reproductive habitat. The unusual air breathing characteristic puts the fish at the water's surface frequently. This surfacing makes gars an easy target for bow hunters who shoot the fish with barbed arrows when they surface.

Few fishermen find gar to be desirable table fare and choose to release these mega-fish of the Bayou City.
Photo by Jennifer Logsdon Kramer

I worked as eco-tour guide captain on the pontoon boats operated by Harris County Parks Department during the 1980s. The free boat tours ran out of Bay Area Park five days per week. Those electric boats had seats that were positioned to the very front edge of the boat. Each trip began with a word of caution: "Please be aware that we are likely to bump a huge fish that will rock the boat, create a gigantic splash and cover you folks in front with water." Those gar interactions occurred regularly for years but have now become very rare. A lack of harvest regulations, loss of reproductive habitat and a bad reputation have all contributed to gar population decline throughout their range. Fifty-seven species of fish have become extinct in North America in the last century. Today fishermen with concern for the future are increasingly embracing catch and release practices.

Diversity of fish-eating bird species is a good indicator of a healthy fishery and a good biological indicator of ecosystem health. Photos by Ann Brinly

Habitat is the specialized assembly of places that a species requires to meet its complete set of needs in every stage of its life. When thinking about an animal's habitat, think about what *you* need as habitat. Habitat for humanity is your home, the place where you get all of your needs met. Your home has different rooms that have special functions to meet your needs. The kitchen fills the need for eating, the bedroom for sleeping, the children's room is a nursery area for developing young. There is the living room, which is the place to lounge and relax. For me that means in the recliner with the remote-control watching Game of Thrones with a piece of pie. Wildlife has similar needs for the species to be healthy. The image above portrays the complex habitat needs for wading birds, which is referred to as a habitat mosaic.

When all of the various required habitats are present, it is high quality habitat and the species thrives. If any one of the habitats is compromised or removed, the species will suffer. For example, imagine that bayou waters are severely polluted and fish populations decline. Without adequate food resources the birds will suffer. Remove two of the required habitats and species population may crash. Each species requires a unique set of habitats. A similar habitat mosaic may be built for each.

Photos by Ann Brinly

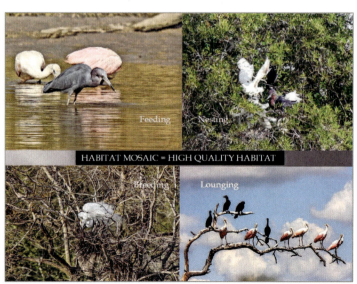

Feeding | Nesting
HABITAT MOSAIC = HIGH QUALITY
Lounging | Breeding

All species require high quality habitat. A similar habitat mosaic may be assembled for any form of wildlife such as the alligators of Armand Bayou.

Heron Shores

Photo by Gary Seloff

There are few places on the Texas coast where nature lovers can expect to see the assembly of wildlife that is concentrated at Armand Bayou Nature Center. ABNC is an island ecosystem, increasingly surrounded by urban and industrial growth. With few other natural areas nearby, ABNC is effectively a "biological greenhouse," concentrating a richness of species difficult to experience elsewhere. To find this located in the most densely populated county in Texas is truly remarkable. The concentration of wading birds along the bayou's wetland edges and tidal flats reaches its peak over the summer months. Almost every species of heron and egret found in Texas may be regularly encountered on a half mile summer paddling or pontoon excursion.

Those birds are drawn to the ideal habitats found in the productive waters and quiet surroundings of the 2500-acre urban wilderness. They find ideal *feeding habitat* in the bayou's estuarine waters. There is ideal *lounging habitat* of the quiet waters of Armand Bayou where a protective city ordinance prohibits the use of gasoline powered boat traffic. The refuge also supports excellent *nursery habitat* and one of the few sites where hundreds of these birds gather to collectively nest as a group. What we have described is a complete mosaic of heron habitat. All species require feeding, lounging, breeding and nursery habitat to thrive. Compromise any one of those elements and a wildlife's population will decline.

The first marsh planting circa 1995.
Photo by Mark Kramer

ABNC staff and volunteers have built an innovative structure to enhance nesting opportunities on the Rookery. Photo by Mark Kramer

The 2020 census counted over 300 birds on the rookery, which is located on an island about the size of your house! Photo by Mark Kramer

ABNC is a rare ecological success story in environmental news in that its habitats have recovered and improved throughout our lengthy restoration history. These efforts have enhanced wetland habitats and encouraged an abundance of Great Egrets, Snowy Egrets, Cattle Egrets, Tri-Colored Herons, Little Blue Herons, Yellow-crowned Night-Herons, Black-crowned Night-Herons, Great Blue Herons, Green Herons and Least Bitterns onto the nature center. I have had many a Bayou Ranger tour where all of these species are seen on a single trip!

Every spring many of these fish-eating bird species gather to raise the next generation. This assortment of different bird species that congregate and nest as a group is referred to as colonial nesting waterbirds. In 2008, one of these "rookeries" of colonial nesting waterbirds spontaneously formed on the nature center. The formation is a testament to the high-quality complete habitat mosaic of the refuge coupled with the presence of nesting alligators on the rookery island. Nesting alligators are commonly associated with rookeries. The strong maternal alligator nesting instinct inadvertently protects bird nests located in the trees overhead. Should a scavenging raccoon swim to the rookery island, it is quickly filled with deep regret. ABNC staff and volunteers have further enhanced nesting opportunities by building an innovative artificial nesting structure on the rookery. In addition to tree nests, there are now over 150 nest boxes available to be occupied by this vertical city of birds.

Many of these elegant colonial nesting species grow a specialized set of feathers used during courtship. These breeding plumes are used as part of a beautiful and sophisticated pair bonding display on the rookery early in the nesting season. At the turn of the 20th century these feathers were

Great Egrets in courtship display.
Photo by Gary Seloff

considered very valuable to the fashion industry. The feathers were collected in huge numbers as birds were shot off of rookeries throughout their range. Some of America's first federal wildlife regulations protected birds from plume hunting and extinction. Slowly their populations have recovered and today herons and egrets find the productive summer waters of Armand Bayou to be ideal habitat. The fishing is always good. The neighborhood is quiet. It's valuable waterbird real estate in an area where it's increasingly difficult for wildlife to get its complex set of needs met.

For a deeper dive into the Armand Bayou Rookery:

Bayou City Eco-Almanac Rookery
youtu.be/3HoobZI9JzQ

ABNC Rookery Guided Tour
www.youtube.com/watch?v=GlV9mWse_PU

ABNC Rookery With Birdsong and Captions
www.youtube.com/watch?v=4pFpxHZNJyM

Huge quantities of water were removed from underground aquifers for agricultural purposes. Notice the contour lines in this eight-hundred-acre rice field, which was seasonally flooded for rice production for several decades. It takes a lot of water to flood that amount of land.

What is Subsidence?

During the 1960s, the Houston area went through an explosion of human growth. Along with people came homes, business and industry, all of which needed water. During much of this period Houston's water needs were met by pumping water from underground aquifers. The upper geology of the Texas coastal plain contains very little rock. You must dig several hundred feet before encountering stone, which serves as a structure or skeleton for the substrate.

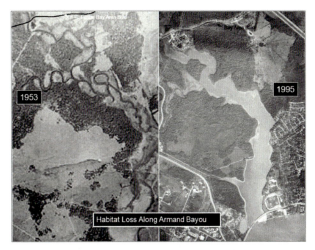

There has been a 90 percent loss of historic wetlands on Armand Bayou since 1950 due largely to the effects of subsidence

When large amounts of well water were removed, a void or cavern was left behind. This empty area created instability in the clayey soils causing the land surface to collapse into the empty void where the well water had once been. This man-made event is called *subsidence* but more easily visualized, it is the sinking of the land surface.

Along Armand Bayou the effects have been dramatic. Some areas have sunk or subsided as much as nine feet. Imagine that when you walked outside this morning that your front yard had sank nine feet! In fact, at one point during the 1970s it was recognized Houston would have to change sources of water supply. Some neighborhoods flooded after every rainfall. During that period the Harris County

Subsidence District was created to regulate the amount of well water withdrawal. Today Harris County's water is largely supplied from surface water sources such as Lake Houston.

Marsh Habitat Loss

Armand Bayou was affected by subsidence as it became wider and deeper. The lush tidal marsh habitats that once lined the bayou edge were inundated with water much too deep for its survival. Remember, tidal marsh thrives in the shallow water tide zone between low and high tide. As the water deepened due to subsidence, most of the marshes drowned, finding themselves in water too deep to survive.

There has been an estimated 90 percent reduction in marsh habitat in Armand Bayou since 1950. The same phenomenon occurred throughout the Galveston Bay complex with an estimated 30,000 acres of tidal marsh loss.

Restoration Ecology

ABNC engaged in marsh restoration activities for over two decades. Photo from ABNC Archives

Restoration is a human act. People take action in order to enhance the ecology of the environment. *Restoration ecology* begins with a well thought out plan. The Restoration Plan will identify the natural history, threats, and actions to be taken to reach identified goals. The plan is also used to help generate the associated costs. The plan is also a useful tool for fundraising. Armand Bayou Nature Center deve-

loped The Natural Resource Management Plan in 2000, which is now used as the guidance document for restoration. Once a restoration has people who produce a plan which is used to solicit project funding, the field work begins. Funds may be used to hire staff, hire contractors, buy tools or equipment.

The largest marsh restoration project on Armand bayou was conducted in 1995 in partnership with The Clear Lake Marsh Restoration Task Force. The project was one of the first "beneficial use" projects around Galveston Bay. Photo by Mark Kramer

As restoration efforts progressed upstream, salinity levels were lower. Lower salinity required new different plant material adapted to the freshwater environment. California bulrush was chosen due to its high value for wildlife. The plant tolerates freshwater and is not palatable to predation from wildlife. It can also grow to greater water depths than other species creating additional marsh acreage.

Soils were moved from the open bayou bottom and pumped into the restoration site. The soils created the critical shallow water depth to support tidal marsh vegetation. Photos by Mark Kramer

Bulrush bomb construction

An innovative restoration technique was developed. Three-gallon containers of bulrush were grown in the ABNC nursery ponds. Plants were removed from the plastic pots. The bulrush root balls were wrapped in cotton cloth and chicken wire. Concrete ballast was placed inside the wire to anchor the propagules to the bayou bottom. Bulrush rhizomes pushed through the wire and secured the plant in place. Over time the wire rusted and disintegrated.

California bulrush

Bombs Away! Photo by Ann Brinly

The beauty of the *bulrush bomb* was deployment. Unlike other manual techniques that require personnel to enter the water, the bombs were simply tossed into the bayou. This allowed planting year-round. It also allowed plant material to be installed into deeper water that was limited by manual techniques.

Photo by Ann Brinly

Over a four-year period, the single propagule expands creating an island of vegetated habitat. This circular marsh shape also maximizes the edge effect of the marsh. Research has shown that the first few feet of marsh are most highly used by juvenile estuarine species.

Combined efforts of marsh restoration produced 26 acres of tidal marsh habitat.

Bayou Wildlife

Wood Duck drakes are one of the most strikingly colorful birds in North America. Photo by Gary Seloff

Most ducks and geese are on the move in the spring, migrating for more northern latitudes with nesting on their minds. Wood ducks are an exception and stay in Texas to raise their young. In early spring they're scouting for nest sites! The birds are cavity nesters and seek out trees or poles hollowed out by pileated woodpeckers to deposit their eggs. These are among the most colorfully striking birds in North America.

Indigo Bunting and other songbirds include a bayou layover on their spring migration. Photo by Gary Seloff

There is a richness of life along coastal Texas. An assembly of plant and animal communities thriving in the climatic sweet spot of warm temperatures, gulf breezes and abundant semi-tropical rain. The birds know this and have built a lifestyle, a culture of globetrotting to take advantage of the seasonal abundance of spring as it spreads across the planet. Tender green grass seeds and spring wildflowers are here in late April and early May. In a few weeks that tender green of spring will be in Massachusetts – and so will many of the migratory birds.

Migration is the name of this ornithological lifestyle. For a few weeks during the spring the forests and grasslands of Armand Bayou Nature Center are filled with the songs and colors of these winged travelers following the annual retracing of the pathways of their ancestors. The Houston area is located on the largest of these migratory bird route superhighways known as the *Central Flyway*. Coastal Texas and ABNC is a "stopover" for some who are making their way further in. For others ABNC is a summer nest site to raise the next generation. During a typical year ABNC documents about 220 bird species. We are at the peak of this avian exodus around mid-April.

Some of the most striking migrants are here only briefly but have the ability to grab the attention of anyone within view. The Indigo Bunting is near the top of that list. These small birds are a vivid blue. For most people, at first viewing the response is a questioning of reality. The list of questions from incredulous pontoon boat tour passengers includes, "Can that really be *that* blue?" "That's a color I've never seen before. Is that a *real* bird?"

I love those moments. In spite of who you are, your age, your education, your income or your level of electronic connectivity—you just had a wildlife moment. A genuine experience where you are totally captured by the natural world. Everything from the peripheral conscious thought of the mind has vanished. You have entered into the pure land of being in the present moment. No more thought of bills, or work issues, or health issues, or nagging global pandemics. Maybe you've had one these moments? Maybe you've had one of these moments at Armand Bayou Nature Center? I have had many. In fact, I've spent a lifetime valuing those moments as some my most cherished possessions. People ask why is Armand Bayou important? What good is nature or wilderness or being outdoors? As a proud graduate of the University of Armand Bayou I remember each of those lessons. It turns out that how we pay attention is everything.

For a Deeper Dive Into More ABNC Genuine Viewing Experiences:

Armand Bayou – Ecological Oasis of the Gulf Coast youtu.be/W3TbrVzUa3M

Wood Storks

Wood Stork In Flight. Photo by Gary Seloff

On rare occasion a special winged visitor passes through the tidal wetlands of Armand Bayou. With a five-foot wingspan, it's surprising that few have ever seen it. As someone who has spent a lifetime on the bayou waters, I can count on one hand my sightings of Wood Storks (*Mycteria americana*). Last April (2020), Gary Seloff captured the image above from a small group of the birds in Horsepen Bayou.

Wood Storks use Armand Bayou briefly as a "stop over" point in their travels. My observations typically see them here for only a day or two as they travel onwards after dispersing from their Mexican breeding grounds. Years may go by without a sighting. However, I suspect that the birds stop every year without being seen in their remote bayou wetland layover.

Members of a flock of more than 70 Wood Storks camp on Armand Bayou. Photo by Gary Seloff

Wood Storks seem to do most actions in slow motion. They soar in spiral perfection at great altitude and I often look up two or three times to convince myself that what I see is actually storks and not White Pelicans. Wood Storks are wading birds that use their heavy bill to dredge the soft sediments with a *grope feeding technique* and feel their way to dinner. This feeding technique also enables nocturnal feeding, which may explain why the birds are seldom seen wading in Armand Bayou waters. Their feeding habitat is very specific and requires shallow pools of concentrated prey. Just like those areas created by years of tidal marsh and tidal flats restoration in Horsepen Bayou. Dinner is easier for those who have little preference. Fish (especially mullet) comprise the vast majority of the menu with shrimp, snakes, juvenile alligators and crabs also on the tidal flats buffet.

Wood Stork sightings are not rare just on Armand Bayou. Their population in the United States has declined by 75 percent since the 1930s. Experts theorize that dredging, draining and water manipulation in Florida altered the Everglades hydrology of seasonal dry periods that concentrated prey of the Wood Stork during nesting period. Current best estimates are that only 8,000 nesting pairs remain in Florida. American Wood Storks were listed as an Endangered Species in 1984. Similar declines in the Mexican population had them listed as endangered in 1991.

All of my Wood Stork sightings have been birds perched high in roosting areas. My notes show a memorable sighting in 2008 where an estimated 80 birds in upper Armand Bayou perched for the evening. April's sighting by Gary counted only four birds but he encountered a flock of more than 70 the previous June (2019). As an animal's population plummets, it puts a different context on each viewing experience. As a species disappears from an area, so does the richness of human experience – an extinction of experience for all. With every sighting of the Wood Stork I ask myself, will this be the last?

Texas Turtles

Common snapping turtle. Photo by Kelli Ondracek

I grew up with a pet turtle as did many of my friends in the 1960s. Turtles were commonly sold in "dollar stores" as a novelty and they came with their own handy plastic container. We kept mine on the kitchen counter. The sale of hatchling Red-eared sliders continued for a handful of years until it was recognized that they may also carry salmonella.

Turtles still carry a fascination for most people and it seems like they live the perfect vacation lifestyle. Their RV is on their back, dinner is fish, which is always eaten slowly and enjoyed one bite at a time. They finish the day alternating between swim breaks and sunbathing. For many who visit Armand Bayou Nature Center, the first encounter with wildlife is on the entry boardwalk. Turtles, commonly sighted basking on the shoreline, are the delight of many visiting school children on their way to explore the depths of the nature center.

Armand Bayou is ideal habitat for these leisure-loving pleasure seekers that spend most of their life in the water. This time of year, there is an exception to their semi-aquatic water loving ways and it can be deadly for them. As with all reptiles, turtles deposit their eggs on dry land. That's where the spring turtle odyssey begins. *Gravid* females leave the safety of their aquatic habitat and travel some distance from the water's edge in search of the ideal location to safely deposit this year's clutch of eggs. Some turtles only move a few feet from the water's edge, but others decide to walk hundreds of yards before laying their eggs. That journey can be perilous in the most densely populated county in Texas.

This is the time when we see Houston's most common turtles (red-eared slider, common snapping turtle, spiny soft-shell turtle) in unexpected locations. You may have seen them crossing the road or walking across the ABNC Parking lot. Please drive slowly as they won't get out of your way. Every year we have the privilege to observe this spectacle and witness the egg laying marvel.

In the recent past ABNC also participated in a research study that is worth reflecting on today. Texas wildlife regulatory agencies had growing concern about the trapping and sale of turtles. The above-mentioned species were being targeted by commercial trappers and sold for meat to the emerging middle class of Chinese consumers. Texas turtles were captured and transported alive and then sold in the "wet markets" that are now familiar to Americans through the Covid 19 Pandemic. Between 2002 and 2005 more than 250,000 wild-caught turtles were shipped from the Dallas airport alone! For three summers ABNC Staff captured, tagged, and released turtles, providing data to better guide policy. Turtles are generally slow to reach sexual maturity. When large numbers of breeding age adults are removed from a waterway, the turtle population can crash, taking decades to recover. We also now know the consequences of selling wildlife in these open-air live wildlife meat markets. All things considered, it's worth reconsidering before putting turtles on the menu.

For a deeper dive into more Texas turtles:

Bayou City Eco-Almanac: Bringing Back Coastal Turtles

www.youtube.com/watch?v=RFGvLmlvU4E

Spiny Soft-Shell Turtle. Photo by Kelli Ondracek

Invasive Species

What is an invasive species?

A plant or animal brought to a new part of the planet in which it did not originally exist can become an invasive species. This could mean the plants originated from another part of the planet. It could also mean that they may have originated from the same state. Many of these species have special strategies that enable the plants to outcompete the native species. Water hyacinth is a perfect example, with a list of multiple strategies that allow it to flourish. Rapid growth rates allow it to expand its footprint. The ability to reproduce both from seed and from cuttings allow it to reproduce quickly. Its free-floating nature allows for the colonization of new territory with every flood event.

Water hyacinth is a free-floating plant.
The leaves serve as sails on windy days
transporting plants into new environs.

Water Hyacinth

Water hyacinth originates in South America and is native to the Amazon basin. It was brought to New Orleans in the late 1800s to be used as an ornamental plant in backyard ponds. Water hyacinth is one of the fastest growing plants on Earth. Armand Bayou is ideal habitat. Summer days are warm, long and bright. Bayou waters are low in salinity and nutrient-rich. Under these ideal conditions water hyacinth may double its surface area every ten days.

Photo by Mark Kramer

Notice the "pup plant" on the lower right side of the plant. This plant will separate from the parent plant creating a clone of the original. This *asexual fragmentation* is an important reproductive strategy. Also note the beautiful purple (hyacinth) colored flower. The flowers produce seeds through sexual reproduction, creating additional offspring.

Being native to the Amazon River, water hyacinth is a freshwater plant. Salinity levels in Armand Bayou fluctuate, driven by rainfall and the freshwater inflows that they create. Higher annual rainfall creates lower salinity (fresher water) and lower annual rainfall creates higher salinity (saltier water). As a result, high rainfall rates create bayou water that is more fresh and hyacinth populations expand. These rainfall rates vary dramatically, and most scientists believe global climate change is a factor in these shifts. The changing climate is driving extreme weather patterns across the globe. For example, 2011 marked Houston's driest year ever recorded and 2017 marked the wettest year (think Hurricane Harvey) ever recorded.

Water Hyacinth has the ability to cause
the collapse of the entire bayou ecosystem.
Photo by Mark Kramer

Left unmanaged, the plants expand their footprint and eventually cover the water surface –
shoreline to shoreline. This blanketing of the water
surface compromises several ecological processes.
The cover suppresses sunlight from penetrating into
the water column. No sunlight means no algae or any
submerged vegetation. The covering of the water surface also minimizes the diffusion of atmospheric
oxygen. Diffusion takes place at the water's surface,
especially during windy days. Atmospheric oxygen is
more highly concentrated than dissolved oxygen in
water. *Diffusion* is essentially the "soaking" of oxygen
from the air into the water. It is a critical process for
the health of all aquatic life. The blanket of water hyacinth suppresses this process.

All invasive species are not created equal. Ecologists rank the danger of the species in relation to the
severity of impact to the environment. With no oxygen in the water there is little aquatic life. The plant
has the ability to cause the collapse of the entire
bayou ecosystem. This places water hyacinth high on
the threat level of risk assessment and requires active
management to minimize these impacts.

The recreational impacts of Water Hyacinth infesta-
tion are also significant. Armand Bayou, which is a
premier paddling destination, is rendered unusable
with high plant populations. Photo by Mark Kramer

Photo by Jerome Matula

Recognizing the ecological and recreational impacts caused by water hyacinth, ABNC works with
contractors and Texas Parks and Wildlife to actively
manage populations. Along all Gulf states, the use
of appropriate herbicide is recognized as the best
management strategy.

Invasive Animals

Channeled Applesnail with egg mass on bulrush stalk.
Photo by Gary Seloff

Channeled Applesnails are another introduced species from the aquarium trade. The snails are large and about the size of an adult human fist. Applesnails are *macrophytes,* which eat plant material, and they have devastated rice crops in Indonesia. Little evidence has been recorded of impacts to wetlands in Armand Bayou. The adult snails are seldom seen under water however, their presence is indicated by the large "bubble gum" egg masses, which are deposited on plants above the waterline.

Our actions are the foundation upon which we stand. From the beginnings of Armand Yramategui's and Hana Ginzbarg's visionary efforts to preserve open space in Harris County, to the decades of habitat restoration and management, to environmental education and programming, to local/state/federal protective legislation, Armand Bayou is a rare success story in the annals of environmental activism.

The Nature of Relative Reality

I spent many hours of my young adulthood sitting around a campfire. It was a priority for personal space, quiet conversations and marveling at the depth of the night sky. There were camping trips to east Texas and all my favorite destinations along Armand Bayou. We would discuss the seemingly impossible, including how the star that projected the light we were witnessing might have died millions of years ago, and yet what we were seeing made it appear that it was still shining bright.

Countless human generations have shared the experience of sitting around a fire and marveling at the depth and mystery of the cosmos. For many, witnessing the motion of the stars overhead convinced them that the stars and galaxies were all traveling around the Earth, that in fact the Earth was the center of the universe. It's a belief that persisted until we began to create viewing tools and sharpen our observation skills to explore the natural world and cosmos through a more rational lens.

Ecologically speaking, we are going through a similar transition right now. Countless generations of humans have looked at the planet as if it were here for the taking. That Earth's resources were put here for humans to use and that the Earth was so big that our footprint of extraction, limitless consumption and a throw-away culture could have no bearing on the mechanisms of such systems. Our behavior reflected the idea that humans were the center of the universe.

But in fact, we are beginning to recognize a similar cultural shift right now. Just as there was initial resistance to the theories of Galileo, there is resistance to acceptance of the Earth's changes underway, which are driven by the cumulative impacts of eight billion people. There is a lot at stake during the transition of a paradigm shift. Those who are invested in old ways of seeing have a lot to lose. Letting go is hard.

It's Later Than You Think

The human footprint of consumption has reached unprecedented levels. We are making a mark that will be captured in the geological record of Earth. When the alien archeologists arrive after the moment of human history has passed, they will find evidence of our short-sighted lifestyle. Recognizing this, archeologists use the term Anthropocene for the era created by what humans are depositing in the

geologic record. Evidence of atmospheric change captured in the air bubbles of Antarctic ice, evidence of chemical change in seawater, and evidence of plastics and other materials which don't decompose in soil profiles.

F Minus 7/23/17 by Tony Carillo

When the meteor that caused the last great extinction event impacted near the Yucatan Peninsula, it spewed a huge volume of debris into the atmosphere. So much in fact, that it was distributed over the entire planet, causing the extinction of the dinosaurs. When geologists dig into the soil today, the zone of this debris scattered by the meteor is clearly visible. Known as the KT Boundary, it divides the age of reptiles from the age of mammals. There has never been a specimen of dinosaur found above the KT Boundary.

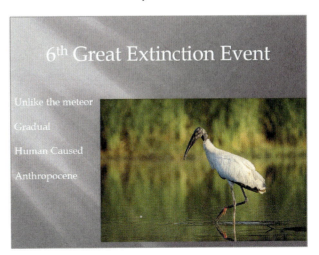

Ghosts of the Past

Habitat Loss

Photo by Gary Seloff

The Anthropocene is also leaving similar evidence and having similar evolutionary consequences. Not only is there evidence of our ecological disruption, but there is a similar extinction event currently underway. Unlike the meteor driven extinction, which happened literally overnight, this event is slower. Slower by comparison in human timescales but still the blink of an eye in geologic time. One is compared to the flipping of a switch, the other is the dimming of the light slowly. This extinction event will be spaced over a dozen human generations. The rate of species disappearance will not be remembered from one generation to the next. The previous extinction was caused by a celestial event, the current event is caused by humans. For the most part, it's as if no one is even noticing.

The landscape of Harris County was historically dominated by coastal prairie. Today due to loss of prairie habitat, many species are losing the habitat required to meet their needs. Remnant populations of the Attwater's Prairie Chicken were numerous in the immediate area when ABNC opened. Today their populations have plummeted with only 50 birds remaining in the wild in 2020 making them one of the most critically endangered birds in the world.

H abitat Loss
I nvasive Species
P ollution
P opulation
O ver Hunting

The list of global impacts is so long that it can be hard to see or remember. Habitat loss, invasive species, pollution, human population and over hunting all rank at the top of the ecological issues list.

Armand Bayou Watershed 2020

POPULATION

Image by Google Earth Pro

Harris County is the most densely populated county in Texas and is the third most populated county in the United States. Approximately 125,000 people live in the 60 square mile Armand Bayou watershed. When human populations are high, the ecological footprint of each of us is magnified.

Plastic pollution is a growing global ecological

threat. During runoff events, this material is carried through ditches and drain ways. It ultimately arrives in Armand Bayou. Current research indicates that plastics break down into small particles called microplastics. Microplastics persist in the environment and are accumulating in many forms of aquatic life.

For the past thirty-five years my driveway home has been a one-mile-long gravel road through the preserve. In addition to being one of the most beautiful scenic views in Texas, it has also offered an opportunity to observe wildlife. Every winter I watch for a lone Loggerhead Shrike perched along the road. The birds have been extirpated throughout portions of their historic range, especially in the Armand Bayou watershed due to habitat loss. Every year now I wonder if the Loggerhead Shrike will return to the winter prairie of ABNC or if the previous year will have been its last.

Before a species becomes extinct, there is a process of listing the decline. Wildlife biologists use the best available science to determine the current status and project anticipated trends of the population. If the population is determined to be at risk, it may receive federal protection and be listed as an *Endangered Species*. Once listed, a Recovery Team is established, which creates a plan to insure the species survival. A typical pathway of decline for any species has it transitioning from (1) locally rare, to (2) threatened, to (3) endangered, to (4) critically endangered, to (5) extinct in the wild, to (6) extinct. Armand Bayou Nature Center has (or has had) species representing each of these stages.

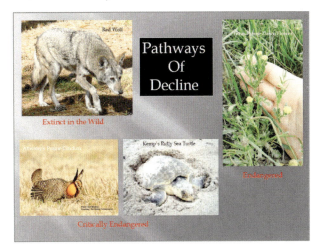

If we look to the geologic record, it's reasonable to assume that all species eventually vanish. It could be concluded that extinction is a normal factor in natural selection. However, the current rate of extinction is far exceeding those historic rates. A number of species that once occupied Armand Bayou habitats have now disappeared. I wonder, will we?

Return of the Endangerds

Bald Eagles, one of the first animals to be placed on the Endangered Species List, have returned and have nested at ABNC since 2004. Photo by Gary Seloff

When ABNC opened in 1974, air and water pollution were regular topics on nightly news programs. Pollution is a tangible reminder to Americans when the air and water smells. A vivid news memory in my mind is that of a river on fire. The Cuyahoga River in Cleveland, Ohio caught fire for the thirteenth time in 1969. During this time, Houston also struggled with some of the nation's most serious air and water quality issues. Growing up in Pasadena, one mile south of the Houston Ship Channel, I have personal air quality memories. In those days my hometown was also referred to as Stinkadena. The first fall cool front's northerly winds were cherished in an era before air conditioning. But the north winds also often brought such potent odors from The Champion Paper Mill that we would have to close the windows.

Those early memories are also filled with wonderful television programing. These were some of the first programs that exposed the beauty and fragility of the natural world to a nationwide audience. Programs from the National Geographic Society showcased the importance of preserving natural areas. *The Undersea World of Jacques Cousteau* brought the first images from the ocean depths. Carl Sagan released the series, *Cosmos*, that guided viewers through the depth and origins of the universe. Think about that. Where we've gone in one lifetime. Cousteau (inventor of scuba diving equipment) and Sagan brought the invisible nature of the ocean and outer space to many wide-eyed Americans. Today, ABNC offers activities and programs to enhance Houstonian's eco-literacy, providing information and experiences to deepen our understanding of the environment in our own backyard.

This juxtaposition of beauty and fragility versus environmental degradation was a motivating force for action. I am proud to say that Pasadena is not often referred to as Stinkadena any longer and is now better known as home to one of the largest urban wilderness areas in the country. At the national level some of the most visionary environmental agencies and policies were established. The Environmental Protection Agency, The Endangered Species Act, The Clean Water Act and The Clean Air Act were all created under President Richard Nixon. These were born from a public awareness and sense of urgency of threat to the environment.

Since that time period, bay and bayou water quality have improved. Over those past 50 years, species that were once threatened or on the brink of extinction have recovered. Habitats under threat have been preserved. These are all testaments to federal regulations that have been and remain effective. The recent regulatory rollback from 2016 to 2020 of environmental programs that have a proven record of success should make us question where our priorities lie.

**Armand Bayou watershed in 1959.
Photo from ABNC Archive**

Have you ever wondered what the Houston area looked like before humans so dramatically altered the landscape? This aerial photograph was taken roughly the year that I was born. In the blink of an eye the Armand Bayou watershed has gone from an area with no human structures to a densely populated urban environment with over 120,000 people living inside the watershed boundaries. Today, we live in a landscape that is almost entirely manmade. Drive around Harris County and when you look out of the car window, what you see is built by man. Armand Bayou Nature Center is a living museum, an island ecosystem located in the midst of one of America's major metropolitan areas.

Habitat loss is the single biggest ecological threat facing the planet. For decades ABNC has worked to preserve and restore these remnant local habitats. Coastal tallgrass prairie, un-channelized bayous and flatwoods forest are the ecological heritage of all Houstonians. Today Armand Bayou Nature Center is a success story in habitat preservation, restoration and long-term management. There is a list of threatened and previously endangered species that are now thriving at ABNC.

This environmental history lesson is important. It's important as context for those who inherit an environment that is healthier now than it was a generation ago. If you were born after 1980 this could all be new information to you. Many a younger person that has ventured onto bayou waters and seen a Brown Pelican or American alligator doesn't feel the sense of struggle required for their monumental species recovery to have taken place. Many don't know that in the 1960s and 1970s there were *legacy pesticides* persisting in America's waterways that were compromising bird reproductive systems. They have no memory of the unregulated hunting pressure and wetland loss that nearly drove the largest reptile in North America as well as our national bird into extinction. There were Acts of Congress, local fund raising/preservation efforts and decades of ecological restoration required for many of these species to be thriving in the heart of the most densely populated county in Texas.

I spent much of my life fishing around Galveston Bay and never saw Brown Pelicans. The birds were listed as an Endangered Species from 1970-2009. ABNC staff participated in the early efforts of the Brown Pelican Endangered Species Recovery Team to return the birds to the Texas coast in the 1970s. My first Brown Pelican sighting on Armand Bayou occurred in 2004. Similarly, Bald Eagles were on the List from 1967 to 1995 following hunting pressure in the early 1900s and exposure to the damaging effects of DDT, which contributed to the bird's dramatic population decline. Eagles have also returned and have nested at ABNC since 2004

where local legislation restricts power boats from entering the bayou from Clear Lake, the third largest recreational boating community in the U.S.

Today pelicans enjoy relaxing in the quiet waters of Armand Bayou. Photo by Gary Seloff

American alligator on the bank of Horsepen Bayou. Photo by Gary Seloff

Along with the Bald Eagle, the American alligator was one of the animals placed on the first Endangered Species List in 1967. They were largely absent from Armand Bayou for several decades. Among the few species that have fought their way back after being listed, they were removed from the Endangered Species List in 1987 and today are commonly sighted on the bayou.

I noticed the first return of alligators
to Armand Bayou while offering eco-tours
from the Hana G Pontoon Boat in 1984.
Photo from the collection of Mark Kramer

The Urban Alligator Part One

Photo by Ann Brinly

It is a unique perspective to observe the ecological change as four decades have passed on Armand Bayou. Air and water quality have improved, grasslands and wetlands have been restored and rare species have returned after a lengthy absence. Their return serves as a significant biological indicator of species recovery and ecological restoration success.

We don't inherit the earth from our ancestors,
we borrow it from our children.

More than any other local species, the American alligator is an animal sure to stimulate discussion, emotion and passion. It certainly does for me. This is in part driven by the fact that they are large powerful predators capable of eating you. Learning to safely appreciate and accept predators in your neighborhood is an act that we are still cultivating. Fortunately, unlike lions, cobras or elephants, the alligator's habitat is in the water. Those gators seen on the Six O'clock News are on their way to a neighboring pond (or newest gator love interest-or both), not on their way to make a meal of your backyard chihuahua.

My high school explorations of Armand Bayou began with my wilderness running buddy Ray. Ray's dad had a canoe that he would haul for us to the bayou and leave us off for the day. As we got old enough to drive, we would meet at the newly opened Bay Area Park in our cars and swim to the rope swing (located where the current boathouse is now). Alligators were then listed as an Endangered Species, which was troubling to the young mind of a developing naturalist. We spent many a summer day swimming the half mile with our belly sliding across the soft, slick mud bottom to the rope swing (hoping barefoot high school girls were already there). With only our eyes and nose above the water, we jokingly suggested this is the life of an alligator.

The urban/gator interface. Photo by Lou Wheatcraft

That was then. Now, things have changed. In a testament to the effectiveness of a positive federal regulation (the Endangered Species Act), the *apex predator* of the Bayou City has returned. I encourage Houstonians to expect the likelihood of an alligator being in *every* bayou, stream, pond and lake. Bayous are biological arteries that run through the massive human population of our area. Bayous are conduits of water, but they are also the conduits of wildlife. Bayous have enabled gators to travel and disperse into any suitable waters of the Houston area. It also means that just because there was no alligator in that pond yesterday, that doesn't mean there won't be an alligator there today.

ABNC is a prime local destination for gator viewing. Whether it's from the boardwalk or a guided pontoon eco-tour, there is no better place to see and learn about alligators in Harris County. Doing it safely means keeping a safe distance, never feeding them and no more swimming.

Basking on a spring day in Alligator Alley. Photo by Gary Seloff

Gator viewing from the Bayou Ranger.
Photo by Mark Kramer

The biology of Armand Bayou alligators follows a predicable seasonal pattern. In early spring (March and April) the animals awaken from a long winter nap. The first order of business is getting warm. Warming of the entire body core temperature is a difficult task for a 500-pound reptile (the largest in North America). On sunny days gators will haul out and bask to raise their body temperature. Rising body temperature also speeds reptilian metabolism enabling the first gator meal of spring. It's a powerful hunger considering the last supper was probably consumed in October or November.

Alligator guarding a big meal, white-tailed deer, in Horsepen Bayou. Predators help to keep wildlife populations in balance. Photo by Gary Seloff

Bellowing signals that courtship is in the air. Photo by Gary Seloff

After awakening and warming, alligators are hungry. *Basking* primes the body for the first meal. Exactly what you eat is driven by your size. That means anything from dragonflies to white-tailed deer are on the menu – depending on how big you are. A gator's life is best described as a sluggish, slow-motion lifestyle punctuated by lightning-fast strikes. Witnessing this predator at work is memorable. Predators help to keep wildlife populations in balance. They are also sometimes responsible for unexpected beneficial ecological outcomes. The establishment of colonial nesting waterbirds at ABNC occurred unexpectedly and spontaneously after nesting alligators appeared in the rookery pond. Alligators found suitable nesting habitat on the pond's island and herons and egrets nested in the trees above with their protection! Waterbird rookeries are commonly associated with the protection of a nesting female alligator serving as an unintentional guardian.

After a good meal or two, alligators begin to think about mating. Alligator mating behavior is amongst the most elaborate in the reptile world. Courtship begins in April/May with a male bellowing or vocalizing with a sub-sonic roar that may make the water dance around his body.

Courting alligator couples may pair for several days. Photo by Gary Seloff

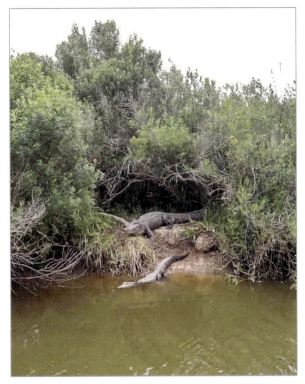

A dominant male and female will partner and mate for several days. These Gator love fests alternate with aquatic reproduction time and pair bonding/basking sessions on land. Photo by Mark Kramer

passed her nest! Sometimes, as we enter Alligator Alley on the Bayou Ranger tour boat and approach one of these nests, it's like traveling upstream on an ancient river with a secret source. It's like looking back in time to see the evolutionary beginnings of motherhood. Many evolutionary biologists suggest that alligators (and all crocodilians) may be a "missing link" in the evolution from the dinosaur to modern birds. This early maternal drive of nest building, egg protection, and care for offspring is carried into the birds of today. In theory, these are similar behavioral adaptations carried from one evolutionary lineage to another.

Today top predators worldwide are challenged to coexist with humans. Alligators are that apex predator in the Bayou City and only exist where we make space for them to survive. Their superior design and lifestyle have enabled them to survive unchanged since the time of the dinosaur, until humans nearly pushed them out entirely and for eternity. As I swam towards that rope swing, I never imagined that 45 years later Armand Bayou would be alive with alligators once more.

Female alligators begin nest building in May and June. She collects material to build what is essentially a compost pile. Grass, twigs and mud are shaped into a three-foot diameter pile into which 30 to 60 eggs are deposited. The temperature of the nest determines if each egg will produce a male or female. The warmer the temperature the more males develop. Several reptile species exhibit this reproductive phenomenon known as *temperature dependent sexual determination*. Then the mother gator waits close to the nest for the reminder of the incubation period (approximately two months). In fact, female alligators are such fiercely protective mothers that this is perhaps the most dangerous time for people to approach an alligator. I have a vivid memory of an eight-foot-long nesting female gator hissing at the 32-foot-long pontoon boat as we

Alligator killed In Lake Mark Kramer.
Photo by Mark Kramer

The Urban Alligator Part Two

Alligators are unusual among reptiles in that the hatchlings remain protected by mom for the first year of life. Photo by Gary Seloff

Imagine it's been two months since we last checked in on our Armand Bayou alligator nest. Over these summer months the eggs have been incubating under mom's watchful eye. Hopefully, there have been no flooding rains. Reptile eggs have a leathery shell and the developing young "breathe" through the eggshell. If they submerge, the young will drown inside the egg. Hopefully, there have been no raccoons or other marauding scavengers.

After a 65-day incubation, hatchlings emerge from the egg. Photo by Mark Kramer

Females may lay 30 to 60 eggs. Photo by Mark Kramer

Mid to late August is the time that alligator eggs begin to hatch on Armand Bayou. Before the young emerge from the eggs, they begin to vocalize. The chirping calls signal to all brethren that today is the day to hatch. As the young begin to dig their way out of the nest, mom is nearby and may offer some assistance if needed. She carefully digs the nest apart and may carry the young in her mouth to the water's edge.

Hatchling alligators are 8 to 10 inches long and are vulnerable to predation. They may be a meal for Great Blue Herons, Wood Storks, raccoons, Bald Eagles or even other alligators.

Even with a fiercely protective two-hundred-pound mother reptile watching over you, the first year of life is the most treacherous. Photo by Gary Seloff

What you eat depends on how big you are. This alligator has caught a Common Merganser. Photo by Gary Seloff

Alligators are carnivores and will eat as large of a prey item that they can kill and tear apart. For a hatchling gator that means a typical meal may be dragonflies or minnows. With adequate food they can grow as much as a foot per year. This growth rate continues until the animals reach sexual maturity which occurs at around six to seven feet long. After that, growth slows down but they never stop growing. This lifelong, slow reptilian growth is called *indeterminant growth*. It also means that the older the animal, the more time you have to grow really big.

Alligator hatchlings will remain with their mom for around a year. Once they lose the protection of their mother, the game changes and becomes even more treacherous. Big alligators will eat smaller alligators. This strategy of cannibalization supports the moving of energy from lower in the food chain up to the breeding size adults. It also means that local alligator populations remain stable.

Big gators will eat smaller gators. Photo by Gary Seloff

Alligators have an incredible bite force when their jaws snap closed. Photo by Gary Seloff

In Cajun Country if you want to make a person disappear, you feed them to the alligators. This is what you will look like. Photo by Mark Kramer

Alligators are ranked at number three of all animals on Earth for strongest bite force. Alligator teeth are cone shaped and designed to grip and puncture flesh (not cut as shark teeth do). After the kill, the teeth are used to perforate tissue and then tear along the dotted line.

Crocodilians have one the most acidic digestion systems of any animal, capable of digesting large bone, like a deer leg. Photo by Gary Seloff

I found this young alligator on the West Bank Road a half mile from the nearest water. He ran into the prairie when he saw I was approaching. He quickly became entangled and stuck in the dense grass and couldn't move. He was relocated to a happy home in the bayou. Photo by Mark Kramer

Leaving home is tough for a juvenile alligator. If you are an alligator under six feet without maternal protection, you are at risk of being eaten by a larger alligator. This is a strong motivation to head out on your own. Many juvenile gators leave their home waters, trekking forth across dry land in hopes of finding another suitable water body that is free of larger alligators. This perilous venture is a great risk. Many youngsters never find water. This behavior also serves the species by promoting dispersal of alligators into new territory. Several of these rogue juveniles show up in Nature Center ponds every summer. Remember, just because there was no alligator in that pond yesterday doesn't mean there won't be one there tomorrow.

Alligators eat turtles but somehow these turtles know that alligators don't eat through the winter.
Photo by Ann Brinly

Houston's first cool fronts arrive in late September. It always amazes me how quickly water temperatures drop in October. Water temperature is the driving regulator behind the level of activity a gator can maintain. As bayou water temperatures drop into the upper 60s in late October, gator activity begins to slow down. In fact, that is when alligators usually have a final fall meal and begin to think about a plan for winter.

Alligator den. Note the gator tracks.
Photo by Mark Kramer

Alligators dig a den or cave in which they spend the winter. Once completed it will be used for years to come. The den is flooded with shallow water and maintains an air space at the top of the cavern. Often the entrance is located below water level and is not clearly visible. A typical den is located in close proximity to the nest site. Alligators exhibit *high site fidelity* and build their nests in relatively the same location every year. It is to the gator mother's advantage to not have to lead her young over a long distance from the nest to reach the den. It is believed that females are the primary builders and users of dens, but the ecology of alligator dens is still poorly understood.

As Fall temperatures drop, mother and hatchings enter the den for a long winter's nap.
Photo by Gary Seloff

Several generations may occupy the den with her. On early Spring sunny days, the young emerge and sometimes create a basking "pile up." Photo by Gary Seloff

Alligators are remarkably resilient and endure extreme winter temperatures. The den buffers the harshest cold temperatures, but conditions are difficult. Alligator winter core body temperatures are approximately the same as the water (that's cold!). There have been numerous documented accounts of alligators trapped in shallow ponds with ice covering the pond with only their nose above the ice!

Armand Bayou gator populations are healthy.
Photo by Gary Seloff

Armand Bayou now has a healthy population of alligators. After decades of recovery, there are abundant gators of all sizes. This diversity of all alligator age classes is one barometer to measure the health of the population. In 2011 and 2012, ABNC partnered with Texas A&M University graduate student Cord Eversole to conduct a research study of Armand Bayou's gator population to better understand its unique characteristics.

Photo by Trudy LeDoux

For two years nighttime spotlight counts were conducted via pontoon boat and canoe. All crocodilians share an unusual characteristic: their eyes have a strongly reflective property when spotlights are shined on them. This "stop sign red" reflective property is visible for several hundred yards. It gives relatively accurate information as to the number of alligators in a field of view, but it does not gauge the size of the animals. The size of an animal in the water can only be estimated by a good look at the size of the gator's head. The distance between the eye and the nose, measured in inches, approximates the number of feet in total body length. For example, six inches between the eye and nose equals a six-foot-long alligator. Following are several graphs that show some of the results.

Staff and volunteers counted alligators throughout the watershed. Photo by Google Earth Pro

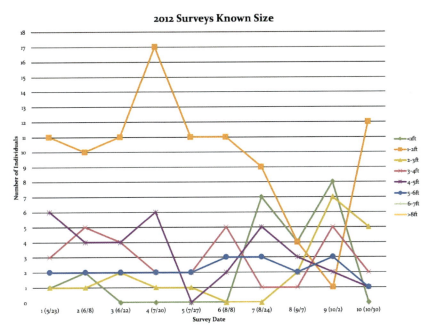

2012 Surveys Known Size

Legend: <1ft, 1-2ft, 2-3ft, 3-4ft, 4-5ft, 5-6ft, 6-7ft, >8ft

While it's clear that the bayou is populated with numerous subadult alligators, those found of breeding age were relatively low. Graph by Cord Eversole

All sightings during the survey both summers. Map by Cord Eversole

My family is from South Louisiana and moved to Pasadena in the early 1950s. The photo below was taken from the banks of the Mississippi River near my mother's childhood home. There were many stories of alligator hunts where hides were sold at market. This unregulated hunting pressure was the primary factor in alligator populations crashing. Their populations have now fully recovered. This *keystone species* plays a critical role in keeping the balance in bayou ecosystems. Today Harris County has altered most every local bayou's hydrology through channelization. Urban alligators only occur where people make room for them to coexist. Habitat loss (in this case alligator habitat) is recognized as the single biggest ecological threat around the world. Armand Bayou remains un-channelized and is the most beautifully preserved and ecologically intact bayou in the Bayou City. Even more beautiful with the return of the Urban Alligator.

Want a deeper dive into Armand Bayou Alligators:
Armand Bayou Nature Center Alligator Research
www.youtube.com/watch?v=2QFG5v6a2Og

Armand Bayou Osprey

The weeks of late September mark the calendar when I begin to watch the sky around Armand Bayou for the return of two iconic birds of prey back to the Texas coast. Ospreys return to coastal Texas after nesting elsewhere. They return at an ideal time. Bayou waters are at their peak of productivity. All summer, juvenile marine fishes have been hiding, feeding and growing in the nursery areas provided by lush green tidal marsh along the shoreline. Ospreys eat only fish. Now these fishes have reached optimal size to begin their migration. The average arrival of our first fall cool front occurs during the last few weeks of September too. Dropping water temperatures and shortening daylength are two key signals that trigger the migration of marine organisms back to the open Bay and Gulf. Ospreys return to the bayou to capitalize on the banquet. The nesting pair of Bald Eagles also returns. For the past two years, my first sighting of the eagle has occurred on September eleventh. That also makes for an easy memory trick to associate the return of the National Symbol with 9-11.

Striped mullet are the primary prey in Armand Bayou. Photo by Gary Seloff

For the Ospreys (*Pandion haliaetus*) of Armand Bayou the diet is focused primarily on one species: striped mullet, which are abundant and spend much of their life near the surface of the water. They are perfect-sized prey averaging about a pound in weight. Some mullets remain in the Bayou all year, critical for Ospreys, which require a fish per day during the cold of winter.

Seeing an Osprey (also called the Fish Hawk) dive and catch a fish is always the greatest thrill of any trip on the water. The birds soar at 60 to 80 feet above the water in search of a meal, always hovering with their head into the wind. Pointing into the wind allows the air to travel over their wings and requires less effort during the focused part of the hunt. If the wind is calm, Ospreys have the ability to "helicopter" in one place. Moving their wings in a "figure eight" allows them to "scull" the air similar to the motion used by paddlers.

Female Ospreys wear a necklace of brown feathers at the base of their neck. Photo by Gary Seloff

Ospreys perform a spectacular aerial display diving into the water from great height. Photo by Gary Seloff

Osprey talons are specially adapted to carry fish. Photo by Gary Seloff

Osprey talons are shaped differently than most other birds of prey. Upon making contact with a fish, one of the talons swivels for a better grip. This places two talons on each side of the fish's body. The inner pads of each toe are covered with rough spicules, which further enhance the grip on a slippery fish.

If it is successful, the real work begins. After being totally submerged in the dive, the Osprey must lift a third of its body weight out of the water and carry the fish to a feeding perch. That's a tall order for a bird that only weighs three pounds.

Just before contact!
Photo by Gary Seloff

Once the bird is locked onto its prey, it folds its wings, diving head-first towards the water. At the very last instant, it thrusts its talons ahead to hit the target. Often, it goes completely underwater in the process of the dive, creating a huge splash.

Ospreys have unusually flexible elbows, which aids the lift. Photo by Gary Seloff

Ospreys are capable of accomplishing the task thanks to several adaptations and a fierce spirit. Osprey wings are built to bend at the shoulder as most bird wings do. However, they also have an unusual range of motion and strength at the bend in the elbow. This enables the birds to gain extra power and lift as they struggle to leave the water with wet feathers along with their catch.

Eagles are kleptoparasites! Photo by Gary Seloff

Both Ospreys and eagles return to the bayou at roughly the same time in September. Eagles are quite capable of catching fish but prefer to rob fish from the Osprey. I believe that a major factor in eagles choosing to return to and nest on Armand Bayou is the large number of Ospreys that eagles can steal from. Some of the most memorable pontoon tours occur when these two birds of prey conduct aerial combat over a meal.

Ospreys have favorite perches that they return to every day for dining or just to survey their domain. These are tree limbs of just the right diameter for the size of their talon, with good texture and preferably a good view.

Once airborne, Ospreys always fly with the fish's head pointed forward to streamline the aerodynamics of flight. Photo by Gary Seloff

Unlike many other birds of prey, Ospreys are quite tolerant of other Ospreys and are one of the most vocal birds of prey in the world. In fact, it's common for a bird to fly along the bayou to trigger a series of the characteristic call from every other Osprey perched along the shoreline. It's a social chorus line of greeting each other.

Ospreys have several distinct calls. The most common is used when other Osprey fly past or when they are lounging and announcing their presence. However, the birds also have a distinct call that is almost frantic and is used when an eagle is approaching. It al most sounds as if the bird's tail is on fire. It's a great auditory cue to look to the sky for a view of one of the most spectacular aerial displays in North America.

Great Blue Herons eat mullet too, but not this time. Photo by Gary Seloff

Ospreys are slow eaters and take small bites.
Photo by Gary Seloff

For many years, I have had the pleasure of watching Ospreys perch and dine from my living room window. They always begin with the head, which minimizes further flapping of the fish. The Osprey's bill is small and only capable of tearing small pieces of fish flesh, about the size of a thimble. It typically takes over an hour to finish the meal.

Ospreys return to Armand Bayou after nesting elsewhere in the U.S. They nest in gulf states east of the Mississippi River, throughout both coasts of Florida and all the way up the East Coast to Maine.

They also nest in the Pacific Northwest. I got a phone call several years ago from a long-lens photographer who had taken a picture of an Osprey that was perched on a tree along the bayou. His picture allowed him to the read the numbers on the band. He followed up with the U.S. Fish and Wildlife Service (USFWS). It turns out that the bird was banded the previous year in Yellowstone National Park. I immediately thought, now that's the life for me, fishing summers in Yellowstone and winters on Armand Bayou.

It's not totally accurate to say Ospreys don't nest in Texas. The USFWS Breeding Bird Survey lists eleven known nests in Texas. Eleven nests are not many for an area the size of Texas. In 1996 ABNC partnered with Houston Lighting & Power to install artificial osprey nesting platforms on top of old telephone poles. These structures have been used with good success throughout the bird's more traditional nesting range. HL&P set the poles and placed the nest platforms (built by ABNC) on top with their equipment. We even placed some nesting twigs on each platform as "chum." Other raptors stole the twigs. After 15 years of no use, we removed all 6 of the nesting platforms.

Eating fish can be messy. Ospreys often skim the water's surface, dragging their talons in an effort to remove blood and slime. Photo by Gary Seloff

Photo by Gary Seloff

Ospreys are very tolerant of humans where they do nest. In Florida I have seen Ospreys nest on streetlights in the center of the freeway and on TV antennae beside homes. There was a brief attempt at nesting in Horsepen Bayou several years ago. I believe that young birds were practicing, playing like children at first love. The nest was very unstable and poorly constructed. No young were produced from the nest. The nest was abandoned the following year and never reoccupied.

Ospreys are one of several bird species whose population declined steeply during the 1960s and 1970s. The *insecticide DDT* was used on crops and farmlands around the country. The toxic chemical washed downstream through the watershed, accumulating in the fish that Ospreys eat. As the chemical is absorbed, it's passed from animal to animal as it works its way up the food chain. This *bioaccumulation* often reaches its most serious impacts with apex predators at the top of the *food web*.

Such was the case for Ospreys. DDT had the effect of compromising the bird's ability to process calcium. Calcium is an important element in the production of bird eggshells. As the birds suffered these effects, their eggshells became very weak and fragile. When parent birds would sit on the eggs for incubation, the eggs would crack. This lack of reproductive ability caused the Osprey's population to steeply decline and nearly resulted in the bird being listed as an endangered species.

This nest in Horsepen Bayou never produced young and was only used once. Photo by Gary Seloff

Dignitaries came specifically to view Armand Bayou Osprey. Photo from ABNC Archives

During the 1980s Armand Bayou maintained a small population of Ospreys, even during the population lows of the DDT era. Prince Phillip of England and renowned naturalist Roger Tory Peterson attended an Osprey tour from the Harris County pontoon tour boat, the Hana G. (It also allowed me to get Tory Peterson's signature in my birding field guide written by him.)

While Ospreys were once threatened by the persistent pesticide, today their numbers have dramatically recovered. This is attributed in large part to the ban of this long-lived legacy pesticide as part of the *Clean Water Act* in 1972. Today the birds have recovered and now occur on every continent except Antarctica. Armand Bayou populations have recovered as well. During a winter pontoon tour or kayak tour, it's not unusual to have four Ospreys in view at the same time.

We counted 23 Ospreys on Armand Bayou during the 2019 Christmas Bird Count. The Audubon Christmas Bird Count happens all around the country. Volunteers gather and count every bird seen, which contributes valuable data regarding population trends in all bird populations. Traveling only three miles and counting 23 Ospreys is an incredible number and a testament to the health of the ecosystem given the quantity of fish that Ospreys require. I wonder if there is anywhere else in America where a person can take a three-mile tour and see that many Ospreys?

Otters Encounters

If you're lucky you may have the opportunity to catch a glimpse of one of the rarest mammals that inhabits the waters of Armand Bayou. The American river otter (*Lontra canadensis*) is seen on rare occasion by those willing to paddle solo, slow and quiet.

Otters are fast, agile swimmers with keen senses and high intelligence. Photo by Gary Seloff

Otters are semiaquatic members of the weasel family with long, flexible bodies. They are very aware of their surroundings, which means that typically they see you before you see them.

Otterly in love. Photo by Gary Seloff

Seeing otters in the act of reproduction is a life memory. As I paddled one morning at first light, I could hear the frantic vocalization. When I paddled around the next bend, they came into view.

Photo by Gary Seloff

In 1995, ABNC installed a 100-gallon saltwater aquarium in the Interpretive Building foyer exhibit area. It was intended as an exhibit of aquatic life in the bayou. I would often start my mornings at the water's edge throwing a cast-net to collect new specimens for the exhibit. One such morning I began to notice a chirping call along the water's edge. It sounded similar to a green treefrog, but somehow new and different. As I paid more attention, I noticed that the sound was moving, and moving towards me, which told me that it was definitely not a tree frog. I stopped throwing the net and laid down flat at the water's edge.

Coming into view was a family of otters with one adult and two pups. I knew instantly that I was viewing a new species on my life list of wildlife.

At first glance, nutrias look a lot like otters.
Photo by Gary Seloff

At first glance I could have mistaken them for nutrias. Nutrias are a non-native rodent from South America. They are of similar size and color and resemble otters to the untrained eye.

Photo by Gary Seloff

Photo by Gary Seloff

Otters have a very high metabolism rate and are almost always eating to supply their needed fuel.
Photo by Gary Seloff

Having observed the nutria in various places through much of my life, I could see that these animals moved differently, more like agile, athletic marine mammals. The tempo of movement in the water was in a higher gear of motion. They swam directly towards me where I was lying undetected and then they disappeared into the bank directly under me! I could have touched them as they swam past.

Otters dig a den where the pups are born. The family unit regularly returns to the den while the pups are small and may remain a family for a year or until the female bears new young.

They mostly eat aquatic organisms, especially fish and crustaceans. Bayou waters are particularly rich in both during the summer months. On several occasions, I have seen shrimp fleeing otters as they swam in quick pursuit. However, I hear otters hidden in the marsh grass far more often than I see them.

Armand Bayou otters have a particular taste for blue crabs, which are abundant during summer. Kayaking the bayou, I have often heard otters crunching crab shells, hidden from view in the grass. The sound is almost like a hungry six-year-old child hurriedly chomping potato chips with mouth open.

The estuarine waters of Armand Bayou provide abundant resources, which are needed for the otter's daily commute. Otters have a home range of 15 to 20 square miles and may travel over 10 miles in a single day.

Here on Armand Bayou, they forage far and wide. There have been confirmed otter sightings on every pond at ABNC on both sides of the bayou. The journey that otters must travel over land to reach any of these ponds is over half a mile. This reinforces their ability to travel long distances equally at home in terrestrial and aquatic environments. They stay in these ponds only briefly before returning home to the bayou. Otters are curious and love to explore. I believe this curiosity promotes their exploring far and wide, which contributes to their occasional pond sightings, as there is no shortage of available food in the bayou.

Otters are equally at home in the water or on land. Photo by Ann Brinly

Over 10 years ago, Stewardship Technicians Cullen and Merari were constructing the first artificial heron nesting platform on the West Bank Pond and had their own life memory otter sighting. Much to their amazement, an otter swam directly past the rookery island with a bluegill sunfish in its mouth. It continued to eat the fish, tail first until it disappeared. I have also found that they can miraculously disappear whenever they choose.

Otter populations plummeted around the Galveston Bay complex during the 1960s, 70s and 80s. During this time the bay lost over 30,000 acres of tidal marsh habitat due to subsidence and erosion. These marshes are critical feeding habitat for otters. When feeding areas are compromised, the population will decline. Additionally, fur trapping was a major impact to the population all around North America. In Texas, otters may be legally hunted or trapped any time of year and may also be killed as nuisance animals. Otter's luxurious fur is valuable to the fur industry, which promoted trappers' wide scale pursuit. While Galveston Bay otter numbers have not rebounded from their previous count, the population seems to be on the rise.

I was initially reluctant to announce the presence of otters in Armand Bayou for several years after the first 1995 sighting. I have found multiple leghold traps set by fur trappers under several bridge crossings in the watershed. In addition to leghold traps being a cruel manner for any animal to die, they could also have a significant impact on the small otter population in Armand Bayou.

Along the West Coast, sea otters are frequently killed as they forage inside of crab traps. The animals enter in search of their favorite crab meal, not finding the escape exit before drowning. Due to their significant daily travel and relatively low numbers around Galveston Bay, otters are very difficult to see, study or monitor. I suspect that similar crab trap mortality is taking place around the bay but collecting meaningful data from commercial crab trappers is difficult.

The one area of obvious impact is from roadkill. I have documented four otters killed by traffic on surrounding roadways since that first sighting in 1995. There are probably more. Two on Bay Area Blvd., one on Red Bluff Road and one on Space Center Blvd. The area covered by these kills is further testament to their wide range over land, away from bayou waters.

Over the past 25 years, during my best years of paddling I have had 8 to 10 otter sightings per year. Recently however, sightings have dramatically declined. The report is similar from Gary Seloff who has also noticed a marked decline.

These elusive animals are often hard to see, however, they may leave evidence of their presence.
Photo by Mark Kramer

Otters are the embodiment of the term charismatic. Here they enjoy playtime in a mudslide.
Photo by Ann Brinly

While I have not had a sighting in over two years, I have seen evidence of their presence twice in the form of otter droppings. While it seems as if their numbers are down in Armand Bayou, they have not entirely disappeared.

Any otter sighting while I paddle the bayou waters is at the very top of my wish list. Otters are extremely playful, which is considered a behavioral indicator of high intelligence. Their presence is always a biological indicator of good ecosystem health. Even though I don't have otter encounters frequently, just knowing that they're here is reassuring that our preservation and conservation endeavors are worth the effort.

Night-Heron Departures

The season is changing. As water temperatures cool in September, a great migration is underway. Unseen by human eyes, small fish, shrimp and crabs are leaving the bayou, headed for Galveston Bay and the Gulf of Mexico. They've spent the first summer of their life in the lush marshes and warm water of Armand Bayou.

This abundant fishery, and especially the presence of juvenile blue crabs, attracts a member of the heron family that specializes in targeting these small crustaceans. Night-Herons have several key adaptations that other herons don't, which allows for their special feeding behavior.

Yellow-crowned Night-Heron (*Nycticorax nycticorax*).
Photo by Gary Seloff

Large, red, light gathering eyes enable Night-Herons to hunt diurnally at dawn, dusk, and into the darkness. The shallow margins of the bayou's water cool quickly as the sun sets. The cooling water and abundant food draws young crabs into the shallows to forage. Into the shallows where Night-Herons hunt.

The second adaptation is a short, stout bill structure. Most herons and egrets have long slender bills evolved for catching fish. Night-Herons have a bill made for crushing. This is an important feature when your primary prey is covered with spiny armor. Can *you* imagine swallowing a whole crab?

Even better, remove claws and tenderize shell first.
Photo by Gary Seloff

The bill allows Night-Herons to crunch the *exoskeleton* of dinner before swallowing. Often, larger crabs are disarmed immediately. Crab claws can produce a painful pinch.

Black-crowned Night-Heron (*Nyctanassa violacea*).
Photo by Gary Seloff

Photo by Gary Seloff

Yellow-crowned Night-Herons are the more common of the two species seen on Armand Bayou. They can be identified by the black and white horizontal stripe running through their eye.

Careful dining is a must when dinner has claws.
Photo by Gary Seloff

They are crustacean-feeding specialists, but don't limit themselves only to crabs. Photo by Gary Seloff

When available, a red crustacean is a tasty addition to the menu. Photo by Mark Kramer

Herons grow special breeding plumes during the nesting season, which are held upright during courtship displays. The plumes may also be raised to warn another bird that it's getting too close to their fishing hole. Photo by Gary Seloff

After a good gully washer last summer, I spotted a Yellow-crowned Night-Heron foraging in the flooded field. I approached for a picture, but the bird flew, dropping this prize catch. Happy to have escaped with his life, I returned the crawfish back to his burrow.

Yellow-crowns are commonly seen when the fields and ditches are filled with water after a good rain. They come to hunt crawfish. They can be so abundant that a friend of mine calls them ditch pigeons (not recommended when you're with birders).

There are 350 species of crawfish in North America. Forty-three species live in Texas. Local crawfish spend the majority of their life burrowed in the moist soil and underground *aquifers* below our feet. When the fields flood after a rain, crawfish come to the surface, foraging on whatever they can find.

As the water recedes, they create a characteristic "crawfish chimney." This chimney closes the entrance to the burrow minimizing evaporation in their moist underground habitat. Some of my fondest childhood memories are of collecting crawfish after a summer rain to put in my red wagon, from the flooded fields around my house. It's also a bonanza for the Yellow-crowned Night-Heron.

Yellow-crowned Night-Herons nest in our area. In fact, they commonly nest in residential neighborhoods. They prefer to nest together with species of their own kind. I have a friend who had one these nesting colonies in his backyard, which contained over 30 nests. While fascinating to watch, it also has some drawbacks. The birds aren't capable of digesting crab or crawfish shell, which means a *bolus* of shell is regurgitated. Also, a massive amount of fishy-smelling poop is delivered into your backyard—free of charge.

Most colonial nesting waterbird rookeries comprise an assortment of species. The colonies are typically on islands in treetops located over nesting alligators. Nesting female alligators possess a strong maternal instinct, protecting their own eggs and inadvertently protecting any egret eggs in the trees overhead from scavenging raccoons. It's theorized that Yellow-crowned Night-Herons may seek out backyards with multiple dogs. The dogs are substituted for alligators as the protective guardian to minimize raccoon raids.

The Black-crowned Night-Heron is less commonly seen on the bayou. This is true in part because they are most active after dark when human activity on the water is low. Most sightings occur during the day while the birds roost in the surrounding trees waiting for nightfall.

Photo by Gary Seloff

Black-crowns are more strictly nocturnal and seldom seen feeding during the light of day. However, they share the same passion for eating crab. Their nesting habits differ from Yellow-crowns in that Black-crowned Night-Herons nest in large rookeries with other species of colonial nesting birds. They are one of the few herons that eat other bird nestlings as a regular part of their diet.

Their distribution is impressive. Black-crowned Night-Herons are the most widely distributed heron in the world. They occur on every continent except Australia and Antarctica.

Their large red eyes are striking and enable them to see well with very limited light. Photo by Gary Seloff

The first cool fronts mark the end of the season that Night-Herons are seen on the bayou. As crabs migrate out of the bayou, so do the Night-Herons. They travel following the food and are commonly seen in winter along the edges of Galveston Bay or further down the Texas coast into Mexico. I always welcome the first sightings of them as the true return of summer.

Kingfishers

Kingfishers are always found adjacent to water. Photo by Gary Seloff

Keep a watchful eye on the powerlines and trees adjacent to local bayous and ditches and you may be fortunate enough to see a Belted Kingfisher (*Megaceryle alcyon*). These small fish-eating birds return to the Texas coast in September/October. After rearing this year's brood, they do a short migration to their winter fishing grounds on Armand Bayou. They're most often seen sitting on an observation perch scanning the water for small fish or other small aquatic morsels.

On close inspection, kingfishers have tiny feet in relation to their body. An oversized shaggy head almost seems out of proportion in relation to the body. Without good optics an observer may never see this, as the birds rarely allow a person to approach and will fly when you are still at a great distance. This long *flight distance* rarely allows the casual observer to gain full appreciation of this magnificent bayou fisherman. Here's another tip of my hat for the intimate photos from Gary Seloff whose images highlight these fabulous details.

Belted Kingfishers are known for their powerful and dynamic dives. Photo by Gary Seloff

Kingfishers most commonly perch, waiting for a fish to surface within diving distance. "Dive," however, is an inaccurate description as it implies a bird falling quickly with motionless wings. "Drive" more accurately describes the spectacle of the kingfisher pursuing fish, driving downward with strong wing beats until impacting the water. They literally fly headfirst into the water. It occurs at such lightning speed that photographers struggle to capture an image of a diving kingfisher.

Kingfishers are birds whose features are noticeably disproportionate. Photo by Gary Seloff

Photo by Gary Seloff

If the dive is successful, the bird returns to the perch and may smash it's catch against the surface to stun the prey before swallowing it.

A fishing tactic less commonly used is hovering in mid-air over a school of fish. The bird has a specific "figure eight" wing motion, which allows it to "helicopter" motionless while accurately locking onto its prey. Like the motion also used by canoe paddlers: the figure eight paddle stroke described as "sculling." The flying motion seems to defy the laws of gravity before the bird drives forcefully down into the water.

Belted Kingfisher male. Photo by Gary Seloff

On Armand Bayou kingfishers are predominantly fall/winter birds. They enjoy the healthy fishery of the estuarine bayou waters until springtime produces the drive to nest. Kingfishers have one of the most unique nesting strategies of any bird in our area. They seek out steep sand embankments, which are typically located in sharp bends of East Texas rivers. Because this critical nesting habitat doesn't commonly occur in the flat coastal plain or in the Bayou City, the birds travel to the rivers where they can meet these reproductive needs. They dig a three- to six-foot deep tunnel in the sand cliff where the young are raised.

Belted Kingfisher female. Photo by Gary Seloff

A composite glimpse of a master of flight. Photo by Gary Seloff

The vertical cliff must be tall enough with unstable sand below to eliminate any scavenging raccoons or rat snakes from entering. On several occasions I have seen these nest tunnels while paddling on Village Creek, a tributary of the Neches River. This short distance migration between nesting habitat and winter feeding habitat is critical for the species survival.

The bird world commonly attributes a distinction between males and females with males displaying vibrant, colorful plumage and females being more dull in color. This *sexual dimorphism* typically provides less vibrant feathers to camouflage females during incubation.

While this is true for the vast majority of birds, the script is flipped with Belted Kingfishers. The males are more drab with females having the most color. Female Belted Kingfishers have a chest patch of rust-red feathers.

Green Kingfisher

On rare occasion, Green Kingfishers (*Chloroceryle americana*) have been seen on Armand Bayou. They are a rare sight here and more commonly seen in the Rio Grande Valley and further south. They seem to prefer the narrow, confined water of extreme upper Armand Bayou where I have seen them twice.

Photo by Gary Seloff

I've enjoyed watching kingfishers both on their wintering grounds and nesting in east Texas. They are fast-flying, loud, animated birds that always put on a good show.

Pelican Outpost

"The pelican, its beak can hold more than its belly can." That was the sage observation from my mother when we would visit South Louisiana in my childhood. My mother was no birder, but she often offered colorful Cajun phrases. Those are standout memories for me, vivid because the birds were very large and had a peculiar bill. The Brown Pelican is the state bird of Louisiana. They're also strong memories because at that time there were no Brown Pelicans to be found in coastal Texas.

Photo by Gary Seloff

Both Brown Pelicans (*Pelecanus occidentalis*) and American White Pelicans (*Pelecanus erythrorhynchos*) now occur on Armand Bayou. They are among the largest and heaviest birds in North America. Pelicans are fish-eating birds and make a good living on the bayou. Once again gulf menhaden, which is the primary forage fish in Armand Bayou, are their main course.

Life is easy on Armand Bayou with abundant food and quiet waters. Photo by Gary Seloff

There are many birds on the bayou that specialize in eating fish. The abundance and diversity of fish-eating bird species is a useful biological indicator of the health of the fishery. Each of these fishermen have evolved their own specialized adaptations to all catch the same short list of fish species, ensuring success in filling their niche and their belly.

Ospreys have sharp vision, powerful wings and large specially adapted talons. Photo by Gary Seloff

Herons have long legs, long spear shaped bill and a long serpentine neck. Photo by Gary Seloff

Kingfishers have fast flight and a bill that effectively grabs or spears individual fish while lunging headfirst into the water. Photo by Gary Seloff

Anhingas have a lithe body and large webbed feet, enabling the bird to swim underwater and capture fish. Imagine a bird being able to outswim a fish! They also have a gular sac that is similar to the pelican's. Photo by Gary Seloff

Pelicans have a very large bill and elastic gular sac that enables the birds to scoop large volumes of water. They then strain the water out, often catching multiple fish. Photo by Gary Seloff

The Louisiana pelicans were special. As a child, I fished all around the Galveston Bay complex and never saw pelicans. The birds were totally absent from the Texas coast for decades. As previously described, with many other birds, the Brown Pelican suffered significant impacts from DDT beginning in the 1960s. The pelican population crashed and the bird was ultimately placed on the newly formed Endangered Species List in 1970.

Adult Brown Pelican plumage is ornate with noticeable white and yellow head feathers. Photo by Gary Seloff

When an animal is Listed, the U.S. Fish and Wildlife Service leads a recovery team that is charged with developing a recovery plan for the species. In 1977, ABNC attended a Brown Pelican Recovery Team meeting in Grande Isle, Louisiana where a remnant pelican population still persisted. We had hoped that Armand Bayou might be considered as a reintroduction site for the upper Texas coast. It was ultimately determined that the bayou lacked quality breeding/nesting habitat and birds weren't moved here. However, Louisiana pelicans were relocated to more promising nesting areas on the Texas coast and were the original colonizers of today's resident population.

Juvenile Brown Pelicans are uniformly drab in comparison. Photo by Gary Seloff

Brown Pelicans prefer nesting on large islands in coastal bays. Many of those historic nesting islands in Galveston Bay (such as Redfish Island) have disappeared from the effects of subsidence and erosion from ship wakes. This loss of nesting habitat has now concentrated their nesting area on North Deer Island. As you approach Galveston Island and begin to cross the causeway, look immediately to the right and North Deer Island is visible. This is the largest collection of colonial nesting waterbirds in Galveston Bay.

Seventeen bird species nest on North Deer Island. In 2009 North Deer Island was designated as a Global Important Bird Area by the National Audubon Society and BirdLife International. Approximately 1,000 nesting pairs of Brown Pelicans use the island as critical reproductive habitat. For several years, I led tours of the colony with fellow conservationist George Regmund. Seeing, smelling and hearing tens of thousands of nesting birds and their young imparts the feeling that you are in the Galapagos. It's likely that if you see a Brown Pelican around the bay, it was born there.

The prohibition of internal combustion engines minimizes disturbance from jet skis and other powerboats. Photo by Gary Seloff

Brown Pelicans were listed as an Endangered Species from 1970 to 2009. After forty years, I had my first sighting ever on Armand Bayou in 2005. It was a memorable moment. The kind of rare moment where you take a deep breath of conservation success.

Photo by Gary Seloff

One of the most spectacular viewing opportunities on Armand Bayou is from the Bayou Ranger tour boat to witness a Brown Pelican dive. The birds make a headfirst entrance creating a huge splash that's audible for some distance.

American White Pelicans have an eight-foot wingspan and an average weight of twenty pounds. Photo by Gary Seloff

In November, large flocks of American White Pelicans may be seen circling in slow-motion spiral perfection high overhead. In North America, only the California Condor is larger. In the fall, the birds return to the Texas coast to overwinter after completing nesting in the central U. S. and southern Canada.

American White pelicans are large, stately and elegant as they swim quietly in bayou waters. Photo by Gary Seloff

White Pelicans' fishing strategy differs from that of their Brown Pelican cousins. They don't dive. Instead, they swim and occasionally dip the large bill into the water grabbing fish. They often work together as a team, swimming in a choreographed fashion that encircles fish schools into a tight ball where they are caught in unison. While they are very large birds, they are graceful and stately in their elegant aquatic dance.

American White Pelican populations also suffered a significant decline from DDT. However, the bird's decline was not significant enough to have it Listed. Why not? Both species inhabit similar habitat and consume fish. One difference is that Brown Pelicans are non-migratory. One theory regarding the contrast of impacts is that the coastal Brown Pelican remained in the receiving bays of watersheds that capture vast agricultural runoff. For example, the main river tributary of Galveston Bay (the Trinity River) captures 18,000 square miles of runoff within its watershed. Any and all pesticides within the area contributed to the toxic runoff load entering the bay, the fish, and ultimately the birds.

American White Pelicans are migratory, spending only the winter along the coast. Winter agriculture is limited in Texas, meaning a reduction of toxic inflow. White Pelicans migrate inland during the summer, which is the peak agriculture period, where they nest around large lakes and reservoirs. This removed White Pelicans from year-round exposure to high levels of toxin in coastal bays.

Pelicans are another success story in environmental management and species recovery. After a forty-year absence, they benefited from the Clean Water Act, which prohibited the use of DDT in America. The Endangered Species Act produced a focused recovery plan for pelicans and many other species on the brink of extinction. They are among a distinguished list of the previously Endangerds now residing on Armand Bayou.

Pelicans find numerous perching opportunities on Armand Bayou where they can relax, preen and allow their feathers to dry. Photo by Gary Seloff

American White Pelicans are a special viewing opportunity for winter Bayou Ranger tours. Photo by Gary Seloff

Chapter Six: *Cultural History*

Archeology

Interest in archeology of the area began with the extensive field surveys conducted by the Houston Archeological Society in the late 1960s. Ultimately, the concentration of prehistoric and historic sites found along Armand Bayou was designated as the Armand Bayou Archeological District on the National Park Services' National Register of Historic Places. Currently, twenty-three sites or features are currently identified within the boundaries of ABNC.

Last of the Akokisa

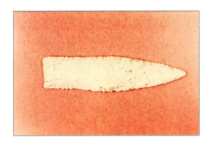

Arrowhead

Author Unknown

First, you must find a rock
That has always wanted to be a bird: to sing, fly
It is hard. Next, you must chip away
Its minor desires respecters
Of ground, moss, the irrelevant
Sparks.

You must shape it into the
Unromanticized heart: tongue
For the deep kiss, shoulders
For holding

Finally
You must teach it to cover
its tracks. Windbreaker,
It must learn
To mend the shards of air
As it goes, swift, tender,
To be the bone
It is hard.

I sit on a shell midden on the edge of the Armand Bayou. Most Houstonians aren't aware that these middens are scattered around the Galveston Bay area. Most Houstonians aren't aware that these shell piles accumulated over thousands of years, left behind by the native peoples of our area. Most Houstonians aren't aware that Native Americans ever lived here. There were a handful of linguistically distinct groups of native peoples once living around Galveston Bay. Now gone with only the faintest trace of their footsteps remaining.

Archeologists estimate the Akokisa occupied these sites along Armand Bayou for approximately 8,000 years. Sitting and overlooking the bayou it's easy to imagine the small band of hunter-gatherers. Easy to imagine a smoldering fire and clams being tossed into the coals. It's harder to imagine how they endured for thousands of years. I thought I wanted to live the back-to-the-land "Indian" lifestyle once. Six months in a tent taught me the harshness of wet winter cold and the relentless nature of mosquitos at "red alert levels." I sit here now with a fragment of Akokisa pottery shard in my hand and wonder, are our people living a lifestyle capable of sustaining us for that long? Can we live this modern lifestyle supporting eight billion people and be here 8,000 years in the future as they were? They were a group of poorly understood people whose story has never been told.

Akokisa ceramic. Photo ABNC archives

The Galveston Bay complex was once home to numerous Native American bands. The Coco, Cujuane, Guapite, Atakapa, and Tonkawa all spoke their own language and occurred along the Bay shores. Karankawa Indians are Texas' most well-known coastal group of native Americans. Once it was believed that they lived around Galveston Bay. Today most experts believe that they primarily occurred further south on barrier islands down the Texas coast. In fact, some previous excavations of Karankawa sites are now determined to have actually been the Akokisa. The Akokisa lived an egalitarian lifeway with no chief, no religion, no permanent housing, no clothing and no written language. They were among the simplest native cultures in North America.

My understanding of the Akokisa has grown through the years. Conversations with archeologist Joan Few and also the book titled "The Karankawa Indians" by Robert A. Ricklis were major sources of valuable information. I had the opportunity to hear Ms. Few speak at the ABNC Volunteer Meeting in March 2008 and collected extensive notes from her presentation. Ms. Few had previously worked on a series of excavations on sites located on Armand Bayou. Her stories were spellbinding and I'll recount several of them here. Further information was gained from reading the technical reports of archeologists Robert Hole, Charles Chandler, and Lawrence Aten who also conducted excavations and field surveys along Armand Bayou in the early 1970s.

The native peoples living along Armand Bayou lived a seasonally nomadic lifestyle. Archeologists estimate their peak population to have been around 2,000 people. It's believed that they ranged from West Bay to the Sabine River. They lived a hand-to-mouth lifeway with their movements being driven by the seasonal availability of food resources. They were a coastal people occurring largely on the eastern shore of Galveston Bay and rarely traveled more than 30 miles inland. Every Spring and Summer they visited Armand Bayou. They did not visit the same campsite every year.

Joan Few excavating Akokisa campsite. Photo ABNC archives

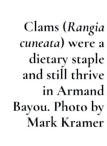

Clams (*Rangia cuneata*) were a dietary staple and still thrive in Armand Bayou. Photo by Mark Kramer

Wild plants, berries, nuts, fish and wildlife were key components of their diet. A detailed faunal survey of the Armand Bayou midden contents includes evidence of oyster, clam, bison, deer, gray wolf, raccoon, gray squirrel, opossum, box turtle, soft-shelled turtle, snake, drum, catfish, alligator, waterfowl, bobcat and rodent. Oysters and clams were a critical dietary component based on excavation evidence. It appears that three- to four-year-old *Rangia* clams were preferred. Clams were a constant dependable food resource. Clam beds always occurred in the same location. They were easy to capture and collect. Preparation was as simple as tossing them into the fire. A returning tribe could arrive at a campsite with confidence clams would be readily available whenever needed. Once consumed the clams' shells were tossed into a pile, which may have accumulated for thousands of years. I have memories from the 1970s of a massive pile of clam and oyster shells (shell midden) in Seabrook near where McHale Park is now. Some archeologists believe that middens were trash piles. Others believe the shell piles provided enhanced drainage and the people lived on top of the shells. Both theories have evidence to support the claims. Note also that oysters were present in the Armand Bayou middens during the excavation. Today oysters do not occur in Armand Bayou or Mud Lake due to low salinity levels. Oysters in the archeological record are a biological indicator reflecting heightened salinity during different climatic conditions in a previous era.

During seasons of abundance different tribal bands would hold large gatherings or "mitotes." Part of the mitote feast and celebration included the brewing of a "black drink" made from the leaf of the yaupon. Yaupon is closely related to the popular South American beverage yerba mate. Yaupon leaves contain caffeine and it is reported that the tea produced was very thick, strong and potent. Often the beverage was consumed to the point of Indians becoming sick and vomiting. Research indicates that gatherings would often proceed around the clock for several days.

Remnants of fine ceramic pottery uncovered during excavation. Photo ABNC archives

Pottery shards account for the bulk of the artifacts found during excavations. On occasion I have found fragments of these broken pots during walks along the bayou's edge during the low tides of winter. It stirs my imagination to hold an artifact made by a human hand from so long ago. Made by a person that lived their whole life on the shores of this bayou. Someone who paddled their canoe to catch fish in these waters. Someone who found beauty in the sun setting over that same portion of prairie. The rising emotions of the similarities of a lifetime of mud beneath my toenails is not lost on me.

Archeologists uncover discarded contents
of cooking pots. Photo ABNC archives

No pottery wheel was used for the ceramic formation. A type of "coil construction" where by a "rope" of clay was looped upon itself and then smoothed to create a vessel. Portions of small bowls, large jars and deep vases were uncovered. Ms. Few recounted the theory that a vessel would remain positioned in a cooking fire for a large portion of the day. As hunters would return to the camp, they would add their contribution to the pot creating an "Indian gumbo." After a period of time the contents would cook beyond being edible. The pot would then be removed from the fire, carried to the edge of camp and the contents tossed. Ms. Few recounted "peeling back" the layers of soil to expose different horizons of cook pot contents being scattered at different angles! Almost as if you could see that someone different had spread the contents on different days from different angles!

Francois De Bellisle, who was shipwrecked on Bolivar Peninsula in 1722, indicated that the Akokisa also raised a "superfine" variety of maize. Further interesting reading from him of his time with the natives includes the description of a prairie fire ignited by Indians, collecting hundreds of bird eggs on islands in the bay, and a winter bison hunt.

Of particular note is an eloquent narrative regarding the beauty of coastal prairie landscapes. Cabeza De Vaca was a Spanish explorer shipwrecked on Galveston Island in 1532. His account of living among the natives is journaled in "Adventures into the Unknown Interior" and provides further insight into the culture.

Painting, "Karankawa Native Americans" by
Frank Weir. Courtesy of Texas Beyond History

I could find little evidence of Akokisa portraits or sketches. However, descriptions of their appearance offer that they were short in stature, had large heads, protruding lips, dark skin and stained teeth. Body and facial tattooing were common in both sexes. They lived in small, dome-shaped wiki-ups thatched in palmetto leaf in winter. A small central fire aided in managing biting insects. Summer dwelling was in the chickee, which consisted of a raised floor, open walls and overhead roof.

Dugout canoes made of cypress or cedar were the primary mode of transportation for the Akokisa. The boats were long, shallow draft, fast and stable. The boats were versatile and carried the entirety of village possessions. Reports describe the boats also being used for hunting fish and wildlife. Early settlers' anger was often driven by Indian raids in which these canoes allowed escape into the shallow marshes and estuaries where pursuit was not possible. Vessels were designed for bay and bayou navigation and were not designed for or used in the open Gulf of Mexico.

Stone does not commonly occur locally and was considered a precious resource. Photo ABNC archives

Early settlers on Armand Bayou.
Photo ABNC archives

Archeological evidence indicated a technological transition through the significant passage of time. Spear and dart points transitioned to the bow and arrow. The bow and arrow were the primary tool for hunting everything from fish to bison in more modern times. Bows were described as being as tall as a man and made from southern red cedar. The Indians prized stone as a very valuable resource recognizing that it does not occur frequently around Galveston Bay. Arrowhead, spear point, and tool making artifacts found in excavations were primarily made of local chert. In my 45 years of hiking and exploring along Armand Bayou, I have found only one arrowhead. Stone was treated as a very valuable material. Fish were harvested with bow and arrow. They were also collected with cane weir fish traps and nets. There was gender division of labor with men hunting and women collecting edible plants.

It is estimated that the population of North American Indians declined by 75% to 95% within the first 100 years of European contact. Cabeza de Vaca reported that during the first winter of contact, half of the natives died from dysentery, infected by the Spaniards. European disease brought by the colonists introduced further illness for which native peoples had no immunity and were unable to survive. Small pox and measles were known to have devastated native populations. Colonization and expansion accelerated around Galveston Bay in the early 1800s. Native peoples were viewed as a hinderance to that process. Numerous conflicts, combats and eradication campaigns were documented. Those Indians not killed in combat died from European infectious disease. Sadly, by 1850 all native peoples around Galveston Bay had completely disappeared.

The Armand Bayou Archeological District was established to recognize, research and preserve the unique cultural heritage of the first people of Armand Bayou. Photo ABNC archives

Armand Bayou is rich in evidence of the native people that once lived here. There are twelve known archeological sites located along Armand Bayou and its tributaries. For this reason, the area received a special designation as The Armand Bayou Archeological District. The designation acknowledges the unique historical nature of the native American sites in the region. Most of the sites are remnant campsites and shell middens. However, one of the sites is more sacred.

An Akokisa burial site exists on the eastern shore of Lake Mark Kramer adjacent to Clear Lake Park. The site is located within the Harris County Youth Village. Referred to as The Harris County Boys Home Cemetery, it is one of the few known burial sites of native peoples on the Texas coast. The site was excavated by Lawrence Aten and Charles Chandler in 1971. Thirty-two native people are buried there. The people resting there were all buried in the sitting position, as was the native custom. Several of the graves contained personal items that

indicated the person's unique tribal skill. Some contained bead making items, another included a flint knapping tool kit used to make arrowheads. Other graves contained jewelry made of shell or bone.

Akokisa burial. Photo ABNC archives

Ceremonial flute. Photo ABNC archives

A flute was also recovered from one of burial sites. Interestingly the flute was crafted from the leg bone of a Whooping Crane. Ms. Few recounted that many native peoples used the flute as part of the matrimonial ceremony. Other native cultures use the flute as part of the burial rites. Often the flute would be intentionally broken and then placed into the grave, as if to indicate that the persons song had been played and would never play again. In either case it harkens back to a time long past when Whooping Cranes still walked the marshes of Armand Bayou. Forensic research into skeletal remains revealed no significant disease or pathology. Teeth were shown to have extensive wear as evidence of the gritty nature of their shellfish diet. Of special interest is that none of the skeletal remains had evidence of violent death. There are historic reports of what was once a much larger burial ground located near the mouth of Clear Lake. Late in the 19th century, large amounts of shell (middens) were removed from the site to provide foundation for railroad track. Over 100 burials were destroyed as part of the shell removal. It is widely believed that this site served as the primary burial ground for native peoples of the Clear Lake region.

Wild places have always served as a place for personal reflection. Their value may also be measured as a sanctuary to reflect on our story as a culture and our own personal story. I'm sitting in an Akokisa campsite beneath the trees overlooking the bayou. The burial grounds are directly across the water. Even though the burial ground is not visible it somehow seems to dignify the view. The southerly breeze in the treetops allows me to almost feel their presence. I imagine voices in an extinct language that will never be spoken again. They tell me from where we came and perhaps where we're going. The pottery shard in my hand is a final crumbling piece of a culture's technology and history. It's a tangible connection to a people's struggle in the face of overwhelming adversity. It deepens the impact of this poignant moment for me as an American.

Racoons are common throughout bayou and prairie. Photo by Gary Seloff

Chapter Seven: *Good Stories*

Memorable Days

Deer on a Tether

Every year since 1982 ABNC has participated in the National Audubon Society Christmas Bird Count (CBC). All around North America people volunteer to go into the field and count every bird that is seen on count day. Over time, the data produced gives biologists a snapshot of bird populations. It's a long day beginning before sunrise and ending at sunset. It's one of my favorite days of the year because I spend all day in the field with friends who all enjoy getting onto some of the most remote portions of the refuge. Count days begin on the water from the pontoon boat. It is often the coldest day of the year for me as we're on the water for three to four hours, often in windy conditions.

One CBC morning in 1998 we were underway at first light. Headed south in Mud Lake (renamed Lake Mark Kramer in 2021) we turned west, into an embayment where we had recently been conducting some of the first tidal marsh restoration projects. At that time there was concern that the projects would be impacted by Grass Carp and Water Hyacinth. Grass Carp had been observed in other areas where they had grazed young marsh plant propagules, undoing weeks of hard work in a few hours. Water Hyacinth is a free-floating plant that travels to new areas with each rising tide or change of wind direction. Large rafts of hyacinth travel on a daily basis. These rafts at times can float on top of a marsh restoration site. As the tide falls, they land on the recently planted marsh site causing impacts to the vulnerable early developmental stages of the project. Because of the damage from carp and hyacinth, it was common practice to install plastic construction fencing as a barrier to mitigate their impacts.

Back to the morning of the bird count. It was a cold and foggy morning. As we turned into the cove, I could see something moving in the distance along the shore, but due to the limited visibility it was obscured. It was large and running back and forth in the same location at a high speed. After years on the bayou, it's unusual for me to see an animal and not know what it is in an instant, but this had me baffled.

Photo by Ann Brinly

As the boat approached through the fog, we could see a deer had entangled its antlers in the marsh fencing. It had somehow ripped a 20-foot-long section of material free from the fence posts. It was essentially running back and forth on a tether. The closer we got, the more we could see it was not just a deer, but a big deer. The closer we got the more the deer panicked. We determined it best to beach the boat a safe distance from the animal and come up with a plan. We knew a local veterinarian who we hoped might have a tranquilizer gun. We made a few calls and got no results. On closer inspection we could count 12 spikes on the animal's antlers.

Photo by Ann Brinly

By this time the animal had worked himself to the point of exhaustion. Slowly and carefully, we approached. He was so tired out that we could now handle him in relative safety. After a ten-minute operation we cut the fencing away. He was free and swam away.

Bobcat on a Tree

For many years I ran nighttime eco-tours on the Bayou Ranger pontoon boat. The bayou at night is a different world. The entire view of the world is captured by the width of the Q-Beam spotlight. One aspect of the spotlight is the reflection it gives off from many different animal's eyes. Alligator eyes reflect a strong "stop-sign" red property that is visible from a good distance. Other animal eyes also have a reflective property, often with a different color.

One summer night we were returning to Bay Area Park after having been on an upstream tour to the north. As we were making the final bend before passing under the Bay Area Blvd. bridge, I saw eye shine. It was not the usual red gator reflection that I was familiar with. I slowed the boat to a crawl and we all focused the binoculars on the spotlight view.

As we got closer, we could see a Muscovy Duck in the water. It is unusual to see park ducks on the water at night due to their vulnerability to alligator attack. I never saw the eyeshine from the duck and began to wonder why. The duck was swimming 5 to 10 feet from the end of a fallen tree that had landed in the water. And then I saw it crouched near the end of the tree—a bobcat. He had his eyes on the duck. He was waiting for the duck to swim within striking distance. We stopped the boat and waited and waited. Nothing. After 10 minutes I began to wonder if the bobcat ever had the nerve to jump into deep water. The duck maintained the 5 to 10-foot space between himself and the cat as if it knew not to get any closer. After a long wait on the edge of our seats, we headed home.

Photo by Gary Seloff

Girl Scout Pontoon Boat Sex Ed

I ran the pontoon boat tours for Harris County out of Bay Area Park from 1981 through 1988. At the height of tour operations, we were offering five trips each day, Monday through Friday. The trips were very popular because they were free.

During the summer months when kids were out of school, we often took children's groups on tours.

On one such trip we hosted a boat-load of Girl Scouts who were all 10 to 12 years old. The trip began as normal and we talked about birds and the bayou and standard boat tour material.

In that era there was a popular spot for canoers to beach their boat and stop for a break near where the ABNC Boathouse is now. Approaching the spot, I could see that a canoe had stopped. As we got closer, I could see a blanket spread out and a pair of boots beside the blanket along with a bottle of wine. The girls were listening to me talk. As we got even closer, I could see a pair of women's feet pointed straight up in the air. Two lovers, buck-naked, were fully engaged. The boat was maybe 30 feet away at this point and they were in plain view. They finally came to their better senses and realized what was happening. The girls giggled and the instructors blushed. I had a memory that is still vivid after 40 years.

Valentine's Day Fire

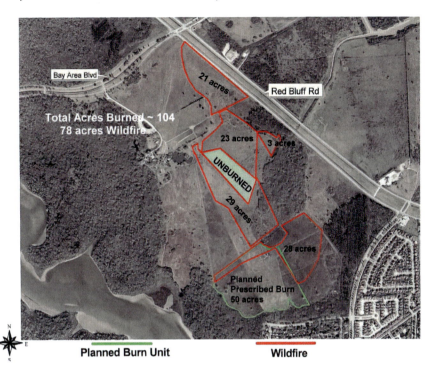

ABNC Prescribed Burn 2/14/06

Photo by Mark Kramer

ABNC began conducting controlled prairie burns from 1979 until 2014. I performed 111 burns as Burn Boss between 1995 and 2014. Leading a group of volunteers into the middle of 300 acres of grass and safely burning only 25 acres of the targeted unit is challenging. During the winter burn season, we would target burning 6 to 8 units. Often reaching the goal was difficult and we were always pushing to try to burn at every favorable opportunity.

One year we had been plagued by drought conditions. Dry soils can create unsafe conditions and in fact this year there had been a burn ban placed on Harris County. Once the ban was finally lifted, we were ready to jump on the chance.

We assembled in the field and began our work. Unfortunately, even though the ban had been officially lifted, the soils were still bone dry. Dry soils and dry fuels increase the probability that any drifting spark or ember could jump out of the designated burn unit and into the adjacent prairie creating a wildfire. Fifteen minutes into the burn we got the call from a volunteer on the radio that the fire had jumped. By the time the water crew arrived, the jumped fire had escaped beyond our control.

We were burning in the south end of the East Bank prairie. The southerly winds were rapidly pushing the wall of flames across the prairie and towards the ABNC buildings. We called the Pasadena Fire Department for assistance. They arrived with bulldozers. The fire burned from one end of the prairie to the other eventually traveling to the corner of Red Bluff Road and Bay Area Blvd. Traffic was stopped on the roads due to limited visibility from the smoke.

Some events leave a mark. This one did for me. Wildland fire fighters call that type of fire a career fire. So large and impactful that you only see one in a lifetime.

It is said that you don't know the measure of a Captain until he hits rough seas. I think you never know the measure of a Burn Boss until there is an escape fire. We continued to conduct controlled burns after the Valentine's Day Fire, but the tone and attention to safety was changed.

Snake Dance

Photo by George Regmund

To be floating on the water at sunrise has been a lifelong passion. In 1984 I purchased a fiberglass solo canoe. The Mad River Ladyslipper was a joy to paddle. It opened the bayou world for me to explore alone. Many mornings I would wake before it was light. I would fish barefoot in cut off blue jeans. Low light and limited visibility are optimal for predators. Their eyes are tuned for sight at diurnal dusk and dawn. Often the sight of prey is not so keenly adjusted. Another reason that the redfish bite is best the hour after sunrise. So too for people, in low light visibility suffers.

One such morning in the pre-dawn hours I was walking out to get the canoe ready for a morning on the water. It was not pitch black, but visibility was difficult. As I walked barefoot towards the canoe to turn it upright, I thought I saw a snake. Stopping in my tracks immediately in the low light I took another look. Yes, a snake, hard to tell what kind but it seemed really small. As I surveyed my domain further, I noticed another snake only five feet from me. It appeared to be small also and of the same species. Sighting two snakes together is rather unusual and it gave me further pause.

The light was slowly gaining and as I looked further, I could now count seven small snakes. I had already walked past several snakes and they were now all around me. It appeared that a snake had given birth. One of the most concerning snake species that gives live birth to their young is the rattlesnake. Rattlesnakes are rare on Armand Bayou. The Pygmy Rattlesnake is the only variety occurring here. I was only several steps away from the canoe and I determined my best course of action was to flip the canoe upright and stand in the boat until the light was adequate to navigate around the venomous newborns.

Before I made my next step, I had a further realization. There was likely a mother Pygmy Rattlesnake also in the vicinity. I scanned and eventually saw a larger snake a few feet away from the boat. I plotted my course carefully, flipped the canoe and stepped inside. I have never felt more relieved to be standing in a boat while on dry land. I took a deep breath and sat down in the canoe waiting for better light.

As time passed, the light increased, and I left the boat to find a bucket and shovel. I scooped up nine newborns and the mother. They were brought to

ABNC where the mother stayed on exhibit for several years. The young were released. When the movie, "Snakes on a Plane" was released, I remembered that feeling. It was almost like one of those bad dreams that you're happy when it's over.

Poaching

When I moved onto the Nature Center in 1985, there was a real issue with poaching. For the first five years of being on site, there were several shots heard every month of the cool season. Most shots would be heard but hard to identify from which direction they had originated. It seems long ago, before Space Center Blvd or Middlebrook Drive had been extended along the boundaries of the refuge. Suburbia hadn't crept in and it felt much more isolated and rural.

In the first week living on the preserve, I was startled awake one night by flashlights shining through my window. My son Aaron was three years old and asleep in bed with me. A voice came through the window stating, "you're trespassing and need to leave." I stood up in bed looking at my 12-gauge shotgun and wondering if I should grab and load it. "Who the hell are you?" I asked back. "We are the police," they said. I told them that I was the resident caretaker now living on site to stop poachers and trespassers. I told them that they were the ones trespassing and asked what business they had being here. I also suggested that waking a person in the middle of the night by shining flashlights in their eyes was not recommended when that person lives in an isolated area and has a shotgun in the corner. I never had direct evidence that law enforcement was shooting wildlife but their behavior was very suspicious. I never saw police there again.

Several years later I was walking one fine winter day. A half mile from home I was lost in thought, slowly walking through the woods. These were the days before cell phones. In fact, I had no phone of any type for the first eight years on the refuge. It was truly an isolated existence with no connectivity. Ideal for my misunderstood, hillbilly-mystic-hermit

lifestyle. As I walked, I noticed something in the distance moving through the woods. Maybe 40 yards ahead was a moving mass that I couldn't identify. That in itself was unusual, to see anything that I didn't have a wild guess as to what I was seeing.

It was the depth of winter. All of the deciduous forest trees were bare and visibility was good. Moving through the isolated trees was a large dark mass, a blob moving at walking speed, away from me. It disappeared slightly out of view. What do I do now? After pondering for a couple of minutes I decided to follow. I moved towards the point from which the thing had originated and determined that I would slowly follow. After walking a few feet, I could see a small backpack at the base of the tree where the blob had originally departed.

It didn't take long to piece together the evidence. The pack meant that what I had seen was a man. "What the hell?" I thought. I felt like the blob was still watching me, just out of view. I began to consider that I had startled a poacher covered in shaggy camouflage who had left his pack behind when he ran. I wondered why would he would run just because a person was walking through the woods, unless maybe he recognized me, knowing who I was.

So there I stood being watched by a poacher trying to determine if I should take his pack. If I didn't take it, it signaled that he could hunt and I would do nothing. If I did take it, it meant that I was not afraid to act. Using my better judgement, I decided not to approach any closer, but to pick up the pack and take it. I got home and drove to the pay phone to get the game warden to come out, but when he arrived it was already over.

Clear Lake

I began leading public pontoon boat eco-tours from Bay Area Park in 1981. There were always new and unexpected visitors. On one such tour, two old men walked onboard the Hana G. I could hear them talking amongst themselves and it soon became apparent that they were local old timers and that they were talking about the bayou.

Hoping to have the chance to get in on their time-traveling moment, I stopped talking. Our conversation soon became the subject of the tour. One of them turned to me and said, "You know, Clear Lake used to be clear." I'd contemplated the question of how Clear Lake could have originally been given that name, considering that today the water clarity resembles that of chocolate milk. They described water where a person could look down three to four feet and see grass growing on the lake bottom.

Their conversation turned to fishing in Clear Lake. Fishing before the invention of the gasoline-powered outboard motor. Their story recounted pulling shrimp nets behind sail boats. It seemed like an impossible feat knowing how hard that it is to run a shrimp boat even with all of today's modern technology.

As if the challenge weren't great enough, their story recounted the difficulty of the nets becoming filled with seagrass. Seagrass in Clear Lake would fill the net, bringing the sailboat to a stop and allowing the shrimp and the remaining catch to escape. I guessed the men might have been in their 80s when we rode down the bayou. By my best estimate, that would have put their fishing story on Clear Lake in the 1920s.

Biologists who study aquatic plants characterize them in relation to where the plants grow within the water column. Some plants, categorized as *Emergent Vegetation*, grow rooted in the bottom with their stems and leaves emerging above water's surface. Examples include marsh plants such as bulrush and cordgrass. Other aquatic plants are free floating. *Floating Vegetation* such as water hyacinth or duckweed have leaves above the surface with roots dangling below. Other aquatic plants such as widgeon grass and turtle grass are rooted in the bottom with stems and leaves remaining below the water surface. This *Submerged Underwater Vegetation* occurs in Texas bays where water clarity is adequate to allow sunlight to penetrate to the bay bottom. Today, this seagrass still occurs along the Texas coast in Matagorda Bay and points south. However, the Galveston Bay complex has lost over 95% of its original seagrass.

So, where has all of the seagrass gone? Ecological experts speculate that several factors contributed to the disappearance of seagrass in Galveston Bay. Some believe that activities associated with the dredging of the Houston ship channel contributed to increased turbidity in bay waters. Some propose that the dredging of oyster reefs further clouded the water. Others suggest that a series of hurricanes scoured the bay bottom disturbing seagrass habitat. It's likely that all of these were contributing factors.

Chapter Eight: *Discover Armand Bayou*

A User's Guide

Acquainting oneself with how to better understand, appreciate and enjoy the largest and most beautiful natural area in the Bayou City is a learning process. Discovering the subtle change of the seasons and how those changes affect wildlife and the viewscape. Getting familiar with how certain outings and activities are best enjoyed at certain times of day or year. Some explorations are better suited to the cold of winter while others are more comfortably enjoyed during the heat of summer. Learning to adjust your activities to optimize wildlife viewing while remaining comfortable are key considerations. For example, the winter woods are prime for hiking. The cool air allows for putting on your hiking shoes, bundling up, and enjoying the chorus of winter songbirds. In contrast, the summer woods are hot, humid and often filled with biting mosquitos. Don't get me wrong; the ABNC forest may be magical at any time of year, but it's true that some seasons are more desirable for certain activities. Learning the best times and places for you will maximize your enjoyment.

What to Do

Hiking

Armand Bayou Nature Center maintains over five miles of hiking trails that lead through forest, prairie and marsh habitats. Many of the trails are surfaced with crushed limestone, which meets ADA standards. Most of the trails are all-season, however some are more primitive and may require appropriate footwear for ankle-deep standing water after a recent rain. Be sure to check with the ABNC Admissions Desk if it is important to keep your feet dry. All trail conditions may fluctuate, especially after one of the Houston area's frequent intense rain events.

Insects

Insect repellent is always a good precaution. Especially a few days after rain, mosquitos may be intense. A walking stick is useful from March through September to assist with any potential spider webs that may cross the trail, but be aware that I have never known a single person to be bitten by a spider along the trails. Please be gentle if moving webs is necessary as spiders are welcome residents of the forest too.

The trails are shaded and make a nice escape during the dry months of summer. They are a great place to escape for some light exercise. Be sure to bring drinking water. Trail running is prohibited to minimize trail wear, avoid conflict with hikers, and to protect from venomous snake bites.

Western cottonmouth.
Photo by George Regmund

Pygmy rattlesnake.
Photo by George Regmund

Snakes

Be aware of every step taken as this is also snake habitat. Twenty-six species of snake have been documented on the refuge with four venomous varieties (above). The trails are well surfaced and paths are kept pruned and clear. Only two venomous snake bites have occurred between 1976 and 2020, and both of these were people who were foolishly handling the snakes.

Observation Points

Prairie, forest and bayou overlook points exist along each trail. Including these as part of any hike allows for time to take a break, hydrate, relax and reflect. Remember that you are in a beautiful surrounding, filled with abundant wildlife and likely only a few minutes from your home. Take a deep breath. Allow yourself to absorb the smells, sights and sounds for as long as needed to take some of it home with you. Maybe you hear the wind swirling through the canopy of the hardwood forest. Ask yourself when was the last time you heard that? Perhaps you find grace in the Great Egret flying across the bayou water. There is no other bayou in the Bayou City as rich with life or as beautiful. If you are so moved, you might consider purchasing an ABNC membership for the benefit of the non-profit preserve and the enjoyment of the next generation of wildlife and people.

Southern copperhead.
Photo by George Regmund

Coral snake.
Photo by George Regmund

Guided Hikes

Guided hikes are offered on weekends. Call or check the website for exact details. Guides are knowledgeable and attending will deepen the experience on your next unguided hike. Participating will allow you learn about wildlife, ecology and the natural history of the area.

Trails

Choosing which trail to walk is the first decision of hiking. Each trail is approximately 1.5 miles in length. However, each trail has unique features, some of which may be more appealing to you. All trails have access to bayou overlooks. One trail has a remote bird blind that enables wildlife observation. Eventually consider walking each trail to pick which is your favorite. Here are two of my favorite routes.

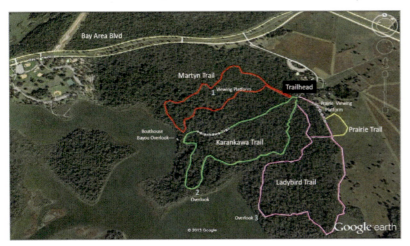

Google Earth Pro

Karankawa Trail

This was the first trail opened to hikers in 1978. The Karankawa trail is driest of all trails and considered all season. It offers access to the Bayou Overlook from a deck which is adjacent to the ABNC Boathouse. There is a bench at this deck that offers access to the panoramic bayou viewscape. The trail runs one-half mile leading from the trailhead to the Bayou Overlook.

Jimmy Martyn, 1959. Photo by Charles McCabe

Walking down this trail segment also carries you back in time. This short trail segment was first constructed by the Martyn family who occupied a long narrow strip of land that included the property you now walk through. The Martyn Road was built in the late 1800s and was used by the family to access the fertile alluvial soils located adjacent to the bayou edge. The Martyns tended a pear orchard and vegetable garden along what is now this trail. Jimmy Martyn, who was the last descendent of the family, lived here until 1965. If you look carefully along the left side of the trail as you head towards the water, you may still see several of the fence posts, which were installed along their property line over 100 years ago. All other evidence of their gardens or presence has now been reclaimed by 50 years of forest growth. The Karankawa Trail is high and dry and is the shortest, fastest route to a view of the bayou.

Continuing further down the path, you travel even further back in time. The trail includes a footbridge that passes over Karankawa Creek. This is the largest freshwater creek on ABNC property. Pause on the bridge and imagine the Akokisa Indians collecting drinking water for their encampment. Archeological evidence confirms that these Native Americans seasonally occupied the campsite for over 8000 years. This water source would have been key to their occupancy.

A nesting pair of Bald Eagles has occupied Armand Bayou since 2010. The Bayou Overlook #2 puts hikers at the best point for a fly by. Photo by Gary Seloff

Northern Cardinal. Photo by Gary Seloff

Leaving the bridge and continuing several hundred yards down the path is access to a second Bayou Overlook (labeled "2" on the Trail Map). This observation point is primitive and overlooks the southern portion of Armand Bayou as it enters into Lake Mark Kramer. This is a good opportunity to sit on the bench at the water's edge. Watch for fish jumping. The striped mullet is the preferred prey for both Osprey and Bald Eagle. If you are fortunate, you may see an Osprey perform a dramatic headfirst dive, extending its talons just before crashing into the water in pursuit. If you are even luckier, you may see the Bald Eagle in pursuit of the Osprey, hoping to steal its meal. This overlook puts visitors at the closest location to the eagle nest and is the best location to hope for a passing eagle.

Leaving the overlook, you are approximately at the halfway point. The trail continues through the Coastal Flatwoods Forest. You are in a hardwood forest primarily composed of several species of oak and elm trees. Listen carefully and you may hear the song of resident songbirds. The Carolina Chickadee, Northern Cardinal and Blue Jay are year-round residents. Cardinals are one of the most vivid songbirds at ABNC, so common that we take them for granted but many birders from outside our area are struck by their intense color.

So, too, is the largest woodpecker in North America. The Pileated Woodpecker thrives in old growth forest. Abundant dead, standing trees harbor grubs that comprise much of the bird's diet. Occasionally the trail will rise over domes of sandy soil. Stop to consider how this microhabitat differs from lower spots along the trail. These mima mounds often contain thick groves of native holly trees. These Yaupon are the dominant understory shrub. The plants produce abundant winter fruit, which attracts large numbers of winter songbirds to coastal Texas to escape harsh northern temperatures and enjoy the feast.

Pileated Woodpecker. Photo by Gary Seloff

Ladybird Trail

This trail was named in honor of Ladybird Johnson, the First Lady who walked the trail in the 1980s. It is a teaching trail that contains interpretive signage describing forest ecology and wildlife. Several hundred yards down from the trailhead, the trail forks to the left and approaches the Coastal Tallgrass Prairie Ecosystem. Taking this turn to the left puts you on the Short Loop, which connects to the Prairie Trail. The Short Loop is approximately one-half mile in length. This trail is often used on school field trips due to its short distance, interpretive signage and inclusion of both forest and prairie ecosystems. The Ladybird Short Loop is a good choice when time is limited and you want to experience both forest and prairie ecosystems.

Coastal tallgrass prairie.

Detouring onto the Prairie Trail takes you directly into the Armand Bayou Prairie, which is one of a very few coastal prairies that is publicly accessible. This is also a teaching trail with interpretive signage describing prairie ecology. The Prairie Trail leads to the Prairie Observation Platform, with an elevated view of one of the rarest vistas remaining in Texas. This panorama gives a glimpse of what the Houston area once was. Coastal Tallgrass Prairie is critically imperiled habitat with less than one percent of its original range remaining. Watch for summer swallows cutting through the prairie air in search of flying insects. During spring and fall, watch for the monarch butterfly. Their population is also declining steeply due to prairie habitat loss. The Armand Bayou Prairie is an important refueling station on their migratory route. If you look intently, far across the prairie following the forest edge, you may even be able to see the waters of Armand Bayou. This is the only observation point where prairie, forest and bayou are all visible together. This shaded observation point is the best place to catch the summer breeze and imagine a time not so long ago when a huge herd of bison grazed peacefully below.

Paddling Armand Bayou

Armand Bayou is the premier paddling destination in Harris County. The waters are protected from the wind and wave heights are rarely an issue. Several launch points make the bayou paddler-friendly for public access. Armand Bayou is a tidally influenced stream that connects to the ebb and flow of the salty tides of the Gulf of Mexico. Paddlers follow the meandering channel, which has never been altered or channelized as most all other bayous have in the area. The paddler is surrounded by several square miles of riparian forest and coastal prairie, which buffer intrusion from the surrounding urban environment. Here you can have a wilderness paddling experience while surrounded by the fourth largest city in America. The bayou edge is lined with lush tidal marsh habitat that supports abundant bird and wildlife viewing. Herons, egrets, pelican, osprey and alligator are expected sightings on every trip. There are occasional sightings of river otter, alligator gar and Bald Eagles. Eagles are winter residents that nest at ABNC.

Photo by Trudy LeDoux

ABNC Guided Canoe Tours – Pasadena Channel

www.youtube.com/watch?v=wLhoHc2Eq_E

Texas Parks and Wildlife Department established the TPWD Paddle Trail on the bayou. The Trail is accompanied by a map and is marked with numbered signs (numbers shown on right). The signs give first time paddlers a reference to get bearings of their location. The map is available for printing at home from the TPWD website. ABNC also sells a durable laminated map in the Gift Shop.

Human power. Photo by Gary Seloff

Armand Bayou also has a prohibition on the use of internal combustion engines. This Pasadena city ordinance creates one of the few places on the Texas coast where paddlers can enjoy a quiet outing free from the noise pollution of jet skis and intrusive boat wakes that disturb wildlife and alter the wilderness experience. But note that all shorelines of Armand Bayou and its tributaries are private property. Going ashore is considered trespassing by all adjacent land owners including ABNC.

Google Earth Pro

Texas Parks and Wildlife Paddle Trail Map

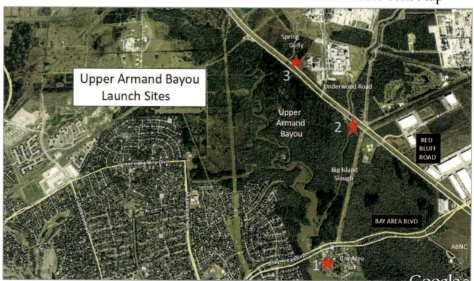

There are five publicly accessible launch sites on Armand Bayou. Three of these are improved asphalt surfaced car access. Each Location has it's benefit and value to the paddler.

Cliff Swallow nest with egg. Photo by Lyman Brown

1.Bay Area Park

This is the launch site most commonly used by all canoers and kayakers. It is located on Bay Area Blvd. in Bay Area Park, which is owned and operated by Harris County Parks Department. This location is midway between Upper and Lower Armand Bayou, allowing excursions in either direction. The launch site allows paddlers to access the ramp by driving their vehicle almost to the water's edge. Parking is adjacent to the launch and patrolled by Park Police. Restrooms and picnic tables are located nearby. Park hours are 7a.m. through 10p.m.

Paddling north under Bay Area Blvd takes paddlers upstream following the original winding streambed. Passing under the bridge, look up and view the largest nesting colony of swallows in the Armand Bayou watershed. They are

actively nesting March through May. Their mud nests resemble "dirt dauber" wasp nests, only larger. You may see small hatchling bird heads peering out. The bayou width constricts, becoming narrower as you progress. The surrounding hardwood forest and narrow channel provide protection from the wind.

2.Big Island Slough

This site has a newly installed (2020) floating kayak launch. The state-of-the-art platform allows for easy put in and take out. The park is owned and operated by the City of Pasadena Parks Department. There is a short distance to portage from the vehicle to the kayak launch. The location offers access to Big Island Slough. A Port-O-Can is located nearby.

3.Spring Gully

This site is a primitive launch located in far upper Armand Bayou. There is a short paddle down Spring Gully before entering Armand Bayou. Turning right (north) you will enter the narrowest portion of paddling opportunity. Continuing north, the channel is covered overhead by a cathedral of trees. This one of my favorite paddling experiences on the bayou.

However, this is often where a population of

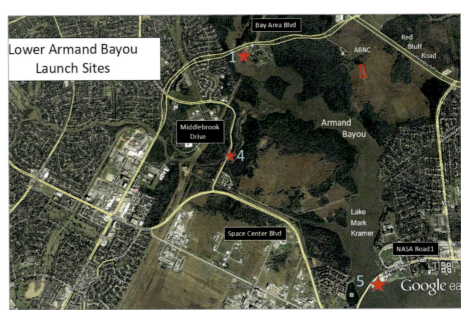

Google Earth Pro

large alligators reside. For your safety, please respectfully appreciate this beautiful apex predator from a safe distance. It is prudent to turn around rather than paddle directly over a large alligator in this narrow channel. I once saw an alligator over thirteen feet long here.

To access the launch point, take Red Bluff Road to Underwood Road. Turn onto the median in between east and west bound traffic driving on the grass until reaching Spring Gully. This route is best accessed under dry conditions or with four-wheel drive vehicles.

An alternate paddle route heads south on Armand Bayou. It's a favorite route for many paddlers. This route takes you past Bay Area Park and enters into property managed by Armand Bayou Nature Center. As you leave the Bay Area Park boundary, hug the right shoreline, which will lead you into Horsepen Bayou.

The confluence of Armand and Horsepen Bayou creates a broad, shallow delta. This is where ABNC has conducted a large program of wetland restoration. Numerous aquatic habitats converge in this small area, concentrating some of the best wildlife viewing on the refuge, creating a biological hotspot. The common marsh plant is California bulrush and is critical habitat for many forms of aquatic life. It also provides shelter for several marsh-dependent bird species. Red-winged Blackbirds and Marsh Wrens nest here. This is also the best site to observe the smallest member of the heron family, the Least Bittern. This small charismatic heron walks through the marsh grasping stem to stem, never getting wet feet. This shallow marsh edge is the best location to view the multitude of wading birds, which are frequently fishing. I encounter every species of heron and egret on the Texas coast here, except for the Reddish Egret. There are many shallow water embayments. Take your time here.

Paddle slowly and explore. This is where River Otters are most frequently encountered.

The Horsepen Bayou Delta is the prime biological hotspot on the refuge. Google Earth Pro

Keeping to the left as you exit the hotspot, notice the opening of a wide channel, which is called Alligator Alley. It's named for good reason. This is prime gator habitat and the most consistent, easily accessible area for alligator sightings. As you enter, to the right is actually an island where alligators frequently nest from April to September. Keep a respectful distance, stay in your boat and always give gators the right of way.

4. Horsepen Bayou Bridge on Middlebrook Drive

This is a primitive launch that requires a fifty-yard portage. On days with a strong southerly or northerly wind, I will paddle one way between this launch site and Bay Area Park. This requires two cars, one at each point. The effort is worth it if you don't want to spend most of the day fighting a headwind. This strategy keeps the wind at your back for the duration.

Launching from this site provides direct access to the best protection on very windy days. The paddle from the bridge, up Horsepen Bayou to Armand Bayou is the most sheltered stream segment on Armand Bayou. It is an excellent place to sight alligator, Wood Duck and river otter.

5.Clear Lake Park

This launch site is located on Clear Lake. It is located on NASA Road 1 in the Clear Lake Park Public Boat Launch. It is owned and operated by Harris County Parks Department. The kayak launch is located near the NASA Road 1 bridge that crosses Lake Mark Kramer. This launch location is at the southern-most point on Armand Bayou. The launch site allows paddlers to access the put-in point by driving their vehicle to the water's edge. Parking is adjacent to the launch and patrolled by Park Police. Restrooms are located nearby.

Passing under the bridge and heading north, paddlers enter the southern-most segment of Armand Bayou, which was previously known as Mud lake, but recently dedicated as Lake Mark Kramer. The area around the bridge and slightly north is a well-known fishing hole for speckled trout

Safety

All water activities carry inherent risk. Following certain measures is important to making every trip as safe as possible.

- **Float Plan**–Let someone know where you're going and when you plan to return.

- **Weather**–Stay current with the forecast. Check the weather the day before your trip and again before departing if there is any uncertainty. I have cancelled many a planned trip after determining that high winds were forecasted. Paddling is an unpleasant activity when struggling with the wind and may become dangerous. Today's devices allow for watching the radar when thunderstorms approach. If you see lightning or hear thunder, the trip should terminate. FYI–your head is the highest point on the water should lightning seek a target.

- **Map**–Bring a TPWD Paddle Trail Map. It gives a reference to where you are. In emergency situations, the number of the closest Paddle Trail sign can be used to direct help to you.

- **Checklist**–A written checklist takes the guesswork out of ensuring that you have everything you need. Arriving at the launch without a paddle is frustrating. At a minimum include life preserver, hat, drinking water, sunscreen, phone, dry box and Paddle Trail Map.

Paddling Solo

I prefer to paddle alone. The quiet nature of going solo allows for a more intimate connection and increases wildlife sightings. However, going alone should be reserved for experienced paddlers with high confidence.

Paddling with large alligators adds a new dimension to the experience. The above photo captures El Jefe, the largest alligator ever documented on the bayou at 13 feet four inches and estimated to be 500 pounds. He was killed by poachers.

Large alligators live here. Apprehension is good initially and respect is good always. I watched these animals slowly recover over four decades and they are now common on the bayou. I enjoy knowing the apex predator of the Bayou City has safe habitat here. In the center of the fourth largest county in America it's increasingly difficult for them to find a place to survive.

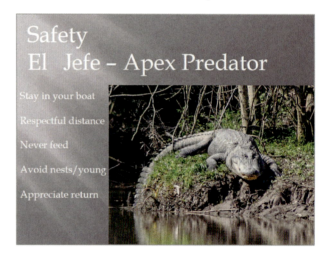

Paddling with alligators

These few tips will ensure your safety while enjoying the view.

1. Stay in your boat.

Alligators are large apex predators that regularly prey on deer and feral hogs. Wading, splashing or swimming is extremely dangerous and will attract alligators to view you as prey. Records show that four alligator fatalities have occurred in Texas since records have been kept. The most recent fatality occurred while a person was standing beside a sign that read, "Warning Alligators No Swimming." He saw a 10-foot alligator and jumped in the water, in front of the animal. He was killed and eaten immediately. In Texas we describe that syndrome as, "Here hold my beer and watch this." The alligator was also killed several days later. The moral of the story is to use common sense when you are in alligator habitat.

2. Keep a respectful distance.

After reaching six to seven feet long, alligators begin to pursue larger prey. Once they reach this size and larger, a safe distance of 20 to 30 feet should be maintained. During the mating and nesting season, alligators may bellow as a means of warning. The vocalization is accompanied by posturing with an arched back, head and tail raised out of the water. When you see it, you'll get the message. The moral of the story is to use common sense when you are in alligator habitat.

3. Never feed.

In Florida, I saw a sign in Everglades National Park that read, "Don't Feed The Alligators———Your Arm." You would never consider tossing tidbits to a grizzly bear and should never feed alligators. In bear country the saying goes, "A fed bear is a dead bear." As apex predators are habituated to associate free food with humans, a natural response is to approach every human they see. Bringing predators into close proximity to people has consequences to both. Additionally, it is against the law to feed a wild alligator in Texas. The moral of the story is to use common sense when you are in alligator habitat.

4. Avoid nests and young alligators.

Female alligators are unusual in the reptile world in that they have a strong maternal instinct to protect their nest and their hatchlings from any threat. This is when alligators may be most dangerous to humans. Keep a safe distance and admire motherhood in one of its earliest forms on the tree of life. The moral of the story is to use common sense when you are in alligator habitat.

5. Appreciate their return.

Today, many paddlers may lack the history behind many of Armand Bayou's most notable forms of wildlife. Alligators were one of the first animals to be placed on the Endangered Species List. When ABNC opened its doors in 1976, alligators were absent from the bayou. Over the past 40 years they have made a comeback. Viewing alligators while on a paddle tour is an environmental management success story and rare treasure for all Texas paddlers.

Guided Kayak Tours

ABNC Kayak Fleet. Photo by Gary Seloff

Armand Bayou Nature Center offers regular guided kayak excursions led by expert guides. Details about schedules are found on the ABNC website. The nature center owns a fleet of boats that were purchased in 2019. A short half mile tour onboard the electric vehicle transports guests through the Coastal Flatwoods Forest to the floating kayak launch site, which allows easy access into the water. Guides lead the way and offer ecological narration and other points of interest. Participating in a guided tour is a great way to "get your feet wet" and explore if owning your own boat is for you. It's also a great way to get your bearings with knowledgeable guides who know the route. Note, ABNC does not offer kayak rentals to individuals.

Electric Pontoon Eco-Tours

ABNC also offers guided pontoon eco-tours onboard the Bayou Ranger II. The vessel is U.S.

Coast Guard inspected, canopy-shaded, and is capable of carrying up to 16 passengers. The boat is a floating classroom, which is solar powered with quiet electric motors. ABNC provides binoculars for passengers twelve years and older. Guides are informative and give an in-depth discussion of ecology, natural history and wildlife sightings.

Wildlife viewing is outstanding from the Eco-Tour Boat. Photo by Gary Seloff

The experience will give a greater depth of understanding and appreciation on your next paddling adventure and is recommended.

A Special Note: Avoid approaching and disturbing wildlife. If you keep a respectful distance, that bird may catch dinner tonight and the next paddler may enjoy the view. Photo by Gary Seloff

ABNC Pontoon Eco-tours - Pasadena Channel
www.youtube.com/watch?v=DOlukBlyQuI

Paddle with a purpose

Corporate groups often partner with ABNC to conduct bayou clean-up projects. These service projects are a great team building activity while doing something meaningful for the environment. Individual paddlers should also feel free to grab any storm water debris to leave the area better for the next person.

Fishing

Kayak paddling and kayak fishing are one of the fastest growing sports in Texas. Fishing solo is a meditative practice for me, allowing me to slow down with a single focus while reconnecting with the bayou, the ecosystem, the planet and the cosmos. Results may vary for you.

Longear Sunfish. Photo by Mark Kramer

The author with a black drum.
Photo by Tommy Sutton

The author with blue catfish, a highly
sought species. Photo by Mike Black

Armand Bayou water is brackish water and the complex fishery reflects that. Forty-five species of fish have been documented. Most fishermen target channel catfish and blue catfish. Sunfish and largemouth Bass are caught in upper Armand Bayou. Sunfish get their name by displaying every color under the sun. This longear sunfish is the most common variety in Armand Bayou and a beautiful specimen.

When conditions are favorable, saltwater species are caught in the southern segment of the bayou. A Texas fishing license with a saltwater stamp is required to fish anywhere on Armand Bayou.

There are no Fish Consumption Advisories unique to Armand Bayou. However, the Armand Bayou watershed is densely populated, including both suburban and industrial landscapes. There is a Consumption Advisory for PCBs and dioxin that covers all of Galveston Bay including Armand Bayou. Further research will produce more detailed and current data. Today, many fishermen choose catch and release.

Birders on the ABNC prairie.
Collection of Mark Kramer

Birding

Today, there are more people engaging in Birdwatching (birding) in America than there are hunters. According to the 2011 report from the U.S. Fish and Wildlife Service National Survey of Fish and Wildlife Based Recreation, there were 13.6 million hunters compared to 22.5 million birders/wildlife watchers. Texas A&M University concluded that nature tourism (dominated by birdwatching) contributed 33.6 million dollars to the Rio Grande Valley economy and created over 4,400 jobs.

ABNC offers excellent birding. With five miles of well-maintained trails that pass through forest, prairie and bayou habitats, a wide diversity of bird species may be seen. In fact, in a typical year, over 220 bird species are documented.

Texas is one of the premier birding destinations in the U.S. Many beautiful year-round avian residents may be seen here including Pileated Woodpecker, Northern Cardinal, Red-Shouldered Hawk and numerous wading birds. Located on the Central Flyway, ABNC also offers excellent birding during spring and fall migration. Numerous species of warblers, vireos and fly catchers are seen in March/April and October/November. The Houston Audubon Society leads monthly bird walks at ABNC, which is a great way to take a relaxing walk with local experts.

Photography

Nature Photography is a great gateway to connect to the natural world. Armand Bayou offers beautiful photographic opportunities for panoramas, sunsets, wildlife and wildflowers. This publication is great testament to the power of photographs to reveal the natural beauty that is typically obscured to our passing eye.

Jerome Matula captures American White Pelicans at sunrise from his Mad River canoe. Photo by Gary Seloff

Nature photographer Gary Seloff in action on Horsepen Bayou. Photo by Jerome Matula

Gary Seloff, the kayak photographer, has provided inspiring images that has allowed me to observe wildlife and their behavior in a manner previously unseen by my eye. His photographs fill this book. Hike the trails, take a pontoon boat tour or visit the Prairie Observation Platform in search of photographic subject matter.

When and Where to Do It

There is a seasonal rhythm to the natural world. Changing seasons reveal new plant growth, guide bird migrations, and shape wildlife behavior. Developing a personal connection to the natural world allows for an appreciation of these annual changes. Understanding these subtle changes and transitions enhances a naturalist's depth of experience. We are a reflection of that world and may begin to recognize the seasons within our own life. Understanding the seasonal rhythm also means that we can be where the focus of beauty and wildlife activity occurs. The following are seasonal activities that I enjoy and recommend.

Winter

December-January

Lesser (left) and Greater (right) Yellowlegs. Photo by Gary Seloff

Winter tides create exposed mud and shallow tidal flats, which are important feeding habitat for shorebirds. Both Greater and Lesser Yellowlegs are common in the Horsepen Bayou Delta.

Swamp Sparrow on mudflat. Photo by Gary Seloff

Northern Flicker. Photo by Gary Seloff

Armand Bayou Prairie is prime habitat for several species of sparrow. Swamp Sparrows are often seen (and heard) from the Prairie Trail.

The first frost/freeze at Armand Bayou typically occurs in early December. These temperatures stop the growth of herbaceous plants. As prairie plants enter dormancy, the character of the prairie is transformed from verdant green into russet brown. Prairie grasses have set seed, which attracts prairie dependent sparrows and wrens. Sparrow and Sedge Wren song fills the prairie air. On calm days with clear sky, flocks of Sandhill Cranes may be heard overhead. Osprey and Bald Eagle are fishing. Often, they perform aerial combat as the eagle intimidates the Osprey to release his catch.

Northern Flickers, a member of the woodpecker family, were previously named the Yellow-shafted Flicker. Viewed in flight from below, the original name seems appropriate. They are a favorite winter woodland species.

Hike

Walk the forest trails with winter boots, trail map and binoculars. One of my favorite destinations is located on the Martyn Trail. A wildlife viewing platform is located here (shown on the trail map). Watch for Brown Thrashers, Northern Flickers, Pileated Woodpeckers and Yellow-rumped Warblers as you hike. These are some of my favorite winter woodland bird species. Upon reaching the viewing

Wilson's Snipe foraging on Horsepen Bayou. Photo by Gary Seloff

platform, take a seat and relax. Look through the viewing portals and you see a large forested wetland in front of you. Take a breath. Listen for the breath of the forest as the winter wind passes through the treetops overhead. If you sit for a few minutes, you'll likely hear the eastern chorus frog resume its song. This amphibian is unusual in that it reproduces in the heart of winter. It uses this wetland as critical reproductive habitat.

After leaving the viewing platform, continue towards the boathouse (shown on the Trail Map). The boathouse is where ABNC houses the Bayou Ranger tour boat. The boathouse also has a public viewing platform that overlooks Armand Bayou. This is one of the best panoramic views of the bayou and a reliable location to see herons and egrets. Take a moment to sit on the bench and listen for the call of the Osprey. Carefully scan the dead trees in the bayou and scan the bayou edges to trace the call to its source.

Wilson's Snipes are a common winter bird found in marsh and prairie wetlands. They are one of the world's longest distance migrants and travel over 3,500 miles to spend winter on the Texas coast. Due to their extreme camouflage and skittishness, they are among the more challenging birds to see or photograph.

Birding

Winter birding has the advantage of cool temperatures and no insects. Walking the full Ladybird Trail will carry you along the prairie edge where winter is the best time to find sparrows in the dormant grass thatch. On a good morning, you might find (or hear) three or four sparrow species. A morning of winter birding averages approximately 60 species. The following are species to be found on a typical half-day January trip. Use this as Your Checklist of Winter Birds At ABNC.

Mottled Duck (*Anas fulvigula*)

Pied-billed Grebe (*Podilymbus podiceps*)

Double-crested Cormorant (*Phalacrocorax auritus*)

Brown Pelican (*Pelecanus occidentalis*)

American White Pelican (*Pelicanus erythrohynchos*)

Great Blue Heron (*Ardea herodias*)

Great Egret (*Ardea alba*)

Snowy Egret (*Egretta thula*)

Little Blue Heron (*Egretta caerulea*)

Tricolored Heron (*Egretta tricolor*)

Cattle Egret (*Bubulcus ibis*)

Black Vulture (*Coragyps atratus*)

Turkey Vulture (*Cathartes aura*)

Osprey (*Pandion haliaetus*)

White-tailed Kite (*Elanus leucurus*)

Northern Harrier (*Circus cyaneus*)

Red-shouldered Hawk (*Buteo lineatus*)

Red-tailed Hawk (*Buteo jamaicensis*)

Killdeer (*Charadrius vociferus*)

Greater Yellowlegs (*Tringa melanoleuca*)

Lesser Yellowlegs (*Tringa flavipes*)

Laughing Gull (*Leucophaeus atricilla*)

Herring Gull (*Larus argentatus*)

Rock Pigeon (Feral Pigeon) (*Columba livia*)

Barred Owl (*Strix varia*)

Belted Kingfisher (*Megaceryle alcyon*)

Red-bellied Woodpecker (*Melanerpes carolinus*)

Yellow-bellied Sapsucker (*Sphyrapicus varius*)

Downy Woodpecker (*Picoides pubescens*)

Northern Flicker (*Colaptes auratus*)

Pileated Woodpecker (*Dryocopus pileatus*)

Crested Caracara (*Caracara cheriway*)

American Kestrel (*Falco sparverius*)

Eastern Phoebe (*Sayornis phoebe*)

Loggerhead Shrike (*Lanius ludovicianus*)

Blue Jay (*Cyanocitta cristata*)

American Crow (*Corvus brachyrhynchos*)

Tree Swallow (*Tachycineta bicolor*)

Carolina Chickadee (*Poecile carolinensis*)

Tufted Titmouse (*Baeolophus bicolor*)

Sedge Wren (*Cistothorus platensis*)

Carolina Wren (*Thryothorus ludovicianus*)

Blue-gray Gnatcatcher (*Polioptila caerulea*)

Ruby-crowned Kinglet (*Regulus calendula*)

Eastern Bluebird (*Sialia sialis*)

Hermit Thrush (*Catharus guttatus*)

American Robin (*Turdus migratorius*)

Gray Catbird (*Dumetella carolinensis*)

Brown Thrasher (*Toxostoma rufum*)

Northern Mockingbird (*Mimus polyglottos*)

Cedar Waxwing (*Bombycilla cedrorum*)

Orange-crowned Warbler (*Oreothlypis celata*)

Pine Warbler (*Setophaga pinus*)

Yellow-rumped Warbler (*Setophaga coronata*)

Le Conte's Sparrow (*Ammodramus leconteii*)

Savannah Sparrow (*Passerculus sandwichensis*)

Swamp Sparrow (*Melospiza georgiana*)

Northern Cardinal (*Cardinalis cardinalis*)

Red-winged Blackbird (*Agelaius phoeniceus*)

Eastern Meadowlark (*Sturnella magna*)

Common Grackle (*Quiscalus quiscula*)

Great-tailed Grackle (*Quiscalus mexicanus*)

Brown-headed Cowbird (*Molothrus ater*)

American Goldfinch (*Spinus tristis*)

American White Pelicans. Photo by Gary Seloff

American White Pelicans are among the heaviest of birds in North America. Their size and stately posture make them a favorite sighting while enjoying a Pontoon Tour.

Bayou Ranger Winter Pontoon Tour

Winter on the bayou is a beautiful time of year. Cold temperatures make kayaking less desirable. Wear more clothing than you think that you'll need, as being over the cool water creates a "feels like" temperature 10 to 15 degrees below the actual temperature. Seasonal winds are predominantly northerly. These north winds produce tides well below normal as the bayou water is pushed out. These low tides create numerous exposed mud flats where shorebirds congregate. Bald Eagle and Osprey activity are at their peak.

Roseate Spoonbill coming in to land on Horsepen Bayou. Photo by Gary Seloff

This is a great time to bring your camera in hopes of catching view of a Roseate Spoonbill. These pink wading birds are often mistaken for Flamingos. Winter is the best time to see them fishing in the tide pools in Horsepen Bayou.

A team of Mottled Ducks on Horsepen Bayou.
Photo by Gary Seloff

Carolina jessamine is an early spring bloomer that
fills the forest air with its floral fragrance.
Photo by Lyman Brown

January is the depth of winter for Houston. Cold temperatures allow hikers to wear their winter boots and bundle up. This is also the wet season and the forested wetlands are filled with water. January is the only month when the deciduous forest is leafless. Some leaves persist late into December and resprout in mid-February, resulting in a "reluctantly" deciduous forest. The forest hiking trails are filled with winter birds. American Robins and Cedar Waxwings in flocks of a thousand birds may be encountered. These fruit-eating species arrive to feast on the abundant berries of the yaupon. Yaupon is the dominant understory shrub producing blood red berries.

Mottled Duck populations have declined around Texas and on Armand Bayou. They are one of the few waterfowl that nest in Texas. They are ground-nesting birds that seek out coastal prairie that is adjacent to tidal marsh habitat. Over the past fifty years, both prairie and marsh habitat has dramatically declined around Galveston Bay and so has the Mottled Duck.

February is a transition month. The first week or two are still winter. However, by the middle of February the plant community shows the first signs of life. Trees begin to grow new leaves. There are two to three weeks at the end of February when the forest is a tender green, unique to this time of year.

This is also the time when the most aromatic of wildflowers blooms in the forest canopy. Carolina jessamine is an evergreen vine that produces a bell-shaped flower. The flower is the color of butter and produces a strong intoxicating fragrance. Hiking through the woods of late winter I often catch its sweet smell before I see it. Pausing, looking up, clusters of bright yellow flowers reveal the source. As the flowers mature, they release from the vine and begin to litter the trail. The Karankawa Trail near the boathouse is a reliable location to catch the experience.

Spring

February-April

Spotted Sandpipers are seen hunting the edges
of the bayou. Photo by Gary Seloff

Late February marks the first subtle indicators of Spring. Trees begin to sprout and grasses show their first signs of green. Alligators emerge from their long winter's nap. After having spent all winter soaking in cold bayou water, the first order of business is to get warm. On calm, sunny days, gators haul out onto the shoreline to sunbathe. This warming of their core temperature speeds their metabolism, which promotes healthy digestion of the first meal. It also means large alligators are fully exposed and in full view. This provides excellent viewing and photographic opportunities. This viewing spectacle occurs during the last two weeks of February and first two weeks of March when afternoons are calm, clear and warm.

March is the prime month to be outdoors and do anything on Armand Bayou. During the first two weeks of March, alligators continue to bask and offer outstanding views. These afternoon pontoon tours also find Ospreys and Bald Eagles fishing and interacting. Eagles have hungry young on the nest, which means more fishing activity is required.

Hike – Ladybird Loop & Prairie Trail

This is also an excellent time to take a hike. The Ladybird Trail Short Loop allows hikers to experience both forest and prairie ecosystems. The Coastal Flatwoods Forest is still at the stage of tender green. Winter songbirds still offer their chorus. Resident songbirds begin to sing their nesting songs. During the spring nesting season many birds advertise their availability by singing elaborate courtship songs. This also marks the arrival of the first returning spring migrants. Warblers and vireos are a prized sighting by birders. One of my favorite songs is the subtle call of the Northern Parula. Nesting songs combined with winter bird song fills the air with a chorus that reminds me of the beauty and diversity of this wild place. However, you must stop and smell the roses (with your ears).

Leaving the forest and emerging onto the prairie, you see the panorama that the first Texas settlers encountered. Today, this is one of the rarest views in Texas. Approximately one percent of Coastal Tallgrass Prairie still survives. This prairie has been actively managed by ABNC since 1976. Mowing, burning, controlling invasive species and reintroducing locally rare prairie plants makes this one of the best prairie walks in Texas. Spider lilies are one the most beautiful and fragrant of all prairie wildflowers and may be encountered here in March. The dramatic spider lily bloom occurs along the ABNC entry road. This is a wetland restoration site where hundreds of these beautiful wildflowers may be viewed as you enter and exit the park. The half mile Prairie Trail Loop is one of the few publicly accessible prairie trails in Texas. The rare nature of this portion of Houston's natural heritage is outlined in the interpretive signage along the trail.

This short prairie hike ends at the Prairie Observation Platform. A great endpoint to relax and watch for monarch butterflies on their long migration to Canada. Have some water and a snack and watch for some of the first swallows returning to the Texas coast. After completing a non-stop trans-gulf migration, they're hungry. They cut through the air, foraging on flying insects. Listen carefully and you may hear the calls of Sedge Wrens and Eastern Meadowlarks.

Kayaking

As temperatures warm, kayaking becomes more attractive. Paddling into the Horsepen Bayou Delta is a prime destination. The key to having the full experience is to paddle slowly. Many marsh dependent birds return to the bulrush marsh to breed, nest and feed. March is the best time of year to hear a surrounding melody of the Marsh Wren's intricate song. These small birds fill the air with song from every direction. It can be mesmerizing. Don't rush your way through.

A male Least Bittern in full breeding plumage fishes in the Horsepen Bayou delta. Photo by Gary Seloff

Due to the convergence of many habitat types, this biological hotspot also attracts many herons and egrets, which visit the delta to collect groceries for hatchlings in the nests on the rookery. The smallest North American heron, the Least Bittern returns to these bulrush marshes to nest. Lingering here for 10 to 15 minutes increases the likelihood of bittern sightings as they return to their normal behavior and feeding from the base of bulrush stems. Scanning the trees may produce sightings of Osprey or Bald Eagles. Proceeding beyond the delta and into Alligator Alley, the forest continues to line both shorelines. This is prime habitat for many neo-tropical songbirds to be seen and heard.

Entering Alligator Alley, basking alligators are often encountered. If you slow down to 0.0001 miles per hour, keeping your boat on the far shoreline (away from the alligator) and minimizing any motion with your arms, these giants will often allow your passage without reentering the water. This slow-motion tactic also offers paddlers outstanding viewing of the large reptiles stretched out in the sun. On occasion, the animals become startled and quickly lunge into the water. Don't misinterpret that the gator is coming to make a meal of you. When threatened alligators seek the safety of deep water. They are merely making haste when they perceive you as a threat and are seeking safe haven. Even knowing this, paddlers often get the drizzles.

The last Saturday in March is scheduled as the big bayou clean-up day – Trash Bash. Trash Bash brings hundreds of people together to collect litter and other storm water debris that has previously accumulated. This is a great paddle for a purpose. Details regarding the event may be found on the ABNC website or the Galveston Bay Foundation website.

Swallow-tailed Kite with Spanish moss.
Photo by Gary Seloff

Birding

April is the prime month for birding. Arrive early as birds are most active early in the day. Walk the trails first and then consider spending an hour on the Prairie Observation Platform. The first two weeks of April are the best weeks to spot the Swallow-tailed Kite. Scan above the forest edge where the birds seek dragonflies, which are an important dietary component. Swallow-tail Kites have an effortless flight. A deeply forked tail, long wings and light body weight give the appearance of being buoyant and floating in mid-air.

Another bird of prey is often seen from the platform. The smallest member of the falcon family is commonly seen perched in the lone trees standing in the prairie. This is the best location to see and hear their distinct call. American Kestrels are a winter resident spending their day in search of grasshoppers and small rodents. Enjoy the view because kestrels depart the Gulf coast in early May returning to their breeding range in more northern latitudes.

FeatherFest birders admire the Rookery.
Photo collection of Mark Kramer

April is also the month for the birding festival called FeatherFest. This annual event held on and around Galveston Island brings birders from around the world. Field trips led by local experts travel to prime birding destinations around Galveston Bay. ABNC hosts a guided tour of the Rookery, which is bustling with activity and supports eight species of colonial nesting waterbirds. At the peak in April, 350 birds may be seen on an island that is smaller than your house. It is one of the most densely populated nesting colonies around Galveston Bay. The birds display courtship, breeding, nest building and chick feeding behavior. Check with FeatherFest and ABNC about Rookery tour details.

American Kestrel. Photo by Gary Seloff

Yellow Warbler. Photo by Gary Seloff

Walk the forest trails, stop at bayou overlooks and rest on the prairie platform. A morning of spring birding averages 60 to 70 species.

The following are species to be found on a typical half-day April trip. Use the list as Your Checklist of Spring Birds At ABNC.

Black-bellied Whistling-Duck (*Dendrocygna autumnalis*)

Wood Duck (*Aix sponsa*)

Mottled Duck (*Anas fulvigula*)

Blue-winged Teal (*Anas discors*)

Northern Bobwhite (*Colinus virginianus*)

Double-crested Cormorant (*Phalacrocorax auritus*)

Anhinga (*Anhinga anhinga*)

Great Blue Heron (*Ardea herodias*)

Great Egret (*Ardea alba*)

Snowy Egret (*Egretta thula*)

Little Blue Heron (*Egretta caerulea*)

Cattle Egret (*Bubulcus ibis*)

Yellow-crowned Night-Heron (*Nyctanassa violacea*)

White Ibis (*Eudocimus albus*)

Black Vulture (*Coragyps atratus*)

Turkey Vulture (*Cathartes aura*)

Osprey (*Pandion haliaetus*)

Bald Eagle (*Haliaeetus leucocephalus*)

Red-shouldered Hawk (*Buteo lineatus*)

Swainson's Hawk (*Buteo swainsoni*)

Northern Harrier (*Circus cyaneus*)

American Coot (*Fulica americana*)

Laughing Gull (*Leucophaeus atricilla*)

Herring Gull (*Larus argentatus*)

Royal Tern (*Thalasseus maximus*)

White-winged Dove (*Zenaida asiatica*)

Mourning Dove (*Zenaida macroura*)

Chimney Swift (*Chaetura pelagica*)

Ruby-throated Hummingbird (*Archilochus colubris*)

Red-bellied Woodpecker (*Melanerpes carolinus*)

Downy Woodpecker (*Picoides pubescens*)

Pileated Woodpecker (*Dryocopus pileatus*)

Great Crested Flycatcher (*Myiarchus crinitus*)

White-eyed Vireo (*Vireo griseus*)

Blue-headed Vireo (*Vireo solitarius*)

Red-eyed Vireo (*Vireo olivaceus*)

Blue Jay (*Cyanocitta cristata*)

American Crow (*Corvus brachyrhynchos*)

Purple Martin (*Progne subis*)

Tree Swallow (*Tachycineta bicolor*)

Carolina Chickadee (*Poecile carolinensis*)

Tufted Titmouse (*Baeolophus bicolor*)

House Wren (*Troglodytes aedon*)

Sedge Wren (*Cistothorus platensis*)

Marsh Wren (*Cistothorus palustris*)

Carolina Wren (*Thryothorus ludovicianus*)

Blue-gray Gnatcatcher (*Polioptila caerulea*)

Ruby-crowned Kinglet (*Regulus calendula*)

Eastern Bluebird (*Sialia sialis*)

Hermit Thrush (*Catharus guttatus*)

Gray Catbird (*Dumetella carolinensis*)

Northern Mockingbird (*Mimus polyglottos*)

Cedar Waxwing (*Bombycilla cedrorum*)

Worm-eating Warbler (*Helmitheros vermivorum*)

Black-and-white Warbler (*Mniotilta varia*)

Orange-crowned Warbler (*Oreothlypis celata*)

Hooded Warbler (*Setophaga citrina*)

Yellow-rumped Warbler (*Setophaga coronata*)

Yellow-breasted Chat (*Icteria virens*)

Swamp Sparrow (*Melospiza georgiana*)

Summer Tanager (*Piranga rubra*)

Scarlet Tanager (*Piranga olivacea*)

Northern Cardinal (*Cardinalis cardinalis*)

Indigo Bunting (*Passerina cyanea*)

Red-winged Blackbird (*Agelaius phoeniceus*)

Eastern Meadowlark (*Sturnella magna*)

Orchard Oriole (*Icterus spurius*)

American Goldfinch (*Spinus tristis*)

Kayaking

April is notorious for strong winds. As the season transitions, southerly winds begin to dominate. This is a great time to consider getting a friend to paddle a one-way trip from Clear Lake Park to Bay Area Park. Having a paddler friend to position a vehicle in Bay Area Park allows for a one-way trip with the wind at your back throughout. This trip may be reversed if strong northerly winds prevail.

Paddling through the lower segment of the bayou offers wide open views where Osprey sightings are common. Passing the signage that prohibits the entrance of internal combustion engines, begin to look across the water to the right (north). The wide view captures a glimpse of the Coastal Tallgrass Prairie. This vantage is the only paddling location on Armand Bayou that provides a view of all three ecosystems that converge at ABNC. This view is representative of what much of the upper Texas coast looked like 200 years ago. Pause here and take in the view.

Steer your boat towards the prairie. This route takes you past the largest marsh creation site on Armand Bayou. This six-acre marsh has a small lake located within it. It's an intimate, quiet setting allowing for a good place to relax, snack and rehydrate. This is also a great place to watch for nesting Red-winged Blackbirds. These iconic wetland birds pull the tops of marsh grass together and weave a nest connecting all of stems.

Nesting Redwing Blackbird. Photo by Gary Seloff

Photographic opportunities are rich on the bayou.
Photo by Gary Seloff

Leaving the created marsh, head into the Horsepen Bayou delta. Linger while looking for marsh birds, wading birds, Osprey, Bald Eagles and alligators. The eagles and Ospreys depart now so enjoy your views and say your goodbyes until the fall. End your trip in Bay Area Park where you can enjoy a picnic lunch with your friend before heading for home.

Summer

May - September

The Purple Gallinule is striking and lives in the dense marshes of Horsepen Bayou. Photo by Gary Seloff

Kayaking

Summer is the hard season on the Texas coast. Daytime high temperatures average between 90-100 degrees for five months. Kayaking and kayak fishing are my preferred outings during the heat. Activities on the water are cooler and insect free. Starting early ensures that you beat the hottest part of the day and paddle while winds are light. Bay Area Park opens at 7a.m. The trip from the Park to Horsepen Bayou is a favorite summer paddle for me.

Start your float with a visit underneath the Bay Area Blvd bridge to view the nesting colony of swallows. In May, the peculiar mud nests will have hatchling bird heads poking out as you pass by. There are often over 100 nests in the colony. After taking in the spectacle, head south to Horsepen Bayou.

Leaping mullet. Photo by Gary Seloff

The Horsepen Bayou delta is in peak activity through the summer. Juvenile fish and shellfish that entered in spring as larvae have now grown large enough to be sought after by herons, egrets and terns. Long days, bright sun and warm water fuel the estuarine production to drive the food web. With peak productivity, life is on full display. On calm days, the water's surface is in constant motion from schools of small fish just below the surface and out of view. Juvenile mullet and menhaden travel in large schools. Adult mullet lazily leap. Bitterns in the bulrush, egrets wading the edges and blackbirds perched in the trees are common. Alligator sightings grow less frequent as these reptilian predators shift gears into nocturnal mode. Many animals become creatures of the night during summer to avoid the intense daytime heat. Bring your fishing rod, camera, and drinking water and jump into your boat. If you don't have one this is great season for a guided kayak tour or pontoon tour at ABNC.

Hiking

Before the heat of the day, step out of the woods onto the prairie platform in early June to witness the sea of Pink Liatris in bloom. A bit later in the season, Mother Nature paints a similar picture, but yellow this time.

As you retreat back into the shaded canopy of the woods, one of the most fascinating forms of summer wildlife emerges for viewing from the hiking trails during the summer. The woods come alive with large spiders, which make huge webs. The golden silk spider is about the size of a human hand. It's hard to hike any full trail without counting 50 of these harmless spiders along the edges of the path.

The Spider Experience

If you walk the trails during the summer months, you are certain to see some arachnids, which may be surprising. I know that many of us have certain feelings about spiders. I hope that as you learn more about these beautiful coastal residents that your feelings may evolve. If you have never had the ABNC spider experience, now is the time. They are one of the most abundant and observable forms of wildlife on the refuge. You won't travel far down any of the trails before you sight what is likely the biggest spider that you have ever seen perched on the biggest web that you have ever seen. But never fear, these massive beasts are generally harmless. The spider's

entire universe is the web. They depend on it for food and safety and never leave it (they won't jump off onto you). More than once I have inadvertently walked into a web during the work day and had one land on my face, but have never been bitten. In fact, in my forty years of hiking the trails, I've yet to hear of one of these spiders biting a visitor, ever. All spiders *can* bite, however, these formidable predators reserve their bite for their prey.

All spiders that build their web in the shape of a wheel are included in the group of orb weavers.
Photo by Gary Seloff

The two species of orb weaving spiders commonly seen from the hiking trails are the golden silk spider (*Trichnephilia clavipes*) and the black and yellow argiope (*Argiope aurantia*). All spiders that build their nests in the shape of a wheel are included in the group of orb weavers. The golden silk spider is the champion orb web builder and creates a web that may span over 20 feet! Their web has a beautiful property that reflects a vivid golden color when the sunlight is caught at just the right angle (hence the name - golden silk). Be sure to take a moment and position the web between you and the filtered sun through the trees. Move a few feet side to side or forward and back and when the angle is just right, you'll have a memorable moment!

Spider silk is a miracle material which is the spider's entire world for life. Photo by Mark Kramer

Spider webs are beyond beauty. They are essentially the spider's whole world for the entirety of their life. The web hosts the spider and provides sensory communication of the surrounding environment or any prey that might have been trapped in the webbing. It's a perception of the world entirely tactile, telegraphed through the line to the spider fingertips.

The web is designed not only to hold the spider, it is also an insect trap made of a sophisticated material. Imagine an insect in flight crashing into the web. First the material must be strong enough to endure the impact without breaking. No problem, the material is stronger than steel. Next the web must flex to bend with the impact absorbing the force as it hits. After flexing with the impact, the web must not trampoline the insect back into space. It accomplishes this in part with a sticky surface that holds the prey in place. These composite web properties are produced from a special set of organs on the spider's abdomen called spinnerets, each spinneret contributing its own element to the composite masterpiece.

The silk and woven web it produces rivals man's strong woven fiber, Kevlar. Kevlar is an industrial product used to make bullet proof vests. It's made from petroleum products, which are then subjected to acid baths under high pressure and high temperature. Spider silk uses grasshoppers as raw material, which is processed through the spider's digestive system then extruded through spinnerets. Spiders may even eat their own web as raw material to make more web! Note to self: there's a lesson here for humans too. Spider's produce poop as a waste byproduct; Kevlar produces industrial waste. Spider silk naturally decomposes; Kevlar does not.

This compared product analysis is increasingly being used by science to shape research. The field of biomimicry is an emerging science that looks to nature as inspiration for product design. It turns out that over millions of years, life has been perfecting her wares in a fashion that supports other life without destroying the environment that supports it. Spiders are just one of the species *biomimicry* is looking to for inspiration.

This year for the first time in many years I have hung hummingbird feeders around the house. Where typically I may find four or five silk spiders or argiopes, this year there is only one. ABNC is an important hummingbird nesting habitat. A major material used in nest building is spider web. I suspect that the webs near my house were harvested by Ruby-Throated Hummingbirds for their nests. I enjoy the hummingbirds but have missed having a friend outside my window.

Golden silk spider. Photo by Lyman Brown

The golden silk spider is the species likely to be encountered on a woodland walk at ABNC. Also known as the banana spider, the species is present during the summer months. Females are large and are slightly smaller than an adult human hand.

My friend and naturalist, George Regmund, relayed a remarkable golden silk spider story. As he walked the forest trail, he saw a bird in the distance behaving very strangely. With his interest peaking he approached the bird and found a Tufted Titmouse trapped and dangling in a web. The titmouse is a small bird about the size of a sparrow. The bird had destroyed the web but had managed to wrap a mass of spider silk around its feet. Despite all its struggles and effort it was not able to break free. Dangling upside-down the bird was doomed, if not for our hero of the story! George carefully removed the bird and untangled the webbing from its feet. The bird was exhausted from the ordeal but managed to fly away. The moral of the story is of course that even nature's strongest natural material is no match for the kind hands of a naturalist.

It is common among spiders for females to be noticeably larger than males. Photo by Lyman Brown

Male silk spiders are about one quarter the size of females. In early September females produce an egg case that resembles a ping pong ball in size and shape. Inside are hundreds of tiny spiders, which remain in the egg case until spring. After egg-laying, the adult spiders begin to decline. All adults die by late October. Essentially, the entire fate of the species lies with the young spiderlings that overwinter in the egg case and emerge in late spring of the following year.

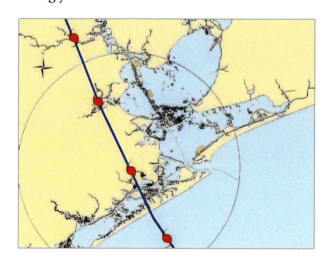

On September 13, 2008 Hurricane Ike made landfall on the Texas coast. The category two storm was broad in size. The eye of the storm passed directly over ABNC and delivered nine continuous hours of hurricane force winds.

Hurricane Ike brought significant impacts to forest dwelling species. Photo by Mark Kramer

The damaging winds brought extreme destruction to the forest, which is critical habitat for the golden silk spider. The hurricane's timing couldn't have come at a worse time. All of the spiders' egg cases had recently been deposited and were lying in the forest canopy. The fate of the next generation of spiderlings was at great risk. Ike laid waste to it all. Best estimates are that there was a 50 percent reduction in the forest canopy. Along with that downfall came a near total destruction of the egg cases. The first year after Ike, the spiders were virtually absent in the woods. In fact, it has taken almost a decade for their numbers to recover to pre-Hurricane Ike levels.

Black & yellow argiope. Photo by Gary Seloff

Black and yellow argiopes are grassland or forest edge species. Also known as the yellow garden spider or zigzag spider, I have never encountered one along a forest hiking trail.

Argiope's weave a unique white silk pattern into the web. Photo by Gary Seloff

The name, zigzag spider, comes from the unique "Z" pattern of white silk woven into the web. Some research indicates that the reflective property of white pattern reflects certain bands of UV light that resemble a similar UV frequency as flowers. The web's UV reflection sends a pattern, which may attract insects into the web. Other research has also suggested the pattern alerts birds in flight to avoid flying through the web.

Many Native American cultures have great reverence for spiders. Some have a creation myth that includes the story of Spider Woman who created the universe.

Song of Spiderwoman

Native American Song

There is a woman who weaves the night sky
See what she spins, how her fingers fly
She is within us beginning and end
Our grandmother, our sister our friend
She is the needle and we are the thread
She is the weaver and we are the web
She changes everything she touches
Everything she touches changes

I had an argiope make its web outside of my living room window last year. The web was inches from the glass, and I could admire its form, color and craftsmanship regularly. At morning's first light, the spider would consume the radial portion of the web and then re-weave new material. Some experts believe this behavior allows the spider to ingest moisture and trace minerals, which adhere to the web. I never expected to develop a bond or friendship to a spider but every morning I would check to see if she was still there. I splashed water on her from my fingers during the dry months of summer and even caught several grasshoppers for her web. It was a sad day in the fall when I woke one morning and she wasn't there. Posted on our Facebook page is a beautiful three-minute video of this spider "re-writing" the zigzag pattern as she did early every morning as I watched in wonder.

White-eyed Vireo. Photo by Gary Seloff

Birding

Walking the summer early in the day often produces sightings of two common vireos. The White-eyed Vireo's call says "quick-bring the beer check-please". The Red-eyed Vireo's call is more lyrical and asks "can you hear me? I'm talkin' to myself–can you hear me?". These calls are frequently heard from a summer hike.

The Scissor-tailed Flycatcher displays the most dramatic tail feathers of any bird. They nest in the prairie in isolated trees and are seen from the Prairie Platform. Photo by Gary Seloff

A typical half-day Summer Birding trip averages 40-50 species. Use the list as Your Checklist of Summer Birds At ABNC.

Black-bellied Whistling-Duck (*Dendrocygna autumnalis*)
Wood Stork (*Mycteria americana*)
Anhinga (*Anhinga anhinga*)
Great Blue Heron (*Ardea herodias*)
Great Egret (*Ardea alba*)
Snowy Egret (*Egretta thula*)
Little Blue Heron (*Egretta caerulea*)
Tricolored Heron (*Egretta tricolor*)
Cattle Egret (*Bubulcus ibis*)

Green Heron (*Butorides virescens*)

Yellow-crowned Night-Heron (*Nyctanassa violacea*)

White Ibis (*Eudocimus albus*)

Black Vulture (*Coragyps atratus*)

Turkey Vulture (*Cathartes aura*)

Osprey *(Pandion haliaetus)*

Cooper's Hawk (*Accipiter cooperii*)

Red-shouldered Hawk (*Buteo lineatus*)

Laughing Gull (*Leucophaeus atricilla*)

Forster's Tern (*Sterna forsteri*)

White-winged Dove (*Zenaida asiatica*)

Mourning Dove (*Zenaida macroura*)

Eastern Screech-Owl (*Megascops asio*)

Chimney Swift (*Chaetura pelagica*)

Ruby-throated Hummingbird (*Archilochus colubris*)

Red-bellied Woodpecker (*Melanerpes carolinus*)

Downy Woodpecker (*Picoides pubescens*)

Pileated Woodpecker (*Dryocopus pileatus*)

Acadian Flycatcher (*Empidonax virescens*)

Empidonax sp. (*Empidonax sp.*)

Great Crested Flycatcher (*Myiarchus crinitus*)

White-eyed Vireo (*Vireo griseus*)

Red-eyed Vireo (*Vireo olivaceus*)

Blue Jay (*Cyanocitta cristata*)

American Crow (*Corvus brachyrhynchos*)

Purple Martin (*Progne subis*)

Barn Swallow (*Hirundo rustica*)

Carolina Chickadee (*Poecile carolinensis*)

Tufted Titmouse (*Baeolophus bicolor*)

Carolina Wren (*Thryothorus ludovicianus*)

Blue-gray Gnatcatcher (*Polioptila caerulea*)

Northern Mockingbird (*Mimus polyglottos*)

Northern Cardinal (*Cardinalis cardinalis*)

Red-winged Blackbird (*Agelaius phoeniceus*)

Common Grackle (*Quiscalus quiscula*)

Fall

September -November

Kayaking

The first cool front of the fall season arrives during the third or fourth week of September. It's not much to write home about, but nighttime temperatures drop into the 60s for the first time in 4 months. It's a signal that there is hope and that the season is changing. It's also a signal to wildlife. Life is on the move as airborne and aquatic migrations are triggered by the cooling temperatures. A procession of aquatic species that have spent the first year of life in the bayou is headed out, headed home to the bay and Gulf where they stay for the remainder of their adult lives. The return of Ospreys and eagles is typically in mid-September, so also keep eyes to the sky. It's a joy to be on the water and all of the paddle tours suggested above are a great choice to consider.

Hiking

There is also a transition underway in the prairie plant community. This is the best season to hike the Prairie Trail. Many of the tall grasses produce seed in the fall. There is a seemingly infinite number of subtle greens and browns spread over the landscape punctuated by the yellows and blues of prairie wildflowers. The cooler temperatures make hiking the Prairie Trail in full sunlight enjoyable. End your hike on the Prairie Observation Platform. Scan the horizon and count fifty shades of green. These prairie landscapes have drawn poets and artists, inspired by the subtle shades and diverse textures. Scan for monarch butterflies. In the spring they were headed north. In the fall, these long distant migrants are headed south, returning from Canada to their wintering grounds in Mexico. American Kestrel, which have been absent during the heat of summer, return in September.

Common Yellowthroat. Photo by Gary Seloff

Birding

Fall birding can be outstanding. A good morning outing can produce a significant species count. The weather is pleasant and it's a short drive to reach your destination. A morning of birding averages 50 to 60 species.

The following are species to be found on a typical half-day October trip. Use the list as Your Checklist of Fall Birds At ABNC.

Pied-billed Grebe (*Podilymbus podiceps*)
Neotropic Cormorant (*Phalacrocorax brasilianus*)
Double-crested Cormorant (*Phalacrocorax auritus*)
Brown Pelican (*Pelecanus occidentalis*)
Great Blue Heron (*Ardea herodias*)
Great Egret (*Ardea alba*)
Snowy Egret (*Egretta thula*)
Little Blue Heron (*Egretta caerulea*)
Tricolored Heron (*Egretta tricolor*)
Cattle Egret (*Bubulcus ibis*)
Green Heron (*Butorides virescens*)
White Ibis (*Eudocimus albus*)
Black Vulture (*Coragyps atratus*)
Turkey Vulture (*Cathartes aura*)
Osprey (*Pandion haliaetus*)
Cooper's Hawk (*Accipiter cooperii*)
Bald Eagle (*Haliaeetus leucocephalus*)
Red-shouldered Hawk (*Buteo lineatus*)
Red-tailed Hawk (*Buteo jamaicensis*)

Laughing Gull (*Leucophaeus atricilla*)
Forster's Tern (*Sterna forsteri*)
Mourning Dove (*Zenaida macroura*)
Yellow-billed Cuckoo (*Coccyzus americanus*)
Barred Owl (*Strix varia*)
Chimney Swift (*Chaetura pelagica*)
Ruby-throated Hummingbird (*Archilochus colubris*)
Belted Kingfisher (*Megaceryle alcyon*)
Red-bellied Woodpecker (*Melanerpes carolinus*)
Downy Woodpecker (*Picoides pubescens*)
Northern Flicker (*Colaptes auratus*)
Pileated Woodpecker (*Dryocopus pileatus*)
American Kestrel (*Falco sparverius*)
Empidonax sp. (*Empidonax sp.*)
Eastern Phoebe (*Sayornis phoebe*)
Scissor-tailed Flycatcher (*Tyrannus forficatus*)
Blue Jay (*Cyanocitta cristata*)
American Crow (*Corvus brachyrhynchos*)
Carolina Chickadee (*Poecile carolinensis*)
Tufted Titmouse (*Baeolophus bicolor*)
House Wren (*Troglodytes aedon*)
Sedge Wren (*Cistothorus platensis*)
Marsh Wren (*Cistothorus palustris*)
Carolina Wren (*Thryothorus ludovicianus*)
Blue-gray Gnatcatcher (*Polioptila caerulea*)
Eastern Bluebird (*Sialia sialis*)
Gray Catbird (*Dumetella carolinensis*)
Brown Thrasher (*Toxostoma rufum*)
Northern Mockingbird (*Mimus polyglottos*)
Common Yellowthroat (*Geothlypis trichas*)
Northern Cardinal (*Cardinalis cardinalis*)
Indigo Bunting (*Passerina cyanea*)
Red-winged Blackbird (*Agelaius phoeniceus*)
Common Grackle (*Quiscalus quiscula*)
Great-tailed Grackle (*Quiscalus mexicanus*)

For more of Gary Seloff's images of birds and other wildlife on Armand Bayou, visit:

www.flickr.com/photos/gseloff

Chapter Nine: *Video Catalogue*

Bayou Ecology

Bayou City Eco-Almanac – Tidal Wetlands
www.youtube.com/watch?v=hwbrxigDUY8

Bayou City Eco-Almanac - Stormwater 2017
m.youtube.com/watch?v=IdCW1RpZPMU

Bayou City Eco-Almanac-Turtles of the Bay Area
www.youtube.com/watch?v=RFGvLmlvU4E

Bayou City Eco-Almanac-Armand Bayou Alligators Pasadena Channel
www.youtube.com/watch?v=2QFG5v6a2Og

Bayou City Eco-Almanac-UHCL Alligators
www.youtube.com/watch?v=0Y33YhF0qPs

ABNC National Estuaries Day with Juv. Alligator
www.youtube.com/watch?v=zjCE1HqBEwA

ABNC Rookery – Pasadena Channel With Birdsong and Captions
www.youtube.com/watch?v=4pFpxHZNJyM

Bayou City Eco-Almanac – Swallows
youtu.be/sN3JQ-1efiI

ABNC Rookery – Pasadena Channel With Mark Kramer Narrating
www.youtube.com/watch?v=GlV9mWse_PU

ABNC Rookery – Pasadena Channel With Birdsong and Captions
www.youtube.com/watch?v=4pFpxHZNJyM

Bayou City Eco-Almanac Rookery UHCL
youtu.be/3HoobZI9JzQ

ABNC Pontoon Eco-tours - Pasadena Channel
www.youtube.com/watch?v=DOlukBlyQuI

ABNC Guided Canoe Tours – Pasadena Channel
www.youtube.com/watch?v=wLhoHc2Eq_E

Bayou City: direct link—password–Houston
filmfreeway.com/BayouCity

Lake Mark Kramer Dedication
www.houstonchronicle.com/neighborhood/pasadena/news/article/Pasadena-lake-renamed-for-longtime-conservationist-15862698.php#photo-20481507

Coastal Prairie

ABNC Prairie Coneflowers – Pasadena Channel With Birdsong and Captions
www.youtube.com/watch?v=_NNQTSbtuhc

ABNC Prairie Ecology Full PowerPoint Lecture— Mark Kramer
www.youtube.com/watch?v=yKFeUXle2Vg

ABNC Prairie Pandemonium – Pasadena Channel
www.youtube.com/watch?v=O73mNUaWZR4

ABNC Prescribed Fire – Pasadena Channel
www.youtube.com/watch?v=_1TyHceRhmQ

Bayou City Eco-Almanac-Coastal Prairie Part 1
www.youtube.com/watch?v=k-hwFjo3B0s

Bayou City Eco-Almanac-Coastal Prairie Part 2
www.youtube.com/watch?v=AUAAYx5aT3U

Bayou City Eco-Almanac - Wetlands, Flooding & You
www.youtube.com/watch?v=EFm2RU_3YJk

Bayou City Eco-Almanac – Service Learning
www.youtube.com/watch?v=ulBOLw1jTvA

ABNC Prairie Builders – Jaime Gonzales
West Side High School Service Learning
www.youtube.com/watch?v=EozILlAf8To

Native Plant Society of Texas – Annual Meeting Keynote - Wildscaping at the Landscape Level
www.youtube.com/watch?v=S0XqcV1W5WI

State of the Prairie Conference 2015
The Prairie Liberation Army Wants You
www.youtube.com/watch?v=RUizOrOxAUg

General Info

Bayou City Eco-Almanac – ABNC an Ecological Oasis
youtu.be/W3TbrVzUa3M

ABNC Hiking Trails Tour – Pasadena Channel
www.youtube.com/watch?v=rpP52cgYtFM

Native Plant Society Conf. -Be A Conservationist 2016
Produced by Nivien Saleh
youtu.be/HyTINcmd0wc

Texas Conservation Corps 2016
youtu.be/t8duim4Qb54

Terry Hershey Bayou Stewardship Award Mark Kramer
www.youtube.com/watch?v=nMlFLkPEVik

Native Plant Society- ABNC 3 Plant Communities
youtu.be/hd34mxFt45o

Nature as Normal-Blog Links

Blog #1 – post week of 3.30.20 – Redwing Blackbirds
www.abnc.org/nature-blog/redwing-blackbirds

Blog #2 – post week of 4.3.20 - Texas Prairie Dawn Flower
www.abnc.org/nature-blog/texas-prairie-dawn-flower

Blog #3 – post week of 4.13.20
Spider Lily – www.abnc.org/nature-blog/spider-lily

March Wren – www.abnc.org/nature-blog/marsh-wren

Blog #4 – post week of 4.21.20-Great Egret and the Rising Tide
www.abnc.org/nature-blog/egret-rising-tide

Blog #5 – post week of 4.24.20-Monarchs on the Move
www.abnc.org/nature-blog/monarchs

Blog #6 – post week of 4.29.20- Buntings Be Here Now
www.abnc.org/nature-blog/bunting

Blog #7 – post week of 5.2.20–Texas Turtles
www.abnc.org/nature-blog/texas-turtles

Blog #8 – post week of 5.14.20-Wood Storks
www.abnc.org/nature-blog/wood-storks

Blog #9 – post week of 5.22.20-Urban Gator
www.abnc.org/nature-blog/2020/5/20/urban-alligator-part-1

Blog #10 – post week of 5.29.20-The Swallows of Summer
www.abnc.org/nature-blog/swallow-of-summer

Blog #11 – post week of 6.2.20-Heron Shores

www.abnc.org/nature-blog/heron-shores

Blog #12 – post week of 6.9.20-Peak Bloom

www.abnc.org/nature-blog/peak-bloom

Blog #13 – post week of 6.16.20-Last of the Akokisas

www.abnc.org/nature-blog/last-of-the-akokisas

Blog #14 – post week of 6.23.20-The Mega-Fish of Armand Bayou

www.abnc.org/nature-blog/mega-fish

Blog #15 – post week of 6.29.20-If Not For Hana- A Founders Tribute

www.abnc.org/nature-blog/if-not-for-hana

Blog #16 – post week of 7.13.20—Avian Acrobats

www.abnc.org/nature-blog/avian-acrobat

Blog #17 – post week of 7.27.20——Return of the Endangerds

www.abnc.org/nature-blog/return-of-the-endangereds

Blog #18 – post week of 8.7.20—The Spider Experience

www.abnc.org/nature-blog/spider-experience

Blog #19 – post week of 8.30.20-The Urban Alligator Part 2

www.abnc.org/nature-blog/urban-alligator-part2

Blog #20 – post week 9.11.20-Armand Bayou Osprey

www.abnc.org/nature-blog/osprey

Blog #21 – post week of 9.23.20-Otter Encounters

www.abnc.org/nature-blog/otter-encounters

Blog #22 – post week of 10.14.20-Night Heron Departures

www.abnc.org/nature-blog/night-heron-departures

Blog #23 – post week of 11.1.20—Kingfishers

www.abnc.org/nature-blog/kingfishers

Blog #24 – post week of 11.16.20—Pelican Outpost

www.abnc.org/nature-blog/pelican-outpost

Blog #25 – post week of 12.10.20—Re-Wilding the Urban Wilderness

www.abnc.org/nature-blog/rewilding-the-urban-wilderness

Blog #26 – post week of 1.5.21—Living Water

www.abnc.org/nature-blog/living-water

Indigo Buntings feed in restored cutgrass marsh in Horsepen Bayou. Photo by Gary Seloff

Chapter Ten: ABNC Species List

(All species listed occur on the refuge and have been identified by credible sources)

Mammals (25)

Common Name	Genus/Species	Family
Armadillo	*Dasypus novemoinctus*	Dasypodidae
Big Brown Bat	*Epesicus fuscus*	Phyllostomidae
Big Free-tailed Bat	Nyctinomops macrotis	Molossidae
Bobcat	*Lynx rufus*	Felidae
Brazilian Free-tailed Bat	*Tadarida brasiliensis*	Molossidae
Coyote	*Canis latran*	Canidae
Eastern Cottontail	*Sylvilagus floridanus*	Leporidae
Eastern Flying Squirrel	*Glaucomys volans*	Anomaluridae
Eastern Gray Squirrel	*Sciurus carolinensis*	Sciuridae
Fox Squirrel	*Sciurus niger*	Sciuridae
Hispid Cotton Rat	*Sigmodon hispidus*	Cricetidae
Hog (Feral)	*Sus Scrofa*	Suidae
Mink (American)	*Neovison vison*	Mustelidae
Norway Rat/Brown Rat	*Rattus norvegicus*	Muridae
Nutria	*Myocaster coypus*	Myocastoridae
Opossum	*Didelphis marsupialis*	Didelphidae
Raccoon	*Procyon lotor*	Procyonidae
Red Fox	*Vulpes fulva*	Canidae
Ringtail	*Bassariscus astutus*	Procyonidae
River Otter	*Lutra canadensis*	Mustelidae
Short-tailed Shrew	*Blarina brevicauda*	Soricidae
Striped Skunk	*Mephitis mehitis*	Mustelidae
Swamp Rabbit	*Sylvilagus aquaticus*	Leporidae
White-footed mouse	*Peromyscus leucopus*	Cricetidae
White-tailed Deer	*Odocoileus virginianus*	Cervinae

Birds (223)

Acadian Flycatcher	*Empidonax virescens*	Tyrannidae
American Bittern	*Botaurus lentiginosus*	Ardeidae
American Coot	*Fulica americana*	Rallidae
American Crow	*Corvus brachyrhynchos*	Corvidae

Common Name	Genus/Species	Family
American Goldfinch	*Carduelis tristis*	Fringillidae
American Kestrel	*Falco spaverius*	Falconidae
American Pipit	*Anthus rubescens*	Motacillidae
American Redstart	*Setophaga ruticilla*	Parulidae
American Robin	*Turdus migratorius*	Turdidae
American White Pelican	*Pelecanus erythrorhynchos*	Pelecanidae
American Woodcock	*Scolopax minor*	Scolopacidae
Anhinga	*Anhinga anhinga*	Anhingidae
Bald Eagle	*Haliaeetus leucocephalus*	Accipitridae
Baltimore Oriole	*Icterus galbula*	Icteridae
Barn Owl	*Tyto alba*	Tytonidae
Barn Swallow	*Hirundo rustica*	Hirundinidae
Barred Owl	*Strix varia*	Strigidae
Bay-breasted Warbler	*Dendroica castanea*	Parulidae
Belted Kingfisher	*Ceryle alcyon*	Alcedinidae
Black Vulture	*Coragyps atratus*	Cathartidae
Black-and-white Warbler	*Mniotilta varia*	Parulidae
Black-bellied Whistling Duck	*Dendrocynga autumnalis*	Anatidae
Black-billed Cuckoo	*Coccyzus erythropthalmus*	Cuculidae
Blackburnian Warbler	*Dendroica fusca*	Parulidae
Black-chinned Hummingbird	*Archilochus alexandri*	Trochilidae
Black-crowned Night-Heron	*Nycticorax nycticorax*	Ardeidae
Black-necked Stilt	*Himantropus mexicanus*	Recurvirostridae
Blackpoll Warbler	*Dendroica striata*	Parulidae
Black-throated Gray Warbler	*Dendroica nigrescens*	Parulidae
Black-throated Green Warbler	*Dendroica virens*	Parulidae
Blue Grosbeak	*Guiraca caerulea*	Cardinalidae
Blue Jay	*Cynocitta cristata*	Corvidae
Blue-gray Gnatcatcher	*Polioptila caerulea*	Sylviidae
Blue-headed Vireo	*Vireo solitarius*	Vireonidae
Blue-winged Teal	*Anas discors*	Anatidae
Blue-winged Warbler	*Vermivora pinus*	Parulidae
Bobolink	*Dolichonyx oryzivorus*	Icteridae
Brewer's Blackbird	*Euphagus cyanocephalus*	Icteridae
Broad-winged hawk	*Buteo platypterus*	Accipitridae
Brown Creeper	*Certhia americana*	Certhiidae
Brown Pelican	*Pelecanus occidentalis*	Pelecanidae
Brown Thrasher	*Toxostoma rufum*	Mimidae
Brown-headed Cowbird	*Molothrus ater*	Icteridae
Canada Goose	*Branta canadensis*	Anatidae
Canada Warbler	*Wilsonia canadensis*	Parulidae

Common Name	Genus/Species	Family
Carolina Chickadee	*Poecile carolinensis*	Paridae
Carolina Wren	*Thryothorus ludocicianus*	Troglodytidae
Caspian Tern	*Sterna caspia*	Laridae
Cattle Egret	*Bubulcus ibis*	Ardeidae
Cedar Waxwing	*Bombycilla cedrorum*	Bombycillidae
Cerulean Warbler	*Dendroica cerulea*	Parulidae
Chestnut-sided Warbler	*Dendroica pensylvanica*	Parulidae
Chimney Swift	*Chaetura pelagica*	Apodidae
Chipping Sparrow	*Spizella passerina*	Emberizidae
Chuck-will's-widow	*Caprimulgus carolinesis*	Caprimulgidae
Cliff Swallow	*Petrochelidon pyrrhonota*	Hirundinidae
Common Goldeneye	*Bucephala clangula*	Anatidae
Common Grackle	*Quiscalus quiscula*	Icteridae
Common Moorhen	*Gallinula chloropus*	Rallidae
Common Nighthawk	*Chordeiles minor*	Caprimulgidae
Common Yellowthroat	*Geothlypis trichas*	Parulidae
Cooper's Hawk	*Accipiter cooperi*	Accipitridae
Crested Caracara	*Caracara plancus*	Accipitridae
Dark-eyed Junco	*Junco hyemalis*	Emberizidae
Dickcissel	*Spiza americana*	Cardinalidae
Double-crested Cormorant	*Phalacrocorax auritus*	Phalacrocoracidae
Downy Woodpecker	*Picoides pubescen*	Picidae
Eastern Bluebird	*Sialia sialis*	Turdidae
Eastern Kingbird	*Tryannus tryannus*	Tyrannidae
Eastern Meadowlark	*Sturnella magna*	Icteridae
Eastern Phoebe	*Sayornis phoebe*	Tyrannidae
Eastern Screech-Owl	*Otus asio*	Strigidae
Eastern Towhee	*Pipilo erythrophthalmus*	Emberizidae
Eastern Wild Turkey	*Meleagis gallopavo silvertris*	Phasianidae
Eastern Wood-Pewee	*Contopus virens*	Tyrannidae
European Starling	*Sturnus vulgaris*	Sturnidae
Field Sparrow	*Spizella pusilla*	Emberizidae
Forester's Tern	*Sterna foresteri*	Laridae
Fox Sparrow	*Passerella iliaca*	Emberizidae
Golden-crowned Kinglet	*Regulus satrapa*	Regulidae
Golden-winged Warbler	*Vermivora chrysoptera*	Parulidae
Grasshopper Sparrow	*Ammodramus savannarum*	Emberizidae
Gray Catbird	*Dumetella carolinensis*	Mimidae
Great Blue Heron	*Ardea herodias*	Ardeidae
Great Crested Flycatcher	*Myiarchus crinitus*	Tyrannidae
Great Egret	*Ardea alba*	Ardeidae

Common Name	Genus/Species	Family
Great Horned Owl	*Bubo virginianus*	Strigidae
Greater White-fronted Goose	*Anser albifrons*	Anatidae
Greater Yellowlegs	*Tringa melanoleuca*	Scolopacidae
Great-tailed Grackle	*Quiscalus mexicanus*	Icteridae
Green Heron	*Butorides virenscens*	Ardeidae
Green Kingfisher	*Chloroceryle Americana*	Alcedinidae
Green-winged Teal	*Anas crecca*	Anatidae
Groove-billed Ani	*Crotophaga sulcirostris*	Cuculidae
Hairy Woodpecker	*Picoides villosus*	Picidae
Harris Sparrow	*Zonotrichia querula*	Emberizidae
Hermit Thrush	*Catharus guttatus*	Turdidae
Herring Gull	*Larus argentatus*	Laridae
Hooded Merganser	*Lophodytes cucullatus*	Anatidae
Hooded Warbler	*Wilsonia citrina*	Parulidae
House Sparrow	*Passer domesticus*	Passeridae
House Wren	*Troglodytes aedon*	Troglodytidae
Inca Dove	*Columbina inca*	Columbidae
Indigo Bunting	*Passerina cyanea*	Cardinalidae
Kentucky Warbler	*Oporornis formosus*	Parulidae
Killdeer	*Charadrius vociferus*	Charadriiae
King Rail	*Rallus elegans*	Rallidae
Lark Bunting	*Calamospiza melanocorys*	Emberizidae
Laughing Gull	*Larus atricilla*	Laridae
Least Bittern	*Ixobrychus exilis*	Ardeidae
Least Flycatcher	*Empidonax minimus*	Tyrannidae
Least Sandpiper	*Calidris minutilla*	Scolopacidae
Least Tern	*Sterna antillarum*	Laridae
LeConte's Sparrow	*Ammodramus leconteii*	Emberizidae
Lesser Scaup	*Aythya affinis*	Anatidae
Lesser Yellowlegs	*Tringa flavipes*	Scolopacidae
Lincoln's Sparrow	*Melospiza lincolnii*	Emberizidae
Little Blue Heron	*Egretta caerulea*	Ardeidae
Loggerhead Shrike	*Lanius ludovicianus*	Laniidae
Long-billed Dowitcher	*Limnodromus griseus*	Scolopacidae
Louisiana Waterthush	*Seiurus motacilla*	Parulidae
Magnificent Frigatebird	*Fregata magnificens*	Fregatidae
Magnolia Warbler	*Dendroica magnolia*	Parulidae
Mallard	*Anas platyrhynchos*	Anatidae
Marsh Wren	*Cistothorus palustris*	Troglodytidae
Merlin	*Falco columbarius*	Falconidae
Mississippi Kite	*Ictinia mississippiensis*	Accipitridae

Common Name	Genus/Species	Family
Mottled Duck	*Anas fulvigula*	Anatidae
Mourning Dove	*Zenaida macroura*	Columbidae
Mourning Warbler	*Oporornis philadelphia*	Parulidae
Nashville Warbler	*Vermivora ruficapilla*	Parulidae
Neotropic Cormorant	*Phalacrocorax brasilianus*	Phalacrocoracidae
Northern Bobwhite	*Colinus virginianus*	Odontophoridae
Northern Cardinal	*Cardinalis cardinalis*	Cardinalidae
Northern Flicker	*Colaptes auratus*	Picidae
Northern Harrier	*Circus cyaneus*	Accipitridae
Northern Mockingbird	*Mimus polyglottos*	Mimidae
Northern Parula	*Parula americana*	Parulidae
Northern Pintail	*Anas acuta*	Anatidae
Northern Rough-winged Swallow	*Stelgidopteryx serripennis*	Hirundinidae
Nothern Waterthrush	*Seiurus noveboracensis*	Parulidae
Orange-crowned Warbler	*Vermivora celata*	Parulidae
Orchard Oriole	*Icterus spurius*	Icteridae
Osprey	*Pandion haliaetus*	Accipitridae
Ovenbird	*Seiurus aurocapillus*	Parulidae
Painted Bunting	*Passerina ciris*	Cardinalidae
Palm Warbler	*Dendroica palmarum*	Parulidae
Peregrine Falcon	*Falco peregrinus*	Falconidae
Pied-billed Grebe	*Podilymbus podiceps*	Podiciedidae
Pileated Woodpecker	*Dryocopus pileatus*	Picidae
Pine Siskin	*Carduelis pinus*	Fringillidae
Pine Warbler	*Dendroica pinus*	Parulidae
Prothonotary Warbler	*Protonaria citrea*	Parulidae
Purple Finch	*Carpodacus purpureus*	Fringillidae
Purple Gallinule	*Porphyrula martinica*	Rallidae
Purple Martin	*Progne subis*	Hirundinidae
Red-bellied Woodpecker	*Melanerpes carolinus*	Picidae
Red-breasted Nuthatch	*Sitta canadensis*	Sittidae
Red-eyed Vireo	*Vireo oivaceus*	Vireonidae
Red-headed Woodpecker	*Melanerpes erythrocephalus*	Picidae
Red-shouldered Hawk	*Buteo lineatus*	Accipitridae
Red-tailed Hawk	*Buteo jamaicensis*	Accipitridae
Red-winged Blackbird	*Agelaius phoeniceus*	Icteridae
Ring-billed Gull	*Larus delawarensis*	Laridae
Rock Dove	*Columba livia*	Columbidae
Roseate Spoonbill	*Ajaia ajaja*	Threskiornithidae
Rose-breasted Grosbeak	*Pheucticus ludovicianus*	Cardinalidae
Royal Tern	*Sterna maxima*	Laridae

Common Name	Genus/Species	Family
Ruby-crowned Kinglet	*Regulus calendula*	Regulidae
Ruby-throated Hummingbird	*Archilochus colubris*	Trochilidae
Rufous Hummingbird	*Selasphorus rufus*	Trochilidae
Sandhill Crane	*Grus canadensis*	Gruidae
Savannah Sparrow	*Passerculus sandwichensis*	Emberizidae
Scarlet Tanager	*Piranga olivacea*	Thraupidae
Scissor-tailed flycatcher	*Tryannus forticatus*	Tyrannidae
Sedge Wren	*Cistothorus platensis*	Troglodytidae
Sharp-shinned hawk	*Accipiter striatus*	Accipitridae
Snow Goose	*Chen caerulescens*	Anatidae
Snowy Egret	*Egretta thula*	Ardeidae
Solitary Sandpiper	*Tringa solitaria*	Scolopacidae
Song Sparrow	*Melospiza melodia*	Emberizidae
Sora	*Porzana carolina*	Rallidae
Spotted Sandpiper	*Actitus macularia*	Scolopacidae
Sprague's Pipit	*Anthus spragueii*	Motacillidae
Summer Tanager	*Piranga rubra*	Thraupidae
Swainson's Hawk	*Buteo swainsoni*	Accipitridae
Swainson's Thrush	*Catharus ustulatus*	Turdidae
Swainson's Warbler	*Limnothlypis swainsonii*	Parulidae
Swallow-tailed Kite	*Elanoides forficatus*	Accipitridae
Swamp Sparrow	*Melospiza georgiana*	Emberizidae
Tennessee Warbler	*Vermivora peregrina*	Parulidae
Tree Swallow	*Tachycineta bicolor*	Hirundinidae
Tricolored Heron	*Egretta tricolor*	Ardeidae
Tropical Parula	*Setophaga Pitiayumi*	Parulidae
Tufted Titmouse	*Baeolophus griseus*	Paridae
Turkey Vulture	*Cathartes aura*	Cathartidae
Veery	*Catharus fuscescens*	Turdidae
Vermillion Flycatcher	*Pyrocephalus rubinus*	Tyrannidae
Vesper Sparrow	*Pooecetes gramineus*	Emberizidae
Virginia Rail	*Rallus limicola*	Rallidae
Warbling Vireo	*Vireo gilvus*	Vireonidae
Western Sandpiper	*Calidris mauri*	Scolopacidae
Whip-poor-will	*Caprimulgus vociferus*	Caprimulgidae
White Ibis	*Eudocimus albus*	Threskiornithidae
White-crowned Sparrow	*Zonotrichia leucophrys*	Emberizidae
White-eyed vireo	*Vireo griseus*	Vireonidae
White-faced Ibis	*Plegadis chihi*	Threskiornithidae
White-tailed Hawk	*Buteo albicaudatus*	Accipitridae
White-tailed Kite	*Elanus leucurus*	Accipitridae

Common Name	Genus/Species	Family
White-throated Sparrow	*Zonotrichia albicollis*	Emberizidae
Wilson's Snipe	*Gallinago delicata*	Scolopacidae
Wilson's Warbler	*Wilsonia pusilla*	Parulidae
Winter Wren	*Troglodytes troglodytes*	Troglodytidae
Wood Duck	*Aix sponsa*	Anatidae
Wood Stork	*Mycteria americana*	Ciconiidae
Wood Thrush	*Hylocichla mustelina*	Turdidae
Worm-eating Warbler	*Helmitheros vermivorus*	Parulidae
Yellow Warbler	*Dendroica petechia*	Parulidae
Yellow-bellied Sapsucker	*Sphyrapicus varius*	Picidae
Yellow-billed Cuckoo	*Coccyzus americanus*	Cuculidae
Yellow-breasted Chat	*Icteria virens*	Parulidae
Yellow-crowned Night-Heron	*Nyctanassa violacea*	Ardeidae
Yellow-rumped Warbler	*Dendroica coronata*	Parulidae
Yellow-throated Vireo	*Vireo flavifrons*	Vireonidae
Yellow-throated Warbler	*Dendroica dominica*	Parulidae

Reptiles and Amphibians (57)

Alligator Snapping Turtle	*Macroclemys temminckii*	Chelydridae
American Alligator	*Alligator mississippiensis*	Crocodylidae
Blanchard's Cricket Frog	*Acris crepitans creptians*	Hylidae
Blotched Water Snake	*Nerodia erythrogaster transversa*	Colubridae
Broad-banded Water Snake	*Nerodia fasciata confluens*	Colubridae
Broadhead Skink	*Eumeces laticeps*	Scincidae
Bullfrog	*Rana catesbeiana*	Ranidae
Common Musk Turtle	*Sternotherus odoratus*	Kinosternidae
Common Snapping Turtle	*Chelydra serpentina serpentina*	Chelydridae
Cope's Gray Treefrog	*Hyla chrysoscelis*	Hylidae
Cricket Frog	*Acris crepitans*	Hylidae
Diamondback Water Snake	*Nerodia rhombifer rhombifer*	Colubridae
Eastern Coachwhip	*Masticophis flagellum*	Colubridae
Eastern Hognose Snake	*Heterdon platyrhinos*	Colubridae
Eastern Narrow-mouth Toad	*Gastrophryne carolinensis*	Microhylidae
Eastern Yellow-bellied Racer	*Coluber constrictor*	Colubridae
Five-lined Skink	*Eumeces fasciatus*	Scincidae
Flathead Snake	*Tantilla gracilis*	Colubridae
Graham's Crayfish Snake	*Regina grahamii*	Colubridae
Gray Treefrog	*Hyla versicolor*	Hylidae
Great Plains Rat Snake	*Elaphe guttata emoryi*	Colubridae
Green Anole	*Anolis carolinensis*	Iguanidae

Common Name	Genus/Species	Family
Green Treefrog	*Hyla cinerea*	Hylidae
Ground Skink	*Scincella lateras*	Scincidae
Gulf Coast Toad	*Bufo valliceps vaiilcpes*	Bufonidae
Gulf Coast Waterdog	*Necturus beyeri*	Proteidae
Leopard Frog	*Rana sphenocephala*	Ranidae
Marsh Brown Snake	*Storeria dekayi limnetes*	Colubridae
Mediterranean Gekko	*Hemidactylus turcicus*	Gekkonidae
Mississippi Mud Turtle	*Kinosternon subrubrum hippocrepis*	Kinosternidae
Northern Spring Peeper	*Pseudacris crucifer crucifer*	Hylidae
Ornate Box Turtle	*Terrapene ornata ornata*	Emydidae
Pallid Spiny Softshell	*Trionyx spiniferus pallidus*	Trionychidae
Prairie Kingsnake	*Lampropeltis calligaster*	Colubridae
Red-eared Slider	*Chysemys scripta elegans*	Emydidae
Rough Earth Snake	*Virginia striatula*	Colubridae
Rough Green Snake	*Ophyodrys aestivus*	Colubridae
Smallmouth Salamander	*Ambystoma texanum*	Ambystomatidae
Southern Copperhead	*Agkistrodon contortix*	Viperidae
Speckled Kingsnake	*Lampropeltis getulus*	Colubridae
Squirrel Treefrog	*Hyla squirella*	Hylidae
Texas Brown Snake	*Storeria dekayi texana*	Colubridae
Texas Cooter	*Pseudemys texana*	Emydidae
Texas Coral Snake	*Micrurus fulvius*	Elapidae
Texas Rat Snake	*Elaphe obsoleta*	Colubridae
Three-toed Amphiuma	*Amphiuma tridactylum*	Amphiumidae
Three-toed Box Turtle	*Terrapene carolina triunguis*	Emydidae
Upland Chorus Frog	*Pseudacris triseriata feriarum*	Hylidae
Western Chicken Turtle	*Deirochelys reticularia miaria*	Emydidae
Western Cottonmouth	*Agkistrodon piscivorus*	Viperidae
Western Lesser Siren	*Siren intermedia nettingi*	Sirenidae
Western Mud Snake	*Farancia abacura reinwardtii*	Colubridae
Western Pygmy Rattlesnake	*Sistrurus miliarus*	Viperidae
Western Ribbon Snake	*Thamnophis proximus proximus*	Colubridae
Western Slender Glass Lizard	*Ophisaurus attenuatus attenuatus*	Anguidae
Yellowbelly Water Snake	*Nerodia erythrogaster favigaster*	Colubridae

Fish (62)

Alligator Gar	*Lepisosteus spatula*	Lepisosteidae
Armored Catfish	*Hypostomus plecostomus*	Loricariidae
Atlantic Croaker	*Micropogon undulatus*	Sciaenidae
Bay Anchovy	*Anchoa mitchelli*	Engradulidae

Common Name	Genus/Species	Family
Bay Whiff	*Citharichthys spilopterus*	Bothidae
Bayou Killifish	*Fundulus pulverus*	Cyprinodontidae
Black Bullhead	*Ictalurus melas*	Ictaluridae
Black Crappie	*Pomoxis nigromaculatus*	Centrarchidae
Black Drum	*Pogomius cromis*	Sciaenidae
Blackcheek Tonguefish	*Symphurus plagiusa*	Cynoglossidae
Blacktail Redhorse	*Moxostoma poecilurum*	Catastomidae
Blue Catfish	*Ictalurus furcatus*	Ictaluridae
Blue Runner	*Caranx crysos*	Carangidae
Bluegill Sunfish	*Lepomis macrochinus*	Centrarchidae
Bull Shark	*Carcharhinus leucas*	Carcharhinidae
Carp	*Cyprinus carpio*	Cyprinidae
Channel Catfish	*Ictalurus punctatus*	Ictaluridae
Creek Chubsucker	*Erimyzon oblongus*	Catastomidae
Diamond Killifish	*Adinia xenica*	Cyprinodontidae
Flathead Catfish	*Pylodictis olivaris*	Ictaluridae
Freshwater Drum	*Aplodinotus grunniens*	Sciaenidae
Gafftopsail Catfish	*Bagre marinus*	Ariidae
Gizzard Shad	*Dorosoma cepedianum*	Clupeidae
Golden Shiner	*Notemigonus crysolecas*	Cyprinidae
Golden Topminnow	*Fundulus chrysotus*	Fundulidae
Green Sunfish	*Lepomis cyanellus*	Centrarchidae
Gulf Killifish	*Fundulus grandis*	Cyprinodontidae
Gulf Pipefish	*Syngnathus scovelli*	Syngnthidae
Hogchoker	*Trinectes maculatus*	Soleidae
Ladyfish	*Elops saurus*	Elopidae
Largemouth Bass	*Micropterus salmoides*	Centrarchidae
Largescale Menhaden	*Brevoortia tryannus*	Clupeidae
Longear Sunfish	*Lepomis megalotis*	Centrarchidae
Longnose Gar	*Lepisosteus osseus*	Lepisosteidae
Mosquitofish	*Gambusia affinis*	Poecilidae
Naked Goby	*Gobiosoma bosci*	Gobiidae
Pinfish	*Lagodon rhomboides*	Sparidae
Rainwater Killifish	*Lucania parva*	Cyprinodontidae
Red Drum	*Sciaenops ocellatus*	Sciaenidae
Redear Sunfish	*Lepomis microlophus*	Centrarchidae
River Carpsucker	*Carpiodes carpio*	Catastomidae
Sailfin Molly	*Poecilia latipinna*	Poecilidae
Sand Seatrout	*Cynoscion arenarius*	Sciaenidae
Sea Catfish	*Arius felis*	Ariidae

Common Name	Genus/Species	Family
Sheepshead	*Archosargus probactocephalus*	Sparidae
Sheepshead Minnow	*Cyprinodon variegatus*	Cyprinodontidae
Smallmouth Buffalo	*Ictiobus bubalus*	Catostomidae
Southern Flounder	*Paralichthys lethostigma*	Bothidae
Southern Puffer	*Sphoerides nephelus*	Tetradontidae
Speckled Seatrout	*Cynoscion nebulosus*	Sciaenidae
Spot	*Leiostoma xanthurus*	Sciaenidae
Spotted Gar	*Lepisosteus oculatus*	Lepisosteidae
Stingray (Atlantic)	*Dasyatis sabinus*	Dasyatidae
Striped Mullet	*Mugil cephalus*	Mugilidae
Threadfin Shad	*Dorosoma petenense*	Clupeidae
Tidewater Silversides	*Menidia berryllina*	Atherinidae
Tilapia	*Tilapia*	Cichlidae
Violet Goby	*Gobiodes broussonetti*	Gobiidae
Warmouth	*Chaenobryttus gulosus*	Centrarchidae
White Crappie	*Pomoxis annularis*	Centrarchidae
White Mullet	*Mugil curema*	Mugilidae
Yellow Bass	*Morone mississippiensis*	Centrarchidae
Yellow Bullhead	*Icatlurus natalis*	Ictaluridae

Plants (263)

Alligator Weed	*Alternanthera philoxeroides*	Amaranthaceae
American Beauty-berry	*Callicarpa americana*	Verbenaceae
American Elm	*Ulmus americana*	Ulmaceae
American Sycamore	*Platanus occidentalis*	Platanaceae
Anglestem Beakrush	*Rhynchospora caduca*	Cyperaceae
Antelope Horn	*Asclepias viridis*	Asclepiadaceae
Arrowhead/Bulltongue	*Sagittaria lancifolia*	Alismataceae
Arrowwood	*Virbunum dentatum*	Caprifoliaceae
Awnless bluestem	*Bothriochloa exaristata*	Gramineae
Baccharis/Sea Myrtle	*Baccharis halimifolia*	Asteraceae
Bahiagrass	*Paspalum notatum*	Gramineae
Bald Cypress	*Taxodium distichum*	Taxodiaceae
Basket Flower	*Centauria americana*	Asteraceae
Basswood	*Tilia caroliniana*	Tiliaceae
Beaked Panicum	*Panicum anceps*	Gramineae
Bermuda Grass	*Cynodan dactylon*	Gramineae
Big Bluestem	*Andropogon gerardii*	Gramineae
Bigtop Lovegrass	*Eragrostis hirsuta*	Gramineae
Bitterweed	*Helenium amarum*	Asteraceae

Common Name	Genus/Species	Family
Black Hickory	*Carya texana*	Juglandaceae
Black Needlerush	*Juncus roemarianus*	Juncaceae
Black Willow	*Salix nigra*	Salicaceae
Black-eyed Susan	*Rudbeckia hirta*	Asteraceae
Blue Sage	*Salvia azurea*	Lamiacieae
Blue Waterleaf	*Hydrolea ovata*	Hydrophyllaceae
Blue-star	*Amsonia glaberrima*	Apcynaceae
Bluets	*Hedyotis nigricans*	Rubiaceae
Brasilian vervain	*Verbena brasiliensis*	Verbenaceae
Broomsedge	*Andropogon virginicus*	Gramineae
Brownseed Paspalum	*Paspalum plicatulum*	Gramineae
Bushy Aster	*Aster dumosus*	Asteraceae
Bushy Bluestem	*Andropogon glomeratus*	Gramineae
Butterfly Weed	*Asclepias tuberosa*	Asclepiadaceae
Button-bush	*Cephalanthus occidentalis*	Rosaceae
Calico Aster	*Aster lateriflorus*	Asteraceae
California Bulrush	*Scirpus californicus*	Cyperaceae
Carolina Buckthorn	*Rhamnus caroliniana*	Rhamnaceae
Carolina Buttercup	*Ranunculus carolinianus*	Ranunculaceae
Carolina Cherry Laurel	*Prunus caroliniana*	Rosaceae
Carolina Horse-nettle	*Solanum carolinense*	Solanaceae
Carolina Jessamine	*Gelsemium sempervirens*	Loganiaceae
Carolina Moonseed	*Cocculus carolinus*	Menispemaceae
Carolina Sedge	*Carex caroliniana*	Cyperaceae
Carolina Wolfberry	*Lycium carolinianum*	Solanaceae
Carpet Grass	*Axonopus affinis*	Gramineae
Cat/Green Briar	*Smilax bona-nox*	Liliaceae
Cedar Elm	*Ulmus crassifolia*	Ulmaceae
Ceeping Spot-flower	*Spilanthes americana*	Asteraceae
Cherokee Sedge	*Carex cherokeensis*	Cyperaceae
Cherrybark Oak	*Quercus falcata*	Fagaceae
Chinese Privet	*Ligustrum sinense*	Oleaceae
Chinese Tallow	*Sapium sebiferum*	Euphorbiaceae
Climbing Hempweed	*Mikania scandens*	Asteraceae
Common Cattail	*Tule espadilla*	Typhaceae
Common Fimbry	*Fimbristylis pberula*	Cyperaceae
Common Goldenrod	*Solidago candensis*	Asteraceae
Common Persimmon	*Diospyros virginiana*	Ebenaceae
Coral Bean	*Eythrina herbacea*	Fabaceae
Creeping Seedbox	*Ludwigia glandulosa*	Onagraceae

Common Name	Genus/Species	Family
Curly-leaf Dock	*Rumex crispus*	Polygonaceae
Dallisgrass	*Paspalum dilatatum*	Gramineae
Deciduous Holly; Possum-Haw	*Ilex decidua*	Aquifoliaceae
Deer Pea	*Vigna luteola*	Fabaceae
Deer Pea Vetch	*Vicia ludoviciana*	Fabaceae
Dog Fennel	*Eupatorium capillifolium*	Asteraceae
Downy Lobelia	*Lobelia puberula*	Campanulaceae
Downy Milk-pea	*Galactia volubilis*	Leguminosae
Drummond Rattlebox	*Sesbania drummondii*	Leguminosae
Duckweed	*Lemna polyrhiza*	Lemnaceae
Dwarf Palmetto	*Sabal minor*	Palmae
Eastern Gama Grass	*Tripsacum dactyloides*	Gramineae
Ebony Speenwort	*Asplenium platyneurin*	Aspleniaceae
Elephant Ear	*Colocasia esculenta*	Araceae
Elliott Lovegrass	*Eragrostis elliottii*	Gramineae
Erect Dayfower	*Commelina erecta*	Commelinaceae
Euthamia	*Euthamia leptocephala*	Asteraceae
False Dandelion	*Pyrrhopappus carolinianus*	Asteraceae
False Garlic	*Nothoscordum bivalve*	Liliaceae
False Jerusalem Cherry	*Solanum capsicastrum*	Solanaceae
Farkleberry	*Vaccimium arboreum*	Ericaceae
Fewflower Nutrush	*Scleria pauciflora*	Cyperaceae
Flattened Sedge	*Carex complanata*	Cyperaceae
Florida Paspalum	*Paspalum floridanum*	Gramineae
Frank's Sedge	*Carex Frankii*	Cyperaceae
Fringe Tree	*Chionanthus virginicus*	Oleaceae
Fringed Sneezeweed	*Helenium drummondii*	Asteraceae
Frog Fruit	*Phyla Sp.*	Verbenaceae
Frost Weed	*Verbesnia virginica*	Asteraceae
Gayfeather/Blazing Star	*Liatris pycnostachya*	Asteraceae
Giant Ragweed	*Ambrosia trifida*	Asteraceae
Globe Beakrush	*Rhynchospora globularis*	Cyperaceae
Goldenrod	*Solidago altissima*	Asteraceae
Grassy arrowroot/Duck Potato	*Sagittaria graminea*	Alismataceae
Green Ash	*Fraxinus pensylvanica*	Oleaceae
Green Flatsedge	*Cyperaceae virens*	Cyperaceae
Green Wild Indigo	*Baptisia spharocarpa*	Fabaceae
Gulf Coast Waterhemp	*Amaranthus australis*	Amaranthaceae
Gulf cordgrass	*Spartina spartinae*	Poaceae
Gulf Muhly	*Muhlenbergia cappillaris*	Gramineae

Common Name	Genus/Species	Family
Hairy Flowered Spiderwort	*Tradescantia hirsutiflora*	Commelinaceae
Hairy Ruellia	*Ruellia humilis*	Acanthaceae
Halberd-leaved Rose-mallow	*Hibiscus militaris*	Malvaceae
Herbertia	*Herbertia lahue caerulea*	Iridaceae
Hercules Club/Tickle Tongue	*Zanthoxylum clava-herculis*	Rutaceae
Hogwort/Wooly Croton	*Croton capitatus*	Euphorbiaceae
Honey Locust	*Gleditsia triacanthos*	Fabaceae
Horned Beakrush	*Rhynochospora corniculata*	Cyperaceae
Huisache	*Acacia farnesiana*	Fabaceae
Indian Grass	*Sorghastrum nutans*	Gramineae
Indian Plantain	*Cacalia lancelolata*	Asteraceae
Iva/High tide Bush	*Iva frutescens*	Asteraceae
Japanese Climbing Fern	*Lygodium japonicum*	Schizaeaceae
Japanese Honeysuckle	*Lonicera japonica*	Caprifoliaceae
Japanese Privet	*Ligustrum japonica*	Oleaceae
Johnson Grass	*Sorghum halepense*	Sorghastrum
Knotroot Bristlegrass	*Seteria geniculata*	Gramineae
Late Thoroughwort	*Eupatorium serotinum*	Asteraceae
Lead Plant	*Amorph fruticosa*	Leguminosae
Leafy Three-square	*Scirpus robustus*	Cyperaceae
Lemon Beebalm	*Monarda citriodora*	Lamiacieae
Little Bluestem	*Schizachyrium scoparium*	Gramineae
Lizard-tail	*Saururus cernuus*	Saururaceae
Loblolly Pine	*Pinus taeda*	Pinaceae
Long-leaf Pondweed	*Potamogenton nodosus*	Potamogetonaceae
Longspike Tridens	*Tridens strictus*	Gramineae
Louisiana Dewberry	*Rubus louisianus*	Rosaceae
Lovegrass/Lace Grass	*Eragrostis capillaris*	Gramineae
Low Aster	*Helastrum henisphericum*	Asteraceae
Lyre-leaf Sage	*Salvia lyrata*	Lamiacieae
Marsh Bedstraw	*Galium tinctorium*	Rubiaceae
Marsh Seedbox	*Ludwigia palustris*	Onagraceae
Marshhay Cordgrass	*Spartina patens*	Poaceae
Maximilian Sunflower	*Helianthus maximiliani*	Asteraceae
Maypop/Passionflower	*Plassiflora incarnata*	Passifloraceae
Meadow Beauty	*Rhexia mariana*	Melastomataceae
Meadow Pink	*Sabatia campestris*	Gentianaceae
Missouri Ironweed	*Vernonia missurica*	Asteraceae
Mohr's Eupatorium	*Eupatorium mohrii*	Asteraceae
Monkey Grass	*Ophiopogon japonicus*	Liliaceae

Common Name	Genus/Species	Family
Muscadine Grape	*Vitis rotundifolia*	Vitaceae
Mustang Grape	*Vitis candicans*	Vitaceae
Narrowleaf Seedbox	*Ludwigia lineraris*	Onagraceae
Narrow-leaf Sumpweed	*Iva angustifolia*	Asteraceae
Narrow-leafed Blue-eyed Grass	*Sisyrinchium angustifolium*	Iridaceae
Needlerush	*Juncus effusus*	Juncaceae
Niaiad	*Najas guadalupensis*	Najadaceae
Nits-and-Lice	*Hypericum drummondii*	Hypericaceae
Noseburn	*Tragia bentonicifolia*	Euphorbiaceae
Osage Orange	*Malclura pomifera*	Moraceae
Parsley Hawthorn	*Crataegus marshallii*	Rosaceae
Partridge Pea	*Cassia fasciculata*	Leguminosae
Pecan	*Carya illinoensis*	Juglandaceae
Pepper-vine	*Ampelopsis arborea*	Vitaceae
Philadelhpia Fleabane	*Erigeron philadelphicus*	Asteraceae
Phragmites/Sea Cane	*Phragmites australis*	Poaceae
Pickerelweed	*Ponterderia cordata*	Pontederiaceae
Pink Mint	*Stachys drummondii*	Lamiacieae
Plains Coreopsis	*Coreopsis tinctoria*	Asteraceae
Plains Lovegrass	*Eragrostis intermedia*	Gramineae
Poison Ivy	*Rhus toxicodendron*	Anacardiaceae
Pokeweed	*Phytolacca americana*	Phytolaccaceae
Pony Foot	*Dichondra carolinensis*	Convolvulaceae
Post Oak	*Quercus stellata*	Fagaceae
Powdery Thalia	*Thlia dealbata*	Marantaceae
Prairie agalinis	*Agalinis heterophylla*	Scrophulariaceae
Prairie Cordgrass	*Spartina pectanata*	Poaceae
Priarie Parsley	*Polytaenia nuttalli*	Apiaceae
Purple Cudweed	*Gnaphalium purpureum*	Asteraceae
Purple Loosestrife	*Lythrum lancelolatum*	Lythraceae
Purple Lovegrass	*Eragrostis spectabilis*	Gramineae
Purple Three Awn	*Aristida purpurascens*	Gramineae
Red Cedar	*Juniperus virginiana*	Cupressaceae
Red Mulberry	*Morus rubra*	Moraceae
Resurection Fern	*Polypodium polypodioides*	Polypodiaceae
Retama/Parkinsonia	*Parkinsonia aculeata*	Fabaceae
River Birch	*Betula nigra*	Betluaceae
Rough agalinis	*Agalinis fasiculata*	Scrophulariaceae
Rough Buttonweed	*Diodia teres*	Rubiaceae
Round Pennywort	*Hydrocotyle umbellata*	Apiaceae

Common Name	Genus/Species	Family
Round-head Rush	*Juncus validus*	Juncaceae
Salt-marsh morning Glory	*Ipomoea sagittata*	Convolvulaceae
Salvinia	*Salvinia minima*	Salviniaceae
Scarlet Pimpernil	*Anagallis arvensis*	Primulaceae
Scribner's Dichanthelium	*Dichanthelium oligosanthes*	Gramineae
Seacoast Sumpweed	*Iva annua*	Asteraceae
Sea-ox-eye Daisy	*Borrichia frutescens*	Asteraceae
Seaside Goldenrod	*Solidago sempervirens*	Asteraceae
Seaside Goldenrod	*Solidago stricta*	Asteraceae
Sensitive Briar	*Schrankia hystricina*	Leguminosae
Shiny Coneflower	*Rudbeckia nitida*	Asteraceae
Showy Dodder	*Cuscuta indecora*	Cuscutaceae
Showy Evening Primrose	*Oenothera speciosa*	Onagraceae
Silk Grass	*Heterotheca graminifolia*	Asteraceae
Silky Evolvulus	*Evolvulus sericeus*	Convolvulaceae
Silver Bluestem	*Bothriochloa saccharoides*	Gramineae
Slash Pine	*Pinus elliottii*	Pinaceae
Slender Blazing Star	*Liatris acidota*	Asteraceae
Slender Copperleaf	*Acalypha gracilens*	Euphorbiaceae
Smallseed Spikesedge	*Eleocharis microcarpa*	Cyperaceae
Smooth Cordgrass	*Spartina alterniflora*	Poaceae
Snow-on-the-Prairie	*Euphorbia bicolor*	Euphorbiaceae
Southern Dewberry	*Rubus trivialis*	Rosaceae
Southern Swamp-lily	*Crinum americanum*	Amaryllidaceae
Sow Thistle	*Sonchus asper*	Asteraceae
Spanish-moss	*Tillandsia useneoides*	Bromeliaceae
Spider Lily	*Hymenocallis liriosme*	Amaryllidaceae
Spikegrass	*Chasmanthium laxum*	Gramineae
Spikegrass	*Chasmanthium sessiliflorum*	Gramineae
Spring Ladies-tresses	*Spiranthes vernalis*	Orchidaceae
Squarestem Spikerush	*Eleocharis quadrangulata*	Cyperaceae
St. Andrew's Cross	*Ascyrum hypericoides*	Hypericaceae
Sucker Flax	*Linum medium*	Linaceae
Sugar Hackberry	*Celtis levigata*	Ulmaceae
Sugarcane Plumegrass	*Erianthus giganteus*	Gramineae
Sundew	*Drosera capillaris*	Droseraceae
Supple-jack/Rattan Vine	*Berchemia scandens*	Rhamnaceae
Swamp Parsley	*Trepocarpus aethusae*	Apiaceae
Swamp Sunflower	*Helianthus angustifolia*	Asteraceae
Sweet Sedge	*Cyperus pseudovegetus*	Cyperaceae

Common Name	Genus/Species	Family
Sweetgum	*Liquidamber styraciflua*	Hamamelidaceae
Switchgrass	*Panicum virgatum*	Gramineae
Tall Dropseed	*Sporobolus asper*	Gramineae
Tall Gaura	*Gaura longiflora*	Onagraceae
Texas Panicum	*Panicum texanum*	Gramineae
Texas Prairie Dawn Flower	*Hymenoxys texana*	Asteraceae
Texas Spear/Wintergrass	*Stipa leucotricha*	Gramineae
Thinfruit Sedge	*Carex flaccosperma*	Cyperaceae
Tick-trefoil/Clover	*Desmonium Sp.*	Leguminosae
Trifoliate Orange	*Citrus trifoliata*	Rutaceae
Tropical Sage	*Salvia coccinea*	Lamiacieae
Trumpet Creeper	*Campsis radicans*	Bignoniaceae
Tuber vervain	*Verbena rigida*	Verbenaceae
Turk's Cap	*Malvaviscus arboreus drummondi*	Malvaceae
Twoflower Rush	*Juncus marginatus*	Juncaceae
Upland Privet	*Forestiera ligustrina*	Oleaceae
Variable Dichanthelium	*Dichanthelium commutatum*	Gramineae
Vasey Grass	*Paspalum urvillei*	Gramineae
Virginia Buttonweed	*Diodia virginiana*	Rubiaceae
Virginia Creeper	*Parthenocissus quinquefolia*	Vitaceae
Wafer Ash/Hoptree	*Ptelea trifoliata*	Rutaceae
Water Hyacinth	*Eichornia crassipes*	Pontederiaceae
Water Lettuce	*Pistia stratiotes*	Araceae
Water Oak	*Quercus nigra*	Fagaceae
Water Pepper	*Polygonum hydopiperoids*	Polygonaceae
Water-milfoil	*Myriophyllum spicatum*	Haloragaceae
Wax-myrtle	*Myrica cerifera*	Myricaceae
Western Ragweed	*Ambrosia psilostachya*	Asteraceae
Western Soapberry	*Sapindus saponaria*	Sapondaceae
White Ash	*Fraxinus americana*	Oleaceae
White Gaura	*Gaura lindheimeri*	Onagraceae
White Snakeroot	*Eupatorium rugosum*	Asteraceae
Whiteflower Mercardonia	*Mecardonia acuminata*	Scrophulariaceae
Whiteroot Rush	*Juncus brachycarpus*	Juncaceae
White-topped Sedge	*Rhynchospora colorata*	Cyperaceae
Whorled Milkwort	*Polygala verticilata*	Polygalaceae
Widgeon Grass	*Ruppia maritima*	Ruppiaceae
Wild Celery	*Apium leptophyllum*	Apiaceae
Willow Oak	*Quercus phellos*	Fagaceae
Winged Elm	*Ulmus alata*	Ulmaceae

Common Name	Genus/Species	Family
Wood Sorrel/Sour Grass	*Oxalis dillenii*	Oxalidaceae
Wooly Dichanthelium	*Dichanthelium acuminatum*	Gramineae
Yankee Weed	*Eupatorium compositifolium*	Asteraceae
Yaupon	*Ilex vomitoria*	Aquifoliaceae
Yellow Puff	*Neptunia pubescens*	Leguminosae
Yellow Wild Indigo	*Baptisia sphaerocarpa*	Leguminosae
Hooker's Eryngo	*Eryngium hookeri*	Apiaceae
False Aster	*Boltonia asteroides*	Asteraceae
Greater Bladder Sedge	*Euthamia pulverulenta*	Asteraceae
Great Plains Goldentop	*Carex intumescens*	Cyperaceae
Fringed Nutrush	*Scleria ciliata*	Aciculare
Needleleaf Rosette Grass	*Dichanthelium aciculari*	Gramineae
Pariguay Panicgrass	*Panicum pilcomayense*	Gramineae

Racoon with blue crab. Photo by Gary Seloff

About the Author

Mark and Charlie

Mark Kramer's career has spanned 25 years at Armand Bayou Nature Center where he served as Conservation Director and Chief Naturalist. He is a native of Pasadena, Texas and began paddling on Armand Bayou as a teenager. He has been a student of Armand Bayou for over 40 years. Mark has been described as a leader, a bayou advocate, a mentor, an educator par excellence and a tireless bayou steward – and all are true.

Mark is a Restoration Ecologist, Lecturer, Writer, Interpretive Naturalist, licensed Master Captain with the U.S. Coast Guard, Prescribed Burn Boss, and avid angler. He is the recipient of the Texas Parks and Wildlife Lone Star Land Steward Award, the Bayou Preservation Association Terry Hershey Bayou Steward Award and the Coastal Prairie Partnership Prairie Excellence Award. Exploring, preserving, restoring and interpreting coastal ecology and wildlife have been his lifelong passion.

Made in the USA
Columbia, SC
13 August 2021

43095157R00115